ACCOUNTING & AUDITING RESEARCH: A PRACTICAL GUIDE

fifth edition

Thomas R. Weirich
Central Michigan University

Alan Reinstein
Wayne State University

South-Western College Publishing
Thomson Learning™

Australia • Canada • Denmark • Japan • Mexico • New Zealand • Philippines
Puerto Rico • Singapore • South Africa • Spain • United Kingdom • United States

Accounting & Auditing Research, 5th edition, by Thomas R. Weirich and Alan Reinstein
Accounting Team Director: Rick Lindgren
Acquisitions Editor: Rochelle J. Kronzek
Developmental Editor: Teresa Dulaney Dewald
Marketing Manager: Dan Silverburg
Media Production Editor: Lora Craver
Production Editor: Mike Busam
Manufacturing Coordinator: Doug Wilke
Internal Design: Joe Devine
Cover Design: Jennifer Lambert
Cover Photographer: Kenvin Lyman/Photonica
Production House: DPS Associates, Inc.
Printer: West Group

Printed in the United States of America
1 2 3 4 5 02 01 00 99

For more information contact South-Western College Publishing, 5101 Madison Road, Cincinnati, Ohio, 45227 or find us on the Internet at http://www.swcollege.com

For permission to use material from this text or product,contact us by
• telephone: **1-800-730-2214**
• fax: **1-800-730-2215**
• web: **http://www.thomsonrights.com**

Library of Congress Cataloging-in-Publication Data
Weirich, Thomas R.
    Accounting & auditing research : a practical guide / Thomas R.
Weirich, Alan Reinstein. — 5th ed.
      p. cm.
    Rev. ed. of: Accounting & auditing research. 4th ed. 1996.
    ISBN 0-324-01627-1
    1. Accounting—Research. 2. Accounting—Research. I. Reinstein,
Alan. II. Weirich, Thomas R. Accounting & auditing research.
III. Title.
HF5630.W39 1999   99–29692
657'.07'2—DC21   CIP

This book is printed on acid-free paper.

B R I E F
C O N T E N T S

C O N T E N T S

....

This enlarged fifth edition of *Accounting & Auditing Research: A Practical Guide* incorporates significant improvements over the prior editions. The new edition of this popular text has been expanded to be a comprehensive reference tool for the practitioner/student who desires to become proficient in conducting accounting and auditing research. Not only will the reader be exposed to the steps of accounting and auditing research, but now will be introduced to tax research and the steps of a fraud investigation. The fifth edition focuses primarily on the major research developments emerging in the new millennium with special emphasis on electronic research techniques and tools, as well as added emphasis on communication and critical thinking skills as recognized by the Accounting Education Change Commission, the AICPA, and other organizations.

The approach of this edition, continued from earlier editions, is that of a do-it-yourself, understand-it-yourself manual that serves as a primer on research methodology to assist the reader in conducting research in order to develop theoretically correct and justifiable solutions to accounting or auditing questions. This text, used by a number of universities and staff training courses in public accounting firms and corporations, guides the reader, step-by-step, through the research process. However, this new edition has expanded the research coverage to include greater use of the Internet, basic tax research, fraud investigations, and discussion of new assurance services and basic consulting steps that include the process of benchmarking or performance measurement.

This text, with the following expanded features, will be an appropriate stand-alone text for a basic accounting/auditing research course, or as a supplemental text for any intermediate accounting, advanced accounting, governmental accounting, tax, or auditing courses. Utilization of the text in these courses is now enhanced with various cases developed for these specific courses which are located at the authors Web site.

New Features of the Fifth Edition

- Expanded discussion of critical thinking and effective writing skills for the professional. This new edition has expanded these topics into separate chapters (Chapters 2 and 3) to reflect the renewed interest by employers, accrediting agencies, and the profession in these topics.
- New chapter on utilizing the Internet in conducting practical applied research (Chapter 4). This chapter provides various Web sites and browsers that the practitioner will find useful in conducting research.
- New chapter on the steps of conducting tax research (Chapter 10). An optional CD-ROM is available for the reader if requested. This CD contains the student version of RIA's OnPoint Tax Service. Selected screen shots are included in the tax chapter concerning the use of this service. Check with South-Western College Publishing representative for details.

- New chapter on the techniques of a fraud investigation (Chapter 11). This topic of forensic accounting is a rapidly growing service offered by professional firms in order to add value to the basic services currently rendered to clients. This chapter provides an overview of fraud and the steps of a fraud investigation.
- Screen shots of the new LEXIS-NEXIS Academic Universe Web site are incorporated in the text. Free access to this Web site is available for those classes that utilize this text.
- Screen shots illustrating the use of the Financial Accounting Standards Board's Financial Accounting Research System (FARS) in conducting research are presented as tutorials throughout the text.
- Added end-of-chapter discussion questions and exercises that require the reader to explore various reference materials in developing solutions.
- New cases to enhance the pragmatic approach in developing efficient and effective research skills. The authors have employed "hands-on" research cases located at the authors' Web site at the South-Western College Publishing home page.
- The introduction of new assurance services and consulting services with related professional standards. Also included is a discussion of the basic process of benchmarking or performance measurement and related tools that the practitioner can utilize in researching an entity's performance (Chapter 9).
- Various "hot-links" are available at the authors' Web site to other appropriate Web sites related to topics in selected chapters of the new edition.

With the growing importance of computer-oriented research tools, expanded discussion has been incorporated into this edition. A more in-depth look at the Internet and other computerized databases are presented throughout the text. In order to provide the reader with a demonstration of selected computerized tools, two CD-ROMs accompany this text. The first CD includes the following three tutorials:

LEXIS-NEXIS Academic Universe—This dynamic research tool, available only to the academic community, is a Web-based subset product of the widely recognized commercial LEXIS-NEXIS database. In addition to various topical areas, this database provides access to U.S. authoritative accounting and auditing literature, and accounting journals, as well as various tax sources. The enclosed CD provides a tutorial for the use of Academic Universe with end-of-chapter questions and cases designed to use this powerful product for research purposes.

PricewaterhouseCoopers' *Edgarscan*—This Internet based applet, *Edgarscan*, created by PricewaterhouseCoopers, is an excellent tool for performance measurement or benchmarking activities. This tool is very powerful for anyone attempting to research a company and make performance comparisons with competitors. The CD provides a demo of Edgarscan with end-of-chapter questions requesting the use of this Web-based product by accessing it at PricewaterhouseCoopers' Web site.

ACL for Windows—This is a major software product available for the fraud examiner. As discussed in Chapter 11, this demo, located on the CD, demonstrates how this product can be used in fraud investigations. Selected end-of-chapter questions will quiz you in the use of ACL for fraud detection.

The second CD accompanying this text provides a demonstration of a product called the *Analyst's Notebook* created by i2, Inc. This software product is also an aid for the fraud examiner. The product provides a link analysis by creating a picture (chart) of the individuals or organizations involved in a fraud, and develops a timeline for the events in the fraud case. The *Analyst's Notebook* is a new and powerful tool for the fraud examiner.

The authors express appreciation to the many faculty members that have utilized previous editions of this text and who have made valuable comments in the development of this new edition. Also, we would like to thank the accounting firms who have incorporated this text into their staff training programs. A specific thank you is extended to Don Marshall, Kevin Misiewicz, and James Parker for granting permission to utilize their materials in the development of Chapter 10 on tax research.

Finally, special thanks go to the technical support provided by the staff of South-Western College Publishing, especially Rochelle Kronzek, Mike Busam, and Teresa Dulaney Dewald. Special thanks also to our family members, who provided special encouragement during the writing of this edition.

Thomas R. Weirich
Central Michigan University

Alan Reinstein
Wayne State University

Thomas R. Weirich, Ph.D., CPA, received his B.S. and M.B.A. degrees from Northern Illinois University, and a Doctorate in Accountancy from the University of Missouri–Columbia. He is currently the Arthur Andersen & Co. Alumni Professor of Accounting in the School of Accounting at Central Michigan University. Dr. Weirich, former chair of the School of Accounting, has served on special assignment as the Academic Fellow to the Office of Chief Accountant at the U.S. Securities and Exchange Commission in Washington, D.C. He has recently completed a sabbatical with Arthur Andersen, LLP, in their Business Fraud and Investigative Services Division, during which he participated in various fraud and background investigations. He has also served as a consultant to the Public Oversight Board's Panel on Audit Effectiveness.

Dr. Weirich has public accounting experience with an international firm as well as with a local firm. He has served on the Editorial Advisory board to the Journal of Accountancy and has been a committee member on the American Accounting Association's Education Committee and the SEC Liaison Committee. He has completed an assignment on the AICPA's SEC Regulation's Committee and the Board of Examiners' Auditing Subcommittee that aids in the development of the CPA examination. Professor Weirich has written numerous articles in professional journals and has served as a business consultant to a manufacturing concern. Dr. Weirich has also served 11 years on the Mt. Pleasant, Michigan, City Commission and as mayor of the city. Professor Weirich has been the recipient of the School of Accounting/Beta Alpha Psi's Outstanding Teacher Award, the College of Business Dean's Teaching Award and the Michigan Association of Governing Boards' Distinguished Faculty Award. He has served as an expert witness for the SEC and other organizations.

Alan Reinstein, DBA, CPA, is the George R. Husband Professor of Accounting and former Chair of the Department of Accounting, School of Business Administration, at Wayne State University in Detroit, Michigan. He received his B.A. and M.S. degrees from the State University of New York (New Paltz), an M.B.A degree from the University of Detroit, and a Doctorate in Accounting from the University of Kentucky. Professor Reinstein conducts many seminars for the AICPA, several State Auditors Generals' Offices, state CPA societies, and other professional groups. An author of about 190 articles, Dr. Reinstein serves on the editorial boards of four major academic and professional journals; he is also Associate Editor of *The Accounting Educators' Journal and Book Review,* and Editor of *Issues in Accounting Education.* Professor Reinstein has also held many board and committee chair positions, and other leadership roles in such professional and academic organizations as the Michigan

Association of CPAs, Financial Executives Institute, Institute of Internal Auditors, and American Accounting Association. He was recently named as a Commercial Panel Member "Neutral" for the American Arbitration Association and to the Board of Arbitrators of the National Association of Securities Dealers (NASD).

CHAPTER 1

Introduction to Professional Research

LEARNING OBJECTIVES

After completing this chapter, you should understand:

- The importance of research in the daily activities of the professional accountant.
- The definition of professional accounting research.
- The nature of professional accounting research.
- The importance of critical thinking and effective communication skills.
- The U.S. Securities & Exchange Commission's view on the importance of research.
- The importance of the economic consequences of standards setting in the research process.
- The role of research within a public accounting firm or within an accounting department of a business or governmental entity.
- The basic steps of the research process.

The accounting profession, like other professions, is witnessing major changes due to new services, technology, and an ever-increasing number of professional standards. In addition to the typical services of tax preparation and auditing, accountants are involved in various forms of assurance services and forensic accounting, or fraud examinations. Today's professional accountant must possess the technical ability to keep current and must be able to critically analyze the ever-expanding knowledge base. Additionally, the accounting professional must be able to listen effectively and understand opposing points of view, and then be able to present and defend his/her own views through formal and informal presentations. A well-developed research methodology is beneficial in this environment.

Varying views and interpretations as to the meaning of the term **research** exist. To many outside a given profession, *research* conveys the picture of an academic researcher preparing a scholarly paper. To others, the term depicts a scientist in a white lab coat experimenting with a new miracle drug. However, in the accounting profession, *research* points to what the accounting practitioner does as a normal, everyday part of his/her job.

The professional accountant, whether in public accounting, industry, or government, frequently becomes involved with the investigation and analysis of an accounting, tax, or auditing issue. Resolving these issues requires a clear definition of the problem, gathering information with various forms of technology, reviewing authoritative literature, evaluating alternatives, and drawing conclusions. This research process often requires an analysis of very complex and detailed issues. Therefore, the researching of such an issue will challenge the **critical thinking** abilities of the professional. That is, the professional must possess the expertise to understand the problem and related facts and render a professional judgment for a situation that, in certain cases, no single definitive answer or solution exists. In such cases, the researcher would apply reasonable and reflective thinking in the development of an answer to the issue or problem at hand.

CRITICAL THINKING AND EFFECTIVE COMMUNICATION

The researcher needs to know "how to think." That is, he or she should be able to identify the problem or issue, gather the facts, analyze the situation or issue, synthesize and evaluate alternatives, and then develop an appropriate solution. Such skills are essential for the professional accountant in providing services in today's complex, dynamic, and changing profession. In this environment, the professional accountant must possess the ability to think critically, which includes the ability to understand a variety of contexts and circumstances, and be able to apply and adapt various accounting, tax, auditing, and business concepts and principles to these circumstances to develop solutions to a given issue. The development and nurturing of critical thinking skills will also contribute to the process of life-long learning.

Certain research efforts may culminate in memos to workpapers, letters to clients, journal articles, company or firm monographs, or even textbooks. The dissemination of your research, in whatever form, will require you to possess **effective communication skills** for both oral presentations and effective writing. Your research output must be coherent and concise, incorporate good use of standard English, and be appropriate to the intended reader. Critical thinking and effective writing skills are the focus of Chapters 2 and 3.

WHAT IS RESEARCH?

The term *research* has frequently been misunderstood by those unfamiliar with the research process. Such misconceptions view research as a mechanical process conducted in a mystical environment by strange individuals. The research approach is anything but mystical or mechanical. The conducting of any type of research, including professional accounting, tax, and auditing research, is simply a systematic investigation of an issue or problem utilizing the researcher's professional judgment.

Below are examples of two generalized research problems which can provide insight as to the types of research questions confronting the accounting practitioner:

1. A client is engaged in land sales, primarily commercial and agricultural. The company recently acquired a retail land sales project under an agreement stating that, if the company did not desire to pursue the project further, the property could be returned with no liability to the company.

    After the company invests a considerable amount of money into the project, the state of the economy concerning retail land sales declines and the company decides to return the land. As a result, the client turns to you, the CPA, and requests the proper accounting treatment of the returned project. In question is whether the abandonment represents a disposal of a segment of the business, an unusual and nonrecurring extraordinary loss, or an ordinary loss.

2. As controller for a construction contracting company you are faced with the following problem. The company pays for rights allowing it to extract a specified volume of landfill from a project for a specified period of time. How should the payments for such landfill rights be classified in the company's financial statements?[1]

Research in general can be classified into two primary categories: pure research and applied research. **Pure research**, often labeled basic or theoretical research, involves the investigation of questions that appear interesting to the researcher, generally an academician, but may have little or no practical application at the present time. For example, a researcher may be interested in developing a model that relates properties of the analysts' information environment to the properties of their forecasts.[2] Such research has little present day practical application and can be referred to as empirical research; i.e., research based upon experiment or observation. However, pure or basic research should not be discounted as worthless. On the contrary, such research adds to the body of knowledge in a particular field and may ultimately contribute directly or indirectly to practical problem solutions. Empirical research studies, for example, are frequently reviewed and evaluated by standard-setting bodies in drafting authoritative accounting and auditing pronouncements.

Applied research, which is the focus of this text, involves the investigation of an issue of immediate practical importance. For example, assume that a public accounting firm has been asked to evaluate a client's proposed new accounting treatment for environmental costs. The client expects an answer within two days as to the acceptability of the new method and the impact it would have on the financial statements. In such a case, a member of the accounting firm's professional staff would investigate to determine if the authoritative literature addresses the issue. If no authoritative pronouncement can be found, the accountant would develop a theoretical justification for, or against, the new method.

The applied research in the preceding example can be categorized as *a priori* (before the fact): The research is conducted before the client actually enters into the transaction. On the other hand, a client may request advice relating to a transaction that has already been executed. Research relating to a completed transaction or other past event is referred to as *a posteriori* (after the fact) research. Frequently, many advantages accrue to conducting a priori rather than a posteriori research. For example, if research reveals that a proposed transaction will have an unfavorable impact on financial statements, the transaction can be abandoned or possibly restructured to avoid undesirable consequences. These options are not available, however, once a transaction is completed.

There is a need to conduct both pure and applied research. When either type of research is conducted properly, the methodology is the same; only the environment differs. Both types of research require sound research design to resolve the issue under investigation effectively and efficiently. No matter how sophisticated an individual becomes in any aspect of accounting or auditing, he or she will always have problems associated with research. In

---

1 *AICPA Technical Practice Aids*, Vol. 1, Chicago, Commerce Clearing House, Inc.
2 Barron, Orie E., et al., "Using Analysts' Forecasts to Measure Properties of Analysts' Information Environment," *The Accounting Review*, Vol. 72, No. 4 (October, 1998): 421–433.

such situations, the basic research approach developed by the novice researcher can demonstrate his or her competence as a trained professional.

RESEARCH QUESTIONS

Individual companies or CPA firms conduct private research to resolve specific accounting or auditing issues relating to a company or client. The results of this research often lead to new firm policies or procedures in the application of existing authoritative literature. In this research process, the practitioner (researcher) must answer the following basic questions:

1. Do I have the knowledge to answer the question without conducting research, or must I consult authoritative references?
2. What is authoritative literature?
3. Does authoritative literature address the issue under review?
4. If authoritative literature does exist, where can I find it and develop a conclusion efficiently and effectively?
5. If there exists more than one alternative or more than one authoritative source, which alternative do I select? In other words, what is the hierarchy of authoritative support?
6. If authoritative literature does not exist, what approach do I follow in arriving at a conclusion?
7. Can I utilize the Internet or computerized databases in the research process?
8. How do I document my findings or conclusions?

The purpose of this text is to provide the understanding and the research skills needed to answer these questions. The "what's," "why's," and "how's" of practical professional accounting research, including tax research and fraud investigations, are discussed with emphasis on the following topics:

- How do I apply a practical research methodology in a timely manner?
- What are generally accepted accounting principles and auditing standards?
- What constitutes substantial authoritative support?
- What are the available sources and hierarchy of authority of current accounting and auditing literature?
- What databases are available for computer retrieval as an aid to researching a particular problem?
- What role can the Internet (the information superhighway) have in the research process?

This text presents a practical research approach along with discussions of various research tools, and demonstrates this research approach through the use of a number of practical problems presented as case studies. The text also addresses the importance of critical thinking and effective writing skills that the researcher should possess in executing the research process. Specific tips on these skills are presented in subsequent chapters.

NATURE OF PROFESSIONAL RESEARCH

This text focuses on professional research within the practicing segment of the accounting profession, in contrast to theoretical research often conducted by academicians. Today's practitioner must be able to conduct properly and systematically the research required to arrive at appropriate and timely conclusions regarding the issues at hand. Efficient and effective accounting, tax, or auditing research is often critical in order to determine the proper recording, classification, and disclosure of economic events; to determine compliance with authoritative pronouncements; or to determine the preferability of alternative procedures.

Additional examples of issues frequently encountered by the practitioner include such questions as

- What are the accounting or auditing implications of a new transaction?
- Does the accounting treatment of the transaction conform with generally accepted accounting principles?
- What are the financial statement disclosure requirements?
- What is the auditor's association and responsibility when confronted with supplemental information presented in annual reports but not as part of the basic financial statements?
- How does the accountant proceed in a fraud investigation?

Responding to these often complex questions has become more difficult and time-consuming as the financial accounting and reporting requirements and the auditing standards increase in number and complexity. The research process often is complicated further when the accountant or auditor researches a practical issue for which no authoritative literature exists, or the authoritative literature does not directly address the question.

As a researcher, the practitioner should possess certain desired characteristics or attributes which aid in the research process. These characteristics include inquisitiveness, open-mindedness, patience, thoroughness, and perseverance.[3] The researcher needs to be inquisitive while gathering the information needed to obtain a clearer picture of the research problem. Proper problem definition is the most critical component in research. An improperly stated issue or problem often leads to the wrong conclusion or solution no matter how carefully the research process was executed. Likewise, the researcher should be open-minded, so as not to draw conclusions before the research process is completed. A preconceived solution can result in biased research in which the researcher merely seeks evidence to support a preconceived position rather than search for the most appropriate solution. The researcher must examine the facts, obtain and review authoritative literature, evaluate alternatives, and then draw conclusions based upon research evidence. The execution of an efficient research project takes patience and thoroughness. This is emphasized in the planning stage of the research process, whereby all relevant factors are identified and all extraneous data or "noise" is controlled. Finally, the researcher must work persistently in order to finish the research on a timely basis.

Perhaps the most important characteristic of the research process is its ability to "add value" to the services provided by the accountant or auditor. A good auditor not only renders an opinion on a client's financial statements, but also identifies available reporting alternatives that may benefit the client. The ability of a researcher to provide such information becomes more important as the competition among accounting firms for clients becomes more intense. Researchers who identify reporting alternatives that provide benefits or avoid pitfalls will provide a strong competitive edge to the firm that employs them. Providing these tangible benefits to clients through careful and thorough research is an outstanding method of differentiating a firm's services from those of its competitors.

---

3   Wallace, Wanda, "A Profile of a Researcher," *Auditor's Report*, American Accounting Association, (Fall 1984): 1–3.

ECONOMIC CONSEQUENCES OF STANDARDS SETTING

It has become apparent that various accounting standards can bring about far-reaching economic consequences, as has been demonstrated by the Financial Accounting Standards Board (FASB) in addressing such issues as restructuring costs, financial instruments, stock options, and postemployment benefits. In evaluating these and other concerns, various difficulties often can arise in the proper accounting for the economic substance of a transaction within the current accounting framework.

In the allocation of resources in today's world-wide capital markets, many different types of information are available. Of particular interest to many allocation decisions is the use of financial information reported via an entity's financial statements. Since these financial statements must conform to generally accepted accounting principles, the standard setting bodies, such as the FASB or the GASB (the Governmental Accounting Standards Board), will conduct careful and comprehensive research in the development of a proposed standard due to its economic impact on the resource allocation decisions of investors and creditors in today's capital markets. Standards-setting authorities are placing greater emphasis upon the cost/benefit issues for the entity and society as a whole when contemplating the issuance of a new accounting standard. For example, the handling of off-balance sheet transactions has at times forced the selection of one business decision over another; this often produces results that may be less oriented to the users of financial statements.

In today's environment, the researcher conducting accounting and auditing research needs to be cognizant of the economic and social impact that various accepted accounting alternatives may have on society in general and the individual entity in particular. Such economic and social concerns are becoming a greater factor in the evaluation and issuance of new accounting standards, as discussed more thoroughly in Chapter 5.

ROLE OF RESEARCH IN THE ACCOUNTING FIRM

Although research is often conducted by accountants in education, industry, or government, accounting and auditing research is particularly important in the public accounting firm. Due to the number and diversity of clients served, public accounting firms constantly engage in research on a wide range of accounting and auditing issues.

As a reflection of today's society, significant changes have occurred in the accounting environment. The practitioner today requires greater knowledge because of greater complexity in many business transactions and the proliferation of new authoritative pronouncements. As a result, practitioners should possess the ability to conduct efficient research. An analogy can be drawn between an accountant's responsibility to conduct accounting/auditing research and an attorney's responsibility to conduct legal research. Rule One of the Model Rules of Professional Conduct of the American Bar Association states:

> *A lawyer should provide competent representation to a client. Competent representation requires the legal knowledge, skill, thoroughness, and preparation reasonably necessary for the representation.*

In a California court decision, this rule was interpreted to mean that each lawyer must be able to completely research the law and is expected to know "those plain and elementary principles of law which are commonly known by well-informed attorneys and to discover the rules which, although not commonly known, may readily be found by standard research techniques."[4]

In this case, the plaintiff recovered a judgment of $100,000 in a malpractice suit that was based upon the malpractice of the defendant lawyer in researching the applicable law.

The U.S. Securities & Exchange Commission (SEC) has also stressed the importance of effective accounting research through an enforcement action brought against an accountant. In *Accounting and Auditing Enforcement Release No. 420*, the SEC instituted a public administrative proceeding against a CPA. The Commission charged that the CPA failed to exercise due care in the conduct of an audit. The enforcement release specifically stated the following:

> *In determining whether the (company) valued the lease properly, the (CPA) failed to consult pertinent provisions of GAAP or any other accounting authorities. This failure to conduct any research on the appropriate method of valuation constitutes a failure to act with due professional care. . . .*

Thus, it is vital that the professional accountant possess the ability to find and locate applicable authoritative pronouncements and to ascertain their current status. The purpose of this text is to aid the researcher in meeting this objective.

Due to this expanding complex environment and proliferation of pronouncements, certain accounting firms have created a specialization in the research function within the firm. Common approaches used in practice include the following:

1. The staff at the local office conducts day-to-day research with industry-specific questions referred to industry specialists within the firm.
2. Selected individuals in the local or regional office are designated as research specialists and all research questions within the office or region are brought to their attention for research.
3. The accounting firm establishes at the executive office of the firm a centralized research function that handles questions for the firm as a whole on technical issues.

The task of accurate and comprehensive research can be complex and challenging. However, one can meet the challenge by becoming familiar with a methodology of conducting selected steps (a research process) in the attempt to solve an accounting or auditing issue.

A more in-depth look at a typical organizational structure for policy decision making and research on accounting and auditing matters within a multi-office firm that maintains a research department is depicted in Figure 1–1.

The responsibilities of a firm-wide accounting and auditing policy decision function include maintaining a high level of professional competence in accounting and auditing matters; developing and rendering high-level policies and procedures on accounting and auditing issues for the firm; disseminating the firm's policies and procedures to appropriate personnel within the firm on a timely basis; and supervising the quality control of the firm's practice. Research plays an important role in this decision-making process.

The Policy Committee and Executive Subcommittee, as shown in Figure 1–1, generally consist of highly competent partners with many years of practical experience. The Policy Committee's primary function is to evaluate significant accounting and auditing issues and establish firmwide policies on these issues. The Executive Subcommittee function is to handle the daily ongoing

---

4   Smith and Lewis, 13 Cal. 3d 349, 530 P.2d 589, 118 Cal Reptr. 621 (1975).

Figure 1–1 Organizational Framework for Policy Decision Making and Research Within a Typical Multioffice Accounting Firm

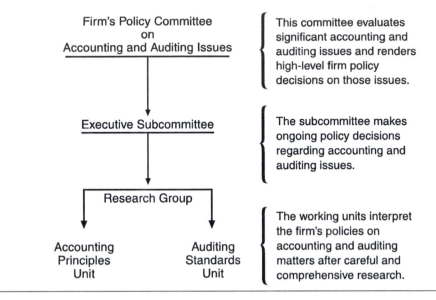

policy decisions (lower-level decisions) for the firm as a whole. The responsibility of the accounting and auditing research units is to interpret firm policies in the context of specific client situations. Frequently, technical accounting and auditing issues that arise during the course of a client engagement can be resolved through research conducted by personnel assigned to the engagement. When a matter cannot be resolved satisfactorily at the local-office level, assistance is requested from the firm's research units. These units conduct careful and comprehensive research in arriving at the firm's response to technical inquiries. This response is then disseminated to the various offices of the firm for future reference in handling similar technical issues.

Practical accounting and auditing research is not confined to the public accounting firm. All accountants should possess the ability to conduct efficient research and develop logical and well-supported conclusions on a timely basis. The research process is identical, whether the researcher is engaged in public accounting, management accounting, internal auditing, educational, or governmental accounting or auditing. Thus the process remains the same; only the environment differs.

OVERVIEW OF THE RESEARCH PROCESS

The research process in general is often defined as the scientific method of inquiry, a systematic study of a particular field of knowledge in order to discover scientific facts or principles. The basic purpose of research, therefore, is to obtain knowledge or information that specifically pertains to some issue or problem. An operational definition of research encompasses the following elements:[5]

1. There must be an orderly investigation and analysis of a clearly defined issue or problem.

---

5   Luck, David J., Hugh C. Wales, and Donald A. Taylor, *Marketing Research* (Englewoood Cliffs: Prentice-Hall, Inc., 1961), 5.

2. An appropriate scientific approach must be used.
3. Adequate and representative evidence must be gathered and documented.
4. Logical reasoning must be employed in drawing conclusions.
5. The validity or reasonableness of the conclusions must be supported.

With this general understanding of the research process, practical accounting and auditing research may be defined as follows:

> *Accounting or auditing research—A systematic and logical approach employing critical thinking skills to obtain and document evidence underlying a conclusion relating to an accounting or auditing issue or problem currently confronting the professional accountant.*

The basic steps in the research process are illustrated in Figure 1–2 with an overview presented in the following sections. As indicated in the illustration, each step of the research process should be documented carefully; the steps in the research process are closely interrelated. In the actual process of executing each step, the researcher may also find it necessary to refine the work done in previous steps. The refinement of the research process is discussed more fully in Chapter 8.

Figure 1–2 The Research Process

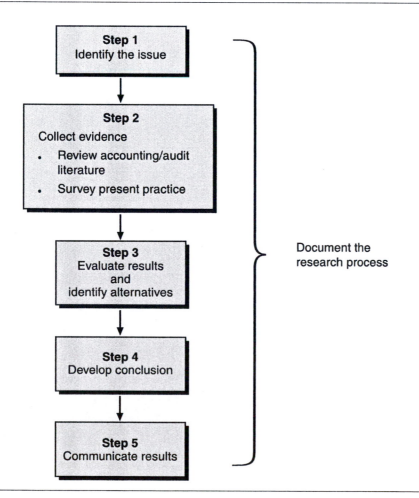

Identify the Issue

The researcher's first task is to gather the facts surrounding the particular problem. However, problem-solving research cannot begin until the researcher clearly and concisely defines the problem. One needs to know the "why" and "what" about the issue in order to begin the research process. Unless the researcher knows why the issue has been brought to his or her attention, he or she might have difficulty knowing what to research. The novice researcher may find it difficult to distinguish between relevant and irrelevant information. When this happens, it is advisable to err on the side of gathering too many facts rather than too few. As he or she becomes more knowledgeable, the researcher will become more skilled at quickly isolating the relevant facts.

In many cases, the basic issue has already been identified before the research process begins; e.g., when a client requests advice as to the proper handling of a specific transaction. However, further refinement of the exact issue is often required. This process of refining the issue at hand is referred to as **problem distillation**, whereby a general issue is restated in sufficiently specific terms. If the statement of the issue is too broad or general, the researcher is apt to waste valuable time consulting sources irrelevant to the specific issue.

Factors to consider in the identification and statement of the issue include the exact source of the issue, justification for the issue, and a determination of the scope of the issue. To successfully design and execute an investigation, the critical issue must be stated clearly and precisely. As explained in Chapter 7, many research tools, especially computerized databases, are indexed by a set of descriptive words. Since keywords aid in reference identification, failure to describe the facts (the key words) in sufficient detail can cause a researcher to overlook important sources. Undoubtedly, writing a clear, concise statement of the problem is the most important task in research. Failure to frame all the facts can, and often will, lead to an erroneous conclusion.

Collect Evidence

As previously stated, problem-solving research cannot begin until the researcher defines the problem. Once the issue is adequately defined, the researcher is ready to proceed with step two of the research process, the collection of evidence. This step usually encompasses a detailed review of relevant authoritative accounting or auditing literature and a survey of present practice. In collecting evidence, the researcher should be familiar with the various sources available, and know which ones to use, which ones not to use, and the order in which they should be examined.

This early identification of the relevant sources will aid in the efficient conduct of the research steps. A number of research tools including electronic databases and the Internet that will aid in the collection of evidence are available and are discussed in detail in Chapters 4 through 7. In cases where authoritative literature does not exist on a specific issue, the practitioner should develop a theoretical resolution of the issue based upon a logical analysis of the factors involved. In addition, the researcher needs to evaluate the economic consequences of the various alternatives in the development of a conclusion. It should also be noted that, in practice, a solution is not often readily apparent. Professional judgment and theoretical analysis will be key elements in the research process.

Evaluate Results and Identify Alternatives

Once a practitioner has completed a thorough investigation and collection of evidence, the next step is to evaluate the results and identify alternatives for one or more tentative conclusions to the issue. Each alternative should be fully supported by authoritative literature or a theoretical justification with complete and concise documentation. One cannot expect to draw sound conclusions from faulty information. Sound documented conclusions can be drawn only when the information has been properly collected, organized, and interpreted.

Further analysis and research may be needed as to the appropriateness of the various alternatives identified. This reevaluation may require further discussions with the client or consultations with colleagues. In discussing an issue with a client, the researcher should be cognizant of the fact that management may not always be objective in evaluating alternatives. For example, the issue may involve the acceptability of an accounting method that is currently being used by the client. In such cases, the research is directed toward the support or rejection of an alternative already decided on by management. The possibility of bias should cause the researcher to retain a degree of skepticism in discussions with the client regarding a conclusion.

Develop Conclusion

After a detailed analysis of the alternatives, including economic consequences, the researcher develops a conclusion. The final conclusion selected from the alternatives identified should be documented thoroughly and be well supported by the evidence gathered. The conclusion is then presented to the client or others as a proposed solution to the issue.

Communicate Results

The most important point in the communication of the conclusion reached, which often takes the form of a research memorandum, is that the words selected must be objective and unbiased. The memorandum should contain a clear statement of the issue researched, a statement of the facts, a brief and precise discussion of the issue, and a straightforward conclusion based upon supported and identified authoritative literature. The written communication should follow the conventional rules of grammar, spelling, and punctuation. Nothing diminishes credibility faster than misspellings, incorrect grammar, or misuse of words.

In drafting the memo, common errors to be avoided include excessive discussion of the issue and facts, which indicates that the memo has not been drafted with sufficient precision; excessive citations to authoritative sources—cite only the main support for the conclusion reached; and appearing to avoid a conclusion by pleading the need for additional facts. Novice researchers too often include information gathered after hours of research that was found to be wholly irrelevant to the issue at hand. The desire to include this information in the memorandum should be avoided since it often distracts from the current solution to the problem. Be careful and precise.

A serious weakness in any part of the research process threatens the worth of the entire research effort. Therefore, each segment of the process should be addressed with equal seriousness as to its impact on the entire research project.

SUMMARY

The importance of research in the work of a practicing professional accountant should now be apparent. Few practitioners ever experience a work week which does not include the investigation and analysis of an accounting or auditing issue. Thus, every professional accountant should possess the ability to conduct practical research in a systematic way. The goal of this text is to aid the practitioner in developing a basic framework, or methodology, to assist in the research process.

The emphasis of the following chapters is on applied or practical research that deals with solutions to immediate issues rather than pure or basic research that has little or no present-day application. Chapters 2 and 3 present an overview of the importance of critical thinking and effective writing skills that every researcher (accountant/auditor) must possess to be an effective professional. Chapter 4 presents how the practitioner can use the Internet for research. Chapters 5 and 9 provide an overview of the environment of accounting and auditing/attestation research, with an emphasis on the standard-setting process. The hierarchy of the authoritative literature that aids in determining where to start and end the research process is also presented in these two chapters. Chapter 6 presents a discussion of the sources of authoritative literature as well as an explanation of access techniques to the professional literature. Chapter 7 discusses other available research tools that may aid in the efficient and effective conduct of practical research, with an emphasis on computerized research via various databases that exist. Chapter 8 concludes with a refinement of the research process by presenting specific annotated procedures for conducting and documenting the research process via a comprehensive problem.

Chapter 10 provides the basic steps of tax research and various Web sites that can be utilized. (Enclosed with this text is an optional CD [On Point] for tax research.) Chapter 11 will provide an overview of fraud and insights into the basic techniques of fraud investigation, since more practitioners are entering the specialized field of forensic accounting.

DISCUSSION QUESTIONS

1. Define the term *research*.
2. Explain what accounting or auditing research is.
3. Why is accounting or auditing research necessary?
4. What is the objective of accounting or auditing research?
5. What role does research play within an accounting firm or department? Who conducts the research?
6. What are the functions or responsibilities of the Policy Committee and Executive Subcommittee within a multioffice firm?
7. Identify and explain some basic questions the researcher must address in performing accounting and/or auditing research.
8. Differentiate between *pure* and *applied* research.
9. Identify the characteristics that a researcher (practitioner) should possess.
10. Distinguish between *a priori* and *a posteriori* research.
11. Explain the analogy of the California court decision dealing with legal research as it relates to the accounting practitioner.
12. Explain how the research process adds value to the services offered by an accounting firm.
13. What economic consequences are considered in the standards setting process?
14. Compare and contrast the varying views of research.
15. Explain the five basic steps involved in the research process.

16. Discuss how research can support or refute a biased alternative.
17. Explain what is meant by problem distillation and its importance in the research process.
18. Your conclusion to the research will often be presented to your boss or client in the form of a research memorandum. Identify the basic points that should be contained in this memo. Also identify some common errors that should be avoided in the drafting of the memo.
19. Explain the necessity of critical thinking in the research process.
20. Why did the SEC bring an Enforcement action against a CPA concerning research?

CHAPTER 2

Critical Thinking in Research

LEARNING OBJECTIVES

After completing this chapter, you should understand:

- The definition of critical thinking.
- The elements of critical thinking.
- Different levels of thinking.
- The universal elements of reasoning.
- How critical thinking skills can help professional accountants "add value" to their services.

Change is accelerating in today's environment and the pressure to respond is intensifying. As new technology and global realities work their ways through the accounting profession, these changes and realities are becoming increasingly complex. Critical thinking is necessary for effectively addressing these dynamic changes.

Clients now expect professional accountants to "add value" to what they observe, read, and write; that is, evaluate complex systems and information, and detect, predict, advise, and recommend appropriate courses of action. Critical thinking is the process enveloping these activities to help provide this added value and to communicate the results effectively to others.

Today's practitioners must respond to the progressive diversity and complexity of accounting practice and develop life-long learning skills which focus on their ability to think critically; i.e., to understand, apply, and adapt concepts and principles in a variety of contexts and circumstances. As the accounting profession continues to evolve, accountants must master critical thinking skills in direct response to their changing roles in information technology and as advisors or decision makers in organizations that face greater competition and become more global in scope. Descriptors of critical thinking have been summarized as follows:

1. Critical thinking is nonalgorithmic. The path of an action is not fully specified in advance.
2. Critical thinking is often complex.
3. Critical thinking often yields multiple solutions (rather than unique solutions) that need to be analyzed with their respective costs and benefits.
4. Critical thinking involves making interpretations.
5. Critical thinking involves the application of multiple criteria.
6. Critical thinking involves uncertainty, and it requires an ability to tolerate ambiguity and uncertainty.

7. Critical thinking involves self-regulation of the thinking process.
8. Critical thinking involves imposing meaning and finding structure in apparent disorder.
9. Critical thinking requires effort. It entails intense elaboration and careful judgment.[1]

The following sections provide some further insights into the development of these skills.

CRITICAL THINKING: A DEFINITION

There is nothing more important or practical to the accounting practitioner than sound thinking. In every circumstance of life, good thinking has its rewards. Poor thinking will inevitably cause problems, waste time, and ensure frustration. Simply stated, critical thinking is the art of utilizing your best thinking given your circumstances and limited knowledge and skills. However, to improve your thinking, you must learn to become a more effective "critic" of your thinking. As you become more proficient in critical thinking, you also become more proficient in using and assessing issues and objectives, problems and solutions, information and data, assumptions and interpretations, and different points of view and frames of reference.

Critical thinking has many definitions. The *American Heritage Dictionary* defines **critical** as "characterized by careful and exact evaluation and judgment." The word is not negative or neutral. "Critical thinking" points to a positive ability in those who possess it. Critical thinking focuses on problem definition and problem solving; it is a rational response to questions that cannot be answered definitively and for which all relevant information may be unavailable. Its purpose is to explore situations to arrive at optimal, justifiable hypotheses or conclusions. It rests on a basic wariness; a willingness to take nothing for granted and to approach each experience as if it were unique. Although it keeps a constant purpose—to understand—its goal usually leads to evaluation and, therefore, to judgment.

This approach is quite different from other methods of thinking. Ideas are always present in our minds; hence we are always "thinking" in one way or another. Daydreaming is one kind of thinking (usually an unfocused kind), as is remembering (focused but uncreative—simple information retrieval). But critical thinking is purposeful, goal-oriented, and creative. It is an active process rooted in a series of qualities that add up to the attitude we call **wariness**, which is taking nothing for granted.

It is an axiom among professional writers that good writing always results from intensive **rewriting**; critical thinking is basically **rethinking**, or refusing the obvious and easy way. The qualities that lie behind rethinking are these:

- A willingness to say "I don't know."
- An openness to alternative ways of seeing and doing—alternatives that are based on understanding how things work.
- An interest in the ideas of others shown by paying attention to them—even when they don't agree with yours.
- Thoughtfulness, or caring, that is shown by genuine curiosity, not just idle curiosity.

---

1 Resnick, Lauren B., *Education and Learning to Think* (Washington, D.C.: National Academy Press, 1987).

- A desire to find out what other people have done and thought.
- An insistence on getting the best evidence before you make up your mind.
- An openness to your own intuition.[2]

The purpose of critical thinking is always the same; to understand. But the goal goes beyond the purpose: critical thinking almost invariably leads to evaluation and therefore to judgment. In the end, you will judge the value of that which you have reflected on.

Critical thinking is a process of understanding how thinking and learning work, using *higher order* skills to comprehend issues, and analyzing, synthesizing, and assessing those ideas logically. Critical thinking focuses on an attitude and the activity of using "higher order" reasoning skills, including:

1. **Analysis** of a problem, or breaking ideas into their component parts to consider each of them separately.
2. **Synthesis** or the connection among different components or ideas in order to derive relationships that tie the parts of an answer together.
3. **Critical assessment** of the conclusions reached, requiring an examination of the conclusions for soundness of reasoning and logic. Accountants must master critical thinking skills to engage effectively in the research and problem solving process.

Thus, the ability to reason critically is an essential, fundamental skill to acquiring knowledge in any discipline, one that new accountants should acquire as soon as possible. To summarize, critical thinking includes:

1. Formulating and identifying deductively- and inductively-warranted conclusions from available evidence.
2. Recognizing the structure of arguments (premises, conclusions and implicit assumptions).
3. Assessing the consistency, inconsistency, logical implications and equivalence among statements.
4. Recognizing explanatory relations among statements.

AN OUTLINE OF CRITICAL THINKING

The difficulty in discussing critical thinking concisely springs from two characteristics of critical thinking itself, as Boostrom explains:

> *First, clear thinking results less from practicing skills than from adopting such attitudes as persistence, open-mindedness, thoroughness, and flexibility. . . . Second, thinking is not a single process that can be divided into a series of steps. Instead, it is a family of processes that enlighten and support each other.*[3]

It is this complexity that Harold Bloom attempted to analyze and define when in 1956 he published his taxonomic table of kinds of thought. An example is presented in Figure 2–1. As a side note, many of the professional accounting examinations (i.e., the Uniform CPA Exam) are modifying their exam questions in order to test the advanced critical thinking skills of candidates (levels 4, 5, 6).

---

2   Boostrom, Robert, *Developing Creative and Critical Thinking: An Integrated Approach* (Chicago: National Textbook Co., 1992), 24–25.
3   *Ibid.*, Teacher's Manual, 1.

Figure 2–1 Example of Applying and Understanding Bloom's Taxonomy

Level No.	Major Categories in Bloom's Taxonomy	Illustrative General Instructional Objectives	Illustrative Behavioral Terms for Stating Specific Learned Outcomes
1.	**Knowledge** represents recalling previously learned materials.	Knows common terms, specific facts, basic concepts and principles.	Defines, describes, labels, lists, reproduces, selects, and states.
2.	**Comprehension** involves "grasping" the material, including translating words into numbers, summarizing or interpreting the materials, and estimating future trends.	Understands facts and principles; translates verbal materials into mathematical formulas; estimates future consequences implied in the data; and justifies methods and procedures.	Converts, defends, distinguishes, estimates, extends, explains, predicts, rewrites, and summarizes.
3.	**Application** of the use of previously learned materials into new situations.	(Correctly) applies laws and theories into new and practical situations.	Changes, computes, demonstrates, discovers, manipulates, modifies, shows, solves, and uses.
4.	**Analysis** breaks down the material into its component parts to understand better its organizational structure.	Recognizes unstated assumptions and logical gaps in reasoning; distinguishes between facts and inferences; and evaluates the relevancy of data.	Breaks down, diagrams, differentiates, discriminates, distinguishes, infers, outlines, selects, relates, separates, and subdivides.
5.	**Synthesis** puts parts together to form a new whole, usually involving creative behaviors and new patterns or structures (e.g., developing a new schema for classifying information).	Writes a well-organized research paper; gives a well-organized speech; integrates learning from different areas into a new plan to solve a problem; and formulates a new schema to classify objects or events.	Categorizes, combines, compiles, composes, creates, devises, assigns, explains, generates, recognizes, plans, revises, reorganizes, rewrites, tells, or writes.
6.	**Evaluation** judges the value of the statement (based upon definite criteria) for a given purpose. The criteria can be internal (organization) or external (relevant to the given purpose).	Judges the logical consistency of the presented material, how well the data "support" the "conclusions" and how well the end product adheres to the internal and external criteria.	Appraises, compares, concludes, criticizes, contrasts, explains, justifies, interprets, relates, summarizes, and supports.

In the nineteenth century, Oliver Wendell Holmes spoke of one-story, two-story, and three-story people: The one-storied were fact collectors with no aims beyond the facts; the two-storied were able to compare, reason, and generalize using the results of the fact-collectors' labors; the three-storied individuals could idealize, imagine, and predict. In our own day, the Illinois Renewal Institute has posited three levels of thought. The lowest level is **recall**, in which one defines, describes, lists, recites, and selects. The second level is **process**, in which one compares, contrasts, classifies, sorts, distinguishes, explains, infers, sequences, analyzes, synthesizes and analogizes. The third level is **application**, in which one evaluates, generalizes, imagines, judges, predicts, speculates, hypothesizes, and forecasts. Useful as this scheme may be, Bloom's taxonomy remains the most detailed and the most widely accepted.

Bloom hypothesized that higher-order knowledge occurs with the use of higher-level skills (which are often called critical thinking skills). Practitioners should use higher-level application skills to complement lower-level recall skills by focusing on "what" successful accountants do (to "add value" to their organizations' goals) and questioning the bases of the provided assumptions and standards.

Bloom's taxonomy implies that the levels of thinking are incremental: one must be able to perform at level four, for example, before moving up to level five. (The ideal reader, writer, accountant, or auditor moves up the levels until he or she can perform at the top level). To exercise the level six skills, one must already possess the skills below that level. To be able to *infer* properly, for example, one must often be able first to define and describe accurately the objects or situations from which one will infer. The skills increase in complexity as the level rises. To analyze a situation, for example, is a far more complicated process than simply to recall a situation, while to evaluate a situation (using definite criteria and for a given purpose) is more complicated than either of the others. It can be argued that the basic differences between the levels are largely a matter of attitude, not procedure. That is, the ability to progress up through the levels depends, first, on one's ability to internalize the qualities noted on pages 15 and 16. Secondly, this progress depends on the ability to make certain specific decisions, some of which are listed below.

THE ELEMENTS OF CRITICAL THINKING

The following list of decisions is freely adapted from a longer list by Robert H. Ennis.[4]

1. Deciding on the meaning of a statement.

    At a low level, grasping the meaning of a statement involves simply not mistaking the intent of a statement, and the evidence of that is the ability to put the statement into one's own words without significantly altering the meaning. But as one moves up the levels, the skill changes. For example, the formula (the statement) for determining the sum of an arithmetic series of numbers is this:

$$(n + 1) \times (n/2)$$

    Being able to recall the formula (one level) and apply it (a higher level) does not demonstrate that one knows what the statement means, i.e., the sum of each of the pairs that can be made in the series multiplied by the number of pairs yields the sum of the whole series.[5] Deriving that meaning takes a higher order of reading skill than simple paraphrase. Thus, grasping a statement's meaning implies that one can apply the statement in a situation and can recognize statements that contradict or support it. This concept forms the basis of all the other logical aspects, each differing only in the particular phase of the entire realm of critical thinking. In accounting and auditing research, a clear and concise meaning of the issue is essential to effective research.

2. Deciding whether a conclusion follows necessarily from the underlying data.

---

4   Ennis, Robert H., "A Concept of Critical Thinking," *Harvard Educational Review*, 32 No. 1 (Winter, 1962), 81–111.
5   *Ibid.*, 96.

Only deductive reasoning yields "necessary" conclusions. "A conclusion follows necessarily if its denial contradicts the assertion of the premises,"[6] and from this one criterion come all the rules of deductive reasoning, whether mathematical, "if-then," or syllogistic reasoning. For example, an auditor must ascertain that the client's accounts receivable balance is both reasonable and collectible before rendering an audit opinion on the (entire) financial statements. This process requires applying generally accepted auditing standards, which, in turn, often relies heavily upon deductive logic.

3. Deciding whether an observation statement is reliable.

Ennis provides what he calls a "combined list of principles from the fields of law, history, and science" that deal with the reliability of observation statements.

Observation statements tend to be more reliable if the observer:

- Was unemotional, alert, and disinterested.
- Was skilled at observing the sort of thing observed.
- Had sensory equipment that was in good condition.
- Has a reputation for veracity.
- Used precise techniques.
- Had no preconception about the way the observation turned out.

Observation statements tend to be more reliable if the observation conditions:

- Were such that the observer had good access.
- Provided a satisfactory medium of observation.

Observation statements tend to be more reliable to the extent that the statement:

- Is close to being a statement of direct observation.
- Is corroborated.
- Is corroboratable.
- Comes from a disinterested source with a reputation for veracity.

Observation statements, if based on a record, tend to be more reliable if the record:

- Was made at the time of observation.
- Was made by the person making the statement.
- Is believed by the person making the statement to be correct.

Finally, observation statements tend to be more reliable than inferences made from them.[7]

In an audit environment, auditors gathering and evaluating audit evidence should apply this taxonomy. For example, externally generated data is generally assumed to be more reliable than those derived from internal sources (e.g., bank or other third-party confirmations are a more reliable source of evidence than internal bank reconciliations, correspondence files, or general ledger details).

4. Deciding whether an inductive conclusion is warranted.

An inductive conclusion is an inference, a probable (but not certain) conclusion drawn from two or more premises. An inductive conclusion can be tested by asking (1) Are the premises reliable? and (2) If the premises are reliable, is the

---

6   *Ibid.*, 87.
7   *Ibid.*, 90.

conclusion convincing? Premises can be judged by whether the evidence that went into their making meets a series of criteria:

- **Sufficient.** Does the accountant have adequate evidence to reach a proper conclusion or should further questions be asked?
- **Representative.** Is the evidence provided objective?
- **Relevant.** Does the evidence relate directly to the provided assertion?
- **Accurate.** Does the evidence come from reliable primary or secondary sources?

Often the researcher conducting accounting research will gather evidence from primary and secondary accounting sources, as explained in Chapter 5.

5. Deciding whether a statement is an assumption.

In one sense, an assumption is simply a presupposition. The statement "The Army's lack of planning caused unnecessary casualties" assumes that the Army did not plan. In such an argument, the lack of planning cannot be assumed but must be proved. In another sense, an assumption is simply a statement that the conclusion follows and depends upon. Such assumptions are checked by deciding if they are plausible and simpler than the alternatives, necessary (in empirical situations) to whatever action or event is posited, and acceptable to experts. For example, auditors spend much of their time assessing the validity of many client assumptions, including the adequacy of the allowance for doubtful accounts and the expected lives of depreciable assets.

6. Deciding whether a definition is adequate.

Persuasive definitions—those that judge a concept, as in " 'liberal' means 'standing up for the right to choose' "—are always suspect in critical thinking. Beyond persuasion, the criterion is simply, "Is this definition good enough for our purposes in this situation?" Auditors generally consider the concepts of materiality and audit risk for a client's assertion in ascertaining the sufficiency of the evidence, recognizing that the more evidence the auditor accumulates the lower the risk of misstatement.

7. Deciding whether a statement made by an alleged authority is acceptable.

There are really two questions here: Is the source an authority? Is the statement acceptable? An authority, as Ennis states, is someone who makes statements in his field, has studied the matter, has a good reputation, is disinterested and in full possession of his faculties, has followed accepted procedures in reaching his conclusions, and is aware that his reputation could be affected by his statements. Whether the statement is acceptable depends on accepting the person as an authority and then checking the specific statements by reference to the other five principles. Auditors often rely on authorities, especially to help satisfy the valuation assertion (e.g., using qualified appraisers to help value precious gems); however, the auditor should ascertain the competence, independence, and "expected reasonableness" of the authority in ascertaining how much reliance to place on the conclusions the authority gives. Also, as explained in later chapters of this text, the accounting profession has developed a hierarchy of authoritative accounting and auditing pronouncements that is utilized in the research process.

Making these decisions is critical thinking. As Boostrom states, in critical thinking "you decide first what the words mean, then whether they make sense, and finally whether you believe them."[8] Figure 2–2 provides a simplified example that will help reinforce the issue of the critical thinking process.

---

8 Boostrom, *op. cit.*, 198.

Figure 2–2 Critical Thinking Accounting Example

Purpose: To prepare a report based upon your research to answer the following client request.

Issue/Question: A major client, who maintains homes in both New York and Florida and uses both frequently throughout the year, asks you, from an economic standpoint, which state would be the best for her to establish residency in.

Answering this question quickly, intelligently, and accurately requires critical thinking to identify all the relevant factors regarding this decision and to develop proper conclusions, including focusing on such issues as (a) state income tax rates of both states, (b) state sales tax rules and rates (e.g., buying and using such "discretionary" assets as a new car), (c) property taxes (e.g., buying or selling a home), unemployment/welfare taxes, municipal taxes, inheritance taxes (e.g., considering the client's age), and (d) costs of other essentials (e.g., food, clothing, and shelter).

After identifying the relevant factors, you should focus this analysis by asking specific questions to narrow the scope of this decision to such relevant issues as:

1. Do you anticipate selling one of the homes? If so, which one?
2. If the client is approaching retirement age, should inheritance tax issues be considered?
3. Where will the client purchase and use her assets (e.g., the new car)?

The answers to these and other similar questions will affect how you proceed with this analysis, while fully considering all of the relevant factors. Considering relevant issues and eliminating irrelevant ones forms the crux of critical thinking.

This example can also help you better understand such critical thinking skills. For example, it should require the researcher to analyze, synthesize and critically assess the relevant factors. This process requires using the available evidence effectively. Specifically, the accountant should ascertain that the evidence is:

1. **Sufficient.** Does the accountant have adequate evidence to reach a proper conclusion or should he or she ask further questions (e.g., are state inheritance tax rates under review by the respective state legislatures)?
2. **Representative.** Is the evidence provided objective (e.g., will the client actually spend the requisite days in Florida to be considered a legal resident of that state)?
3. **Relevant.** Does the evidence relate directly to the provided assertion (e.g., will the client's plans to spend much time visiting her grandchildren in California impact her legal residence status)?
4. **Accurate.** Does the evidence come from reliable primary or secondary sources (e.g., can CPA firm employees observe the times spent in Florida or New York)?

Thus, the ability to reason critically is essential to the acquisition of knowledge in any discipline and may, therefore, be appropriately regarded as a fundamental skill, one that new accountants should acquire as soon as possible. Critical thinking includes:

1. Formulating and identifying deductively- and inductively-warranted conclusions from available evidence.
2. Recognizing the structure of arguments (premises, conclusions and implicit assumptions).
3. Assessing the consistency, inconsistency, logical implications, and equivalence among statements.
4. Recognizing explanatory relations among statements.

UNIVERSAL ELEMENTS OF REASONING

It is helpful for the professional accountant/researcher to concentrate on the universal elements of reasoning when using critical thinking to reason out a solution to a problem. These eight elements provide a central focus in critical thinking.[9] Whenever we think, we should proceed through these eight elements of reasoning or basic categories of questions at depicted in Figure 2–3.

AN EXAMPLE OF USING CRITICAL THINKING SKILLS

Goldratt (and Cox)'s[10] best selling business book, *The Goal*, provides another example of using critical thinking skills in a business organization. The book

---

9   Paul, Richard, *Critical Thinking: Basic Theory & Instructional Structures*, Foundation for Critical Thinking, 1998.
10   Goldratt, E.M., and J. Cox, *The Goal* (New Haven, Conn.: North River Press, 1992).

Figure 2–3 Eight Elements of Reasoning

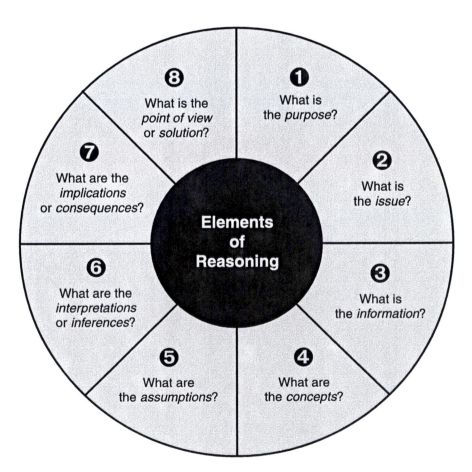

1. **Purpose.** You reason things out in order to meet some specific end, goal, or objective. If the purpose or goal is unclear or unrealistic, various problems can occur as you proceed. As an accountant/researcher, your primary goal or purpose is to complete accounting/auditing research in order to develop an answer to a particular

describes a company that has "floundered" because it conducted its business under certain constant, time honored assumptions, such as:

1. Keep all employees busy all of the time.
2. Order materials in the largest quantities possible to receive the lowest price.
3. Keep the manufacturing robots working all the time (to minimize down-time).
4. Measure the "cost" of an idle machine as its depreciation expense.
5. Allow management to change the priority of jobs in process to meet customer pressure.

Goldratt demonstrates that the company could operate much more profitably by challenging these assumptions (i.e., by using higher-order critical thinking skills), thereby yielding dramatically improved results. He showed that adhering to these "old" policies slowed efficiency rather than enhancing it. Some "new" results included:

1. Because busy employees produce unneeded inventory, thus wasting large resources, have certain production employees perform quality control and preventive maintenance rather than produce non-essential parts.
2. Because large materials orders increase unnecessary inventory, order smaller quantities of parts inventory.
3. Because robots, like employees only increase unneeded inventory, consider the cost of the inventory they produce in deciding whether to allow the robots to work.

Figure 2-3 Eight Elements of Reasoning (continued)

practical issue/problem. You should select clear and realistic purposes and evaluate your reasoning periodically to make sure you still are on target with your stated purpose.

2. **Issue.** The second element is to reason out a question or issue. This requires the formulation of the issue in a clear and relevant way. Because accounting/auditing authoritative literature is organized on keywords or concepts, clearly identifying the issue will greatly aid you in researching it.

3. **Information.** Data or information exists concerning the issue about which you are reasoning. Any defect in the data or information is a possible source of problems in conducting research. As an accounting practitioner, you will use client provided data and both authoritative and non-authoritative sources in reasoning out a solution. Therefore, you need to be mindful that the data or information may contain defects or contradictions, especially in the client data or non-authoritative sources.

4. **Concepts.** Reasoning uses concepts that include theories, principles, or rules. A basic understanding of the concepts is important as you reason out an accounting/auditing issue.

5. **Assumptions.** All reasoning begins somewhere. Incorrect assumptions in your reasoning can be a source of problems and can bias your research. You must determine that your assumptions are justifiable and how they will shape your point of view in conducting research.

6. **Interpretation.** The sixth element of reasoning requires that what you infer from your research is based upon the evidence gathered. All reasoning requires some type of interpretation of the data in order to draw conclusions from the research process.

7. **Implications.** As you conclude the research process and begin to develop conclusions, you need to consider the various implications or consequences that arise from your reasoning. Consider both negative and positive implications as you develop your conclusions.

8. **Conclusion.** The final element of reasoning is the conclusion to the research question or issue. As you develop the conclusion, be careful to have the proper point of view; one which is not too narrow or broad, or based on misleading information or contradictions.

4. Because "bottlenecks" often prevent a factory from working to its full potential, focus on reducing such operating bottleneck constraints.
5. Because rush orders generally impair the optimal timing of the production process, alter the normal work flow for "special" jobs only rarely.

Based upon the above discussion, professional accountants should develop and use critical thinking skills to add value to their services, an important task for all professionals—including newly hired employees. A summary of some necessary, basic critical thinking skills appears in Figure 2–4.

SUMMARY

Accounting professionals, whether in public accounting, management accounting, or not-for-profit accounting, provide value-added services to others in a dynamic, complex, expanding, and constantly changing profession. You should thus learn to *rethink*; to develop lifelong learning skills to think critically (to grasp the meaning of complex concepts and principles), and to judge and apply these concepts and principles to specific issues. A summary of the basic critical thinking skills is presented in Figure 2–4.

Figure 2–4 Basic Critical Thinking Skills

Skill	Description
Value Added Services	Advise, predict, detect, recommend, and evaluate.
Wariness	Take nothing for granted. Approach each experience as a "unique" event.
Rethinking	Do not perform tasks in an obvious and routine manner. Use innovative, alternative ways to perform the necessary jobs. Insist on obtaining the "best" available evidence, considering the related costs.
Evaluation and Judgment	Use definitive criteria to obtain the goal of the assignment, then apply reasonable judgment after this evaluation.
Incremental Levels of Thinking	Apply lower levels of thinking before progressing to higher ones.

DISCUSSION QUESTIONS

1. Define *critical thinking*.
2. Discuss the highest level of thinking according to Bloom's taxonomy.
3. Discuss what *grasping the meaning of a statement* implies.
4. There are five houses in a row, each of a different color, and inhabited by five people of different nationalities, with different pets, favorite drinks, and favorite sports. Use the clues below to determine who owns the monkey and who drinks water. Utilize the chart to develop your answer.

   a. The Englishman lives in the red house.
   b. The Spaniard owns the dog.
   c. Coffee is drunk in the green house.

d.   The Russian drinks tea.
e.   The green house is immediately to the right of the white house.
f.   The hockey player owns hamsters.
g.   The football player lives in the yellow house.
h.   Milk is drunk in the middle house.
i.   The American lives in the first house on the left.
j.   The table tennis player lives in the house next to the man with the fox.
k.   The football player lives next to the house where the horse is kept.
l.   The basketball player drinks orange juice.
m.   The Japanese likes baseball.
n.   The American lives next to the blue house.

	HOUSE 1	HOUSE 2	HOUSE 3	HOUSE 4	HOUSE 5
Color					
Country					
Sport					
Drink					
Pet					

5.   What kind of statement or reasoning yields a necessary conclusion?
6.   List some of the characteristics of a reliable observation statement.
7.   Discuss how one tests an inductive conclusion.
8.   Distinguish between two meanings of an assumption.
9.   Provide an example of a persuasive definition.
10. Define an authority.
11. Show how critical thinking relates to the term *professional skepticism*.
12. Show how to apply critical thinking concepts to the "theory of constraints" as dis-
     cussed in Goldratt's book *The Goal*.
13. Critical thinking applications:
     a.   Critically analyze why an asset is an asset.
     b.   Critically evaluate the pros and cons of the following statements:
          1.   Financial statements are useless because they are incomplete. Not all assets
               or liabilities are included.
          2.   Financial statements are useless because they present assets at historical
               cost rather than fair market values.
     c.   When should a liability first be reported? When should reporting of a liability
          cease?
     d.   What benefits exist for utilizing a contra "accumulated depreciation" account
          rather than crediting the asset account directly?
14. Develop a chart similar to Figure 2–3 for the following assignment: Your client,
     Baxter Controls, has requested your advice as to when a contingent liability should
     be booked (recorded) as a liability.
15. Develop a chart similar to Figure 2–3 for the following assignment: Johnson
     Electronics has requested your advice as to when assets need to be classified as cur-
     rent assets.

Writing Skills for the Professional Accountant

LEARNING OBJECTIVES

After completing this chapter, you should understand:

- How competent writing forms a key element of critical thinking skills.
- How to strengthen your writing skills.
- Elements of effective writing.
- Guidelines to word selection and sentence structure.
- The U.S. Securities and Exchange Commission's "Plain English" initiative.

As discussed in the previous chapter, accounting professionals are providing more *value-added* services to others in today's dynamic, complex, expanding, and constantly changing profession. Thus, accountants are expected to elevate their critical thinking skills—to grasp the meaning of increasingly complex concepts and principles, to judge and apply these concepts and principles to specific issues, and then to communicate the results effectively to others. All professionals must know how to write effectively. This chapter provides professional accountants with some insights to help develop their writing skills.

EFFECTIVE WRITING

Today's practitioner must demonstrate an ability to communicate effectively, in both oral and written communication. Good communication skills are emphasized in the following personal anecdotes as shared by two business professionals:

> *In accounting and all other professions, we must have the appropriate technical skills. But if we cannot communicate what we know, the value of technical skills is lessened. For example, knowing how to compute corporate income taxes is a valuable skill. Being able to tell others how to do it magnifies the value of that technical skill. Others can capitalize on your knowledge only if you can communicate it.*
> **Dennis R. Beresford, Former Chair of the Financial Accounting Standards Board**
>
> *Learning to communicate well should be a top priority for anyone aspiring to lead or advance in a career. Strong technical skills are needed, but technical ability alone will not result in career advancement. Those who develop only*

technical skills always will work for people who have both technical and leadership abilities, and communication is the key ingredient in leadership.[1]
Hugh B. Jacks, President, BellSouth Services

One popular view of the relationship between thinking and writing is that first one determines what it is he or she wants to say (thinking) and then sets these ideas down (writing). That's a misconception, but like many popular misconceptions, it contains a grain of truth: we should have some idea of where we are going before we begin a draft. But we don't carry the draft in memory and then put it into language. After all, we think in language; hence, the difference between thinking and writing is not so great as we might imagine. In addition, writing is not just a matter of putting down a complete draft; it involves putting down isolated ideas, writing reminders to ourselves, making outlines, and charting different sides of an issue. We usually write based on some form of what has already been written, not from pure thought.

Since thinking and writing are intimately related, it follows that critical thinking and effective writing are also. Effective writing is not just a matter of form but of content—garbage in, garbage out applies to more than computers. One must think critically in order to write effectively.

Writing as a Process

Writing is a way to make meaning of our experiences; in other words, it is a form of learning that occurs as a complicated chain of processes. The complication stems from the fact that writers do many things at the same time. They:

- Remember past experience (including their reading) while they plan what they intend to write (from the next word to the total document).
- Try to convey large concepts while at the same time supplying supporting evidence and details.
- Consider what they know while they consider what the audience needs to know for its unique purposes.
- Continually change their minds and revise while they try to keep their main focus, or their central idea and purpose, in mind and in the text.

Perhaps the best way to bring some order to the subject is to envision first the intended, final product. The AICPA defines effective writing *in essay answers for the CPA examination* as a series of document characteristics:

1. **Coherent organization.** Responses should be organized so that the ideas are arranged logically and the flow of thought is easy to follow. Generally, knowledge is best expressed by using short paragraphs composed of short sentences. Moreover, short paragraphs, each limited to the development of one principal idea, can better emphasize the main points in the answer. Each principal idea should be placed in the first sentence of the paragraph, followed by supporting concepts and examples.
2. **Conciseness.** Conciseness requires that candidates present complete thoughts in as few words as possible, while ensuring that important points are covered adequately. Short sentences and simple wording also contribute to concise writing.
3. **Clarity.** A clearly written response prevents uncertainty concerning the candidate's meaning or reasoning. Clarity involves using words with specific and

---

1   Himstreet, William C., Wayne M. Baty, and Carol M. Lehman, *Business Communications*, Wadsworth Publishing Co., 1993, xxxiv.

precise meaning, including proper technical terminology. Well-constructed sentences also contribute to clarity.

4. **Use of standard English.** Standard English is characterized by exacting standards of punctuation and capitalization, by accurate spelling, by exact diction, by an expressive vocabulary, and by knowledgeable usage choices.

5. **Responsiveness to the requirements of the question.** Answers should directly address the requirements of the question and demonstrate the candidate's awareness of the purpose of the writing task. Responses should not be broad expositions on the general subject matter.

6. **Appropriateness for the reader.** Writing that is appropriate for the reader takes into account the reader's background, knowledge of the subject, interests, and concerns. The requirements of some essay questions may ask candidates to prepare a written document for a certain reader, such as an engagement memorandum for a CPA's client. When the intended reader is not specified, the candidate should assume the intended reader is a knowledgeable CPA.[2]

It seems fair to assume that any professional accountant should apply the same criteria to his/her writing as suggested by the AICPA. So let us inspect these six criteria.

Of the six characteristics, three are linked to **editing** skills and three to **composing** skills. (Composing is what one does before and during the actual drafting of a paper; editing is what one does to the draft.) The editing components are conciseness, clarity, and the use of standard English. All three of these are largely matters of rewriting. That is, writers (except under unreasonable time restraints, as in some poorly timed examinations) should not trouble themselves about conciseness, clarity, and standard English in a first draft; it is only confusing and self-defeating to attempt too many tasks at once.

The three composing components are coherent organization, responsiveness to the requirements of the question, and appropriateness for the reader. That is, those three elements must be taken into consideration and dealt with before commencing the first draft. That is not to say that changes relative to these three elements will not be made in revision, but one cannot write a focused first draft without dealing with these elements first.

Composing Elements

Organization. Let us begin by considering coherent organization. Organizing requires something to organize, such as information gathered about a specific question. Effective writing begins with a question; the efficient writer begins, not with a topic or a problem, but with a question that necessitates an answer. Often the client or situation supplies the question: Where can the client get the best after-tax return on investment? Which branches should be sold? What is the best way to report unexpected earnings? A question helps focus the research that the writer must do; a topic opens up vast sources of information that requires asking specific questions.

Since this text deals with the "how to" of retrieving important and relevant information in other chapters, we will not discuss gathering information here but will assume that it was gathered. Now comes the task of evaluating the information—using critical thinking skills—and coming to a general answer to the posed question. If the writer cannot immediately discern a definitive answer, a general answer will usually emerge by the time he or she has read

---

2   Examination Division, AICPA, *Report of the Testing of Writing Skills Subtask Force of the CPA Examination Change Implementation Task Force,* September 18, 1990.

the information gathered several times. In any case, the answer helps determine what material is put into the paper.

Organizing material goes beyond putting some shape into all the information gathered; it also includes sorting material which is important and relevant to the issue and to the audience's special needs. This process is much easier if the writer commits each step to paper, even in informal notes. Often, while writing down the answer (i.e., the "focus" of the work), writers unconsciously discover or invent their organization. For example, using Figure 2–2 information, suppose a client asks which of two states she should establish residency in, New York or Florida, from an economic standpoint. Suppose that after examining the issues of state income taxes, sales and property taxes, unemployment/welfare taxes, municipal and inheritance taxes, and the cost of food, clothing, and shelter, the CPA concludes that Florida is the better choice because the tax advantages more than outweigh the higher food, clothing, and shelter costs. If the response is something like "Mrs. X would benefit more financially by establishing residency in Florida than in New York . . .," the writer normally realizes a need to spell out the reasons: ". . . because the tax advantages far outweigh the higher costs of food, clothing and shelter." Part—if not most—of the answer is now organized: the writer discusses the tax advantages, one by one, then presents the comparative costs of food, clothing, and shelter, and then moves to a conclusion showing the net differences that favor Florida.

A writer should select the pattern of organization before writing the first draft. Only four basic patterns of organization exist—which rhetoricians (e.g., Lauer and Montague)[3] call **modes**:

1. **The descriptive mode.** Description, whether physical or conceptual, moves from the whole to the part or from the part to the whole. A student facing a question about the economic causes of the American Civil War may opt for a descriptive organization with a focus that forecasts that pattern: "There were three major economic causes of the American Civil War: the struggle for control of the textile trade, the battle for the British markets, and the cost of slavery." The whole (economic causes) has been broken down into its parts.

2. **The narrative mode.** Narrative arranges objects or events in a sequence in time, usually chronological. The simplest pattern here is a chronological sequence without flashbacks for explanation. **Cause and effect** is a narrative arrangement that emphasizes the causal relationship between one part of the chronology and another. **Process** is a narrative arrangement that emphasizes repeated and repeatable chronological sequences.

3. **The classification mode.** Classification puts an object or event into a larger group, defines the group, shows how the subject shares features with the group and perhaps how it differs. Classification can be used as a kind of definition.

4. **The evaluation mode.** Evaluation consists of (a) setting standards or criteria by which something can be judged; (b) relating the subject to the criteria to show how it meets or does not meet the criteria; and (c) drawing the conclusion that follows. All patterns of organizations are members of these four modes, which are, of course, not artificial designs but **modes of thought**; they imitate patterns of human thinking. The writer needs to be consistent in following one pattern; shifts confuse the reader.

Responsiveness. The second composing element in the AICPA list is "Responsiveness to the requirements of the question." In fact, except for

---

3 Lauer, Janice, and Eugene Montague, *Four Worlds of Writing*, 3rd ed., (New York: Harper Collins, 1991), 38–39.

reasons of emphasis, this item could have been collapsed into the first composing element, "Coherent organization," or into the last, "Appropriateness for the reader."

A paper should never attempt to incorporate all that a writer knows about the subject because the answer the writer gives should include only material that is relevant and important to the issue and/or specific to the needs of the reader. (Therefore, determining what is responsive is part of the process of determining what should be included in the early stages of selecting material for organization.) Most readers don't need or want to hear about the writer's discovery process; they want the results of the process. Generally, they want application, not theory. If the writer carefully selects material by using his or her answer and his or her knowledge of the audience's needs as a selection device, the question of responsiveness will evolve on its own. For example, a staff accountant would omit much more detail in preparing a report for a subordinate than for a superior.

Appropriateness. The third composing element is "appropriateness for the reader." It is important that the writer know the level and type of experience the reader has had with the subject so that he or she does not write "down" to the reader or overestimate his knowledge. Furthermore, the writer will profit from knowing what values the reader has that relate to the subject so that he or she does not offend unknowingly. The reader's experience, level of knowledge, and attitude toward the subject help determine what the writer says. For example, a tax specialist would use different degrees of technical jargon in composing a memorandum to describe a highly technical tax issue for a client, a subordinate in the organization, or a superior in the organization.

Once the writer has a plan of organization, a rough list of the materials to be included, and a profile of the reader in mind, it is time to draft the first version. The first draft should be done without regard for mechanics (spelling, punctuation, grammar, usage); the important thing is to get the important and relevant information on paper in organized form. Once the draft is completed, it can be edited.

Editing Elements

If we use the AICPA list as a guide, editing is a matter of polishing the prose so that it possesses conciseness, clarity, and standard English.

Conciseness. A concise paper contains no extraneous matter and does not repeat itself. Hence the first editorial sweep should be for unity and coherence; that is, the writer looks for ideas, examples or facts that wander beyond the boundaries set by the focus and then removes that dross. (It is then proper for the writer to ask whether the paper now has **sufficient** material.) Accountants/auditors can best make their writing concise by eliminating unnecessary words. Writing should function like a machine in that the fewer parts needed to make it run smoothly, the better. For example, an accountant can reduce a 14-word statement: "We hope the entire staff will assist us in our efforts to reduce costs," to the eight words: "We hope the staff will help reduce costs." The second sweep should be for coherence: Does the paper follow the organizational plan? Do the pieces fit together and flow properly?

Clarity. A clear paper contains the right word choices (diction) and the most effective sentence patterns (syntax). Such choices have been made much easier by currently available software. Computer-based style checkers such as

RightWriter or one of the **Grammatik** series can identify probable trouble spots, such as overuse of the passive voice, long or esoteric words, and sentence fragments. In the end, the writer, of course, must judge what is proper and effective; the style checker only warns of problems. Furthermore, style checkers generally cannot detect dangling modifiers, squinting modifiers or lapses in subject-verb and pronoun-antecedent agreement. Style checkers are usually helpful, but they are not solutions.

Precision forms an additional important element of clear writing. That is, the meaning of the sentence must be clear. An example of poor diction may be: "While wearing a new three-piece suit, I was unable to detect the cause of the client's decline in revenues and become worrisome." This statement contains several problems including:

1. Who was wearing the three-piece suit—the client or the accountant?
2. Why make mention of the suit at all, since it bears little relationship to the accounting problem?
3. Who was being worrisome; the client or the accountant?
4. Is "worrisome" a proper term to use?

A revised, more precise version of this sentence might be: "I became worried about being unable to detect the cause of the client's decline in revenues."

Business writing suffers generally from inflation, as if the writers were secretly afraid that what they have to say is not important enough to be said plainly. Inflation produces confusion and misunderstanding, which in turn causes anger and separation between writer and reader, which is exactly the opposite of what business writing intends. Moreover, it is expensive, since inflated writing takes longer to read and understand and often is misunderstood.

One kind of inflation is the overuse of prepositional phrases, facilitated by using some form of the verb *to be*. Lanham quotes an actual sentence from a business report:

> *Normal belief is that the preparation and submission of a proposal in response to a Request for Proposal (RFP), Request for Quotation (RFQ), or a bid in response to an Invitation for Bids (IFB) is no different than that of an unsolicited proposal for a grant from the National Science Foundation or another government agency; and that if such a proposal or bid is hand-delivered to the Office of Extramural Support on a Friday afternoon, it will get mailed the same day to reach Washington, D.C. by 4:00 p.m. of the following Monday. Having read this article, however, the reader, we hope, will agree that this is an erroneous belief which has led and, if continued to be believed, will lead to unhappy experiences for all concerned.[4]*

A more precise rewriting and meaning is as follows:

> *Unsolicited grant proposals differ from ones solicited by a Request for Proposal (RFP), a Request for Quotation (RFQ), or an Invitation for Bids (IFB). If you bring a solicited proposal to our office on Friday afternoon, thinking it will be mailed that day and reach Washington by Monday at 4:00 p.m, you will be disappointed. We hope this article has shown you why.[5]*

Effective writers strive for economy and, therefore, for clarity.

Standard English. The use of standard English means both usage (which is discussed above) and mechanical exactness, has also been made easier by

---

4   Lanham, Richard, *Revising Business Prose* (New York: Charles Scribner's Sons, 1981), 1.
5   *Ibid.*, 6.

software. Writers should run their drafts through a spell checker without depending entirely on it: spell checkers will not pick up omitted words, nor do they know the difference between "their" and "there" and other homonyms. But they are invaluable in picking up simple misspellings, typographical errors, and doubled words. The writer also needs to reread carefully for punctuation errors; a good handbook is a helpful companion in this kind of editing. Some basic suggestions for word selection and sentence structure for effective writing are presented in Figure 3–1.

Success in critical thinking and effective writing comes from life-long learning. The skills come with experience and practice when the endeavors are taken seriously and when the professional realizes how intimately the two are related. Research that is not properly thought through and evaluated is useless; conclusions that are not communicated are lost. Moreover, there are dimensions to "satisfying the client" that often go unremarked. Richard Lanham writes that ". . . this is why we worry so much about bad writing. It signifies incoherent people, failed social relationships."[6]

KEY ACCOUNTING ORGANIZATIONS DEMAND IMPROVED WRITING SKILLS

Many key accounting organizations, including the AICPA, the National Commission on Fraudulent Financial Reporting [Treadway Commission], and the managing partners of the country's largest public accounting firms, have focused on the need to improve communications skills. In 1994, the AICPA changed the format, length, and content of the Uniform CPA Examination to assess writing skills. Similarly, a joint Institute of Management Accountants and the Financial Executives Institute study, as well as the Institute of Internal Auditors, have suggested that improved writing skills will improve productivity and lower training costs.

Additionally, the Securities and Exchange Commission (SEC) has entered the discussion. Its Task Force on Disclosure Simplification has chided the dense writing styles, legal jargon, and repetitive disclosures in various prospectuses and issued Rule #33-7380: "Plain English Disclosures," which requires registrants to use "Plain English" in a prospectus' cover page, summary, and risk factor sections. A prospectus is a document that outlines the main features and principal purposes for the use of the proceeds of a security offering. The SEC also issued *A Plain English Handbook: How to Create Clear SEC Disclosure*, which specifies six principles for clear writing: active voice, short sentences, everyday language, tabular presentation of complex material, no legal jargon, and no multiple negatives. An elaboration of these items follows.

---

6   Ibid., 10.

Figure 3–1 Word Selection and Sentence Structure Guidelines

1. Visualize your reader and select words familiar to him or her.
2. Use the active voice in your writing.
3. Choose short words.
4. Use technical words and acronyms with caution.
5. Select your words for precise meanings.
6. Limit your sentence content. Use short sentences.
7. Use proper punctuation in sentence development.
8. Arrange your sentences for clarity and unity.

Active Voice

The SEC noted that, in writing, the active voice with strong verbs is often easier to understand than the passive voice. In the active voice, the subject of the sentence performs the action described by the verb. Such writing follows how we think and process information. In the passive voice, the action is done to somebody or something by another agent that might not always be identified in the sentence. In documents with long and complex sentences, the passive voice often forces the reader to reread information, as in the following "before" and "after" example. The "before" material is from an actual filing. The Commission rewrote the original material as an example of how to apply the effective writing principle.

> *Before:* No person has been authorized to give any information or make any representation other than those contained or incorporated by reference in this joint proxy statement/prospectus, and, if given or made, such information or representation must not be relied upon as having been authorized.

> *After:* You should rely only on the information contained in this document or incorporated by reference. We have not authorized anyone to provide you with information that is different.

Short Sentences

The requirement for short sentences addresses a major writing problem in most disclosure documents, along with such other problems as sentence fragments and run-on sentences. A sentence fragment is just part of a sentence. Typically, in a sentence fragment either the subject or verb is left out. Also common in legal documents are run-on sentences—two independent clauses joined without any punctuation, making the sentence difficult to read. The Commission suggests that a registrant should strive to use shorter sentences of 25 to 30 words, as in the following "before and after" example.

> *Before:* Machine Industries and Great Tools, Inc., are each subject to the information requirements of the Securities Exchange Act of 1934, as amended (the "Exchange Act"), and in accordance therewith file reports, proxy statements, and other information with the Securities and Exchange Commission (the "Commission").

> *After:* We must comply with the Securities Exchange Act of 1934. Accordingly, we file annual, quarterly and current reports, proxy statements, and other information with the Securities and Exchange Commission.

Definite, Concrete, Everyday Language

Clearer communication results when writers and readers use definite and concrete words. Similarly, providing examples using one investor helps make complex information more understandable. The Commission provided the following "before and after" example to help registrants communicate in clearer, less vague language, stressing the specific identification of the transactions in the "after" example.

> *Before:* History of Net Losses. The Company has recorded a net loss under generally accepted accounting principles for each fiscal year since its inception, as well as for the interim nine months of this year. However, these results include the effect of certain significant, non-cash accounting transactions.

After: *History of Net Losses. We have recorded a net loss under general accounting principles for each year since we started business, and for the interim nine months of this year. Our losses were caused, in part, by the annual write-off of a portion of the goodwill resulting from the ten acquisitions we made during this period.*

Tabular Presentation

Tabular presentations often help organize complex information. SEC registrants using "if-then" tables also presented a clearer presentation of complex information, as in the following before and after example.

Before: *"Events of Default" under the Indenture— (i) failure to pay any interest on any Note when it becomes due and payable, and such failure shall continue for a period of 30 days; (ii) failure to pay the principal of (or premium, if any) on any Note at its Maturity (upon acceleration, optional or mandatory redemption, required repurchases or otherwise); (iii) there shall have been the entry by a court of competent jurisdiction of (a) a decree or order for relief in respect of the Company, in an involuntary case or proceeding under any applicable Bankruptcy Law or (b) a decree of order adjudging the Company bankrupt or insolvent, or seeking reorganization, arrangement, adjustment or composition of or in respect of the Company, under any applicable federal or state law, or appointing a custodian, receiver, liquidator, assignee, trustee, sequestrator . . . or any such other decree or order shall be unstayed and in effect, for a period of 60 consecutive days, the Trustee or the holders of not less than 25% in aggregate principal amount . . . shall declare all unpaid principal of (and premium, if any, on) and accrued interest on all the Notes to be due and payable immediately. . . .*

After: *(If-then presentation)*

Event of Default (If)	Remedy (Then)
Interest payment 30 days late.	*Trustee or holders of at least 25% of these notes outstanding may notify the company in writing that the principal, premium, if any, and accrued interest are immediately due and payable; or*
Upon written request of the holders of at least 25% of these notes outstanding, the Trustee shall notify the company in writing that the principal, premium, if any, and accrued and unpaid interest are immediately due and payable.	
Failure to pay principal or premium at maturity, acceleration, redemption, or repurchase.	*Same as above*
Court ordered bankruptcy, insolvency, reorganization, liquidation, or similar action continuing for 60 consecutive days.	*Neither the Trustee nor holders are required to act. The principal, accrued and unpaid interest will be immediately payable.*

Minimize Legal Jargon and Highly Technical Terms

Registration statements should use legal jargon sparingly, since it often forces readers to learn a new vocabulary that inhibits the investor's understanding of the information. In certain circumstances, jargon is unavoidable when it is necessary to communicate technical information as efficiently as possible; however, technical terminology should be defined or explained. The Commission suggests clear and common terms for better understanding as demonstrated in the following example.

> *Before: The following description encompasses all the material terms and provisions of the Notes offered hereby and supplements, and to the extent inconsistent therewith replaces, the description of the general terms and provisions of the Debt Securities (as defined in the accompanying Prospectus) set forth under the heading "Description of Debt Securities" in the Prospectus, to which description reference is hereby made.*

> *After: We disclose information about our notes in two separate documents that progressively provide more detail on the notes' specific terms: the prospectus, and this pricing supplement. Since the specific terms of notes are made at the time of pricing, rely on information in the pricing supplement over different information in the prospectus.*

No Multiple Negatives

The SEC suggests that registrants' filings avoid multiple negatives, which often makes comprehending documents more difficult, as readers must "decipher" the meaning of the negatives. Avoidance of negatives clarifies the writing, as in the following example.

> *Before: Except when an applicant has submitted a request for withdrawal without the appropriate tax identification number, the request will be honored within one business day.*

> *After: We will send your money within one business day if you include your tax identification number in your withdrawal request.*

Elements of Plain English

The Commission also stated that using plain English, or plain language, means writing well. Plain English does not consist only of one-syllable words and one-clause sentences, and it is not simplified or reduced English. It is the opposite not of elaborate language but of obscure language, for it seeks to have the message understood on the first reading. The plainness of a passage is defined in terms of the audience for that passage; it is clear, straightforward language for that audience. To put it simply, the SEC states that the use of plain English aids in writing well, and has identified four basic plain English requirements.

1. **Know your audience.** Successful communicators first identify the investor groups for whom they write. Effective writing includes analyzing the readers' needs and expectations. Writers should tailor their tone and style to their intended audience; select words that contribute to an effective writing style; and choose language based on current and future investors' educational and financial knowledge.

   Other pertinent factors in audience targeting include investor demographics (e.g., job experience, age, and income) and how the investors will read and use the document. Authors should remember that the least sophisticated investors often have the greatest need for an "understand-able" disclosure document.

2. **Know what material information needs to be disclosed.** After identifying the readers' needs and expectations, the author should gather the necessary information to be communicated. The SEC has stated that too many disclosure documents combine material and immaterial information into long, dense sentences; they do not prioritize the information and organize it logically for the reader. The Commission notes that prospectus cover pages typically includes very dense printing with sentences running 60 to 100 words in length with superfluous information—which do not "invite" the investor to read the remainder of the prospectus for key information concerning the offering.

   In coherent writing, main points should stand out. Registrants should emphasize these main points by placing them where they will attract the reader's attention. Therefore, the cover page should provide a clear, concise, and coherent "snapshot" of the offering. Subsequent sections of the prospectus would then present the details in a logical fashion.

3. **Use clear writing techniques.** Two overriding themes in clear and effective writing are **conciseness** and **clarity**. In writing documents, one should eliminate digressions and irrelevant detail. Precise diction is an important element of clear writing.

4. **Design and structure the document for ease of readability.** Readers demand properly designed documents, but typical dense printing in most prospectuses discourages reading them. Good use of white space and margins increases the readability of documents. Headings, bullet points, and graphic illustrations make a "long" document more pleasing to the eye.

   Plain English writing does not mean deleting complex information. Rather, it presents documents in an orderly and clear fashion so that the reader can better understand it.

SUMMARY

Good writing, like any craft, must be practiced continuously and correctly. Just as SEC registrants must recognize the importance of developing strong writing skills, accountants too should expect to follow many of the above suggestions throughout their careers to better meet their profession's needs.

Critical thinking and effective writing are essential tools for accounting, tax, and auditing research. A summary table of some elements of effective writing is presented in Figure 3–2. In conclusion, professional accountants should focus on developing effective writing skills to enhance their everyday practice. The concepts outlined in this chapter will be exemplified throughout the remainder of this text.

Figure 3–2 Key Points of Effective Writing

Content	Effective writing should contain relevant, "value added" content matter, a process enhanced by using critical thinking skills.
Chain of Processes	To add meaning from your experiences, convey "large" concepts, while supplying supporting evidence to these ideas.
Coherent Organization	Organize ideas logically, making the flow of thought easy to follow.
Conciseness	Use as few words as necessary to convey "complete thoughts."
Clarity	Select "effective" words to state ideas with "certainty."
Use of Standard English	Use appropriate punctuation and grammar, perhaps with the help of a computer-based spell/grammar checker.
Responsiveness	Ascertain that the answers directly address the research question.
Appropriateness for the Reader	Consider the intended reader's background and experience.

DISCUSSION QUESTIONS

1. Discuss the AICPA list of effective writing characteristics. Which are editing skills and which are composing skills?
2. What are the four basic modes of thought that can be used to develop into organizational patterns?
3. What does a writer need to know about the reader?
4. What do *unity* and *coherence* mean when applied to a piece of writing?
5. Discuss the problem of "inflation" in business prose.
6. What six principles of clear writing does SEC Rule #33-7380 identify?
7. Show why plain English writing does not mean deleting complex information.
8. What are the guidelines for word selection and sentence structure?
9. Outline how improved writing techniques help improve critical thinking skills.

Professional Research Via the Internet

LEARNING OBJECTIVES

After completing this chapter, you should understand the following:

- The role of the Internet in society.
- Uses of the Internet for the professional accountant.
- How to navigate the Internet.
- Popular search engines.
- Web sites for the professional accountant.

As the professional accountant begins a research project, he or she attempts to gather relevant information in an efficient and effective way. With the recent developments in information technology, new tools are available to aid the researcher with the task of gathering information on a timely basis; whereas in the past, library or archival searches were very time consuming. This chapter provides you with an overview of one important information technology development that will be beneficial in your search endeavors—the Internet. Information about the Internet and how to access information through the Internet will be explained. This tool and other computerized tools will be discussed throughout this text. End-of-chapter questions will allow you to utilize these tools in your search for information.

The Internet is a tool that will have significant impact on the way accounting professionals will do business and, in particular, accounting, tax, and auditing research. The Internet, often referred to as the Information Superhighway, is a global resource that connects millions of users through intercommunicating networks. Currently, the Internet contains what appears to be an unlimited amount of information that can be utilized by an individual for various projects, including research by the professional accountant. Such a resource permits an accounting professional to accomplish the following major tasks:

- **Send and receive electronic mail.** *E-mail* is the term that describes the transmitting of a message from one user to another via an electronic network. E-mail is generally text data, but graphics, pictures, and audio and video data can also be sent. Currently, auditors use e-mail to communicate with other auditors to request assistance in audit planning, share audit techniques, or even transfer audit programs.
- **Discuss various accounting, tax, or auditing issues by participating in discussion groups.** Figure 4–1 presents a sample of discussion groups on Anet, a joint venture between Australian and American academics that provides Internet services to accountants around the world. Accountants have

Figure 4–1 Sample of Anet Discussion Groups

Mailing List Name	Purpose
AAccSys–L	Provides discussion concerning matters of accounting information systems theory and practice.
AAudit–L	Provides discussion on issues related to external and internal auditing.
AEthics–L	Provides discussion on the ethical dimensions of accounting and auditing.
AFinAcc–L	Provides discussion dealing with issues of financial accounting.
AIntSysL	Provides discussion relating to the application of artificial intelligence and expert systems in accounting.
ATaxL	Provides discussion on all aspects of tax accounting.

used newsgroups to confer with fellow experts to obtain answers to technical questions. Currently, various industry groups are on the Internet and many CPA firms, both large and small, are providing information concerning their firms via the Internet.

- **Search for accounting, tax, or auditing information.** Accountants have used the Internet to search for federal and state legislation that may have an impact on clients. Another way in which accountants use the Internet is to retrieve financial statements from SEC filings through the SEC's EDGAR (Electronic Data Gathering and Retrieval) System. Accountants and individuals can also download tax forms, or even file tax returns electronically. Figure 4–2 illustrates just one example of how the Internet can help a small CPA firm provide practical services to clients.

The Internet is changing society on a worldwide basis. Now is the time to become familiar with the Internet in order to be prepared for the twenty-first century. The following sections will aid you in becoming more proficient with

Figure 4–2 An Example of a Small CPA Firm Utilizing the Internet

Mark Jensen, CPA, states that the Internet has become the "greatest equalizer" because it provides his small practice with many of the research tools utilized by the Big Five accounting firms. "It lets me offer resources and services to my clients and future clients that the big firms have to offer," says Jensen.

Mark was asked by a would-be entrepreneur to help write a business plan to open a computer software store in southern New York. Both Jensen and the client were computer literate, but neither of them knew much about the software business. So Mark accessed the Internet, and within an hour was deluged with information about software stores.

A word search for "software" yielded more than 100 articles about computer stores, including one from the *Washington Post* about a software store start-up. Jensen also gleaned information about software stores from the small business forums on the Internet. Mark and his client used the information to prepare a business plan that helped secure financing for the business.

Being online via the Internet allows Jensen to search through news sources throughout the world. Publications and news services such as the *New York Times*, Associated Press, United Press International, Reuters, *Financial Times of London*, and the Dow Jones News Service are just a few of the sources available on the Internet.

Mark also retrieves news items for clients as an effective way to maintain relationships and attract new clients. One of his clients is involved in the machine tools industry and he frequently notifies the client when a major industry event takes place.

Besides tracking news, Jensen uses the Internet to exchange e-mail with clients and associates. He also can access the SEC's Edgar System and obtain recent SEC filings of major public companies, such as their 10-K, 10-Q, or other filings.

this exciting and dynamic tool. You will be astounded by the data that is available on the Internet.

THE INTERNET

The Internet can be thought of as a spider-web of thousands of communications networks that physically cover the world. It began in 1969 in the U.S. Department of Defense under the acronym ARPANET (Advanced Research Project Agency Network). Its purpose was to make military networks less tolerant to failure by providing many paths among computers. This design made the system mode reliable in that the computer connected to the system could send messages by any path. Therefore, if one part of the system failed, the other computers redirected the message by another route, resulting in no lost connection or data. Throughout the last 30+ years, additional networks were added to ARPANET and the system has grown to its present size with various acronym changes to the current name *Internet*. This system is utilized by millions of users daily around the world.

The first Internet navigation tool was developed by researchers at the University of Minnesota, who appropriately entitled it "Gopher" after Minnesota's mascot. This tool provided users easy access to the information on the Internet. However, a major weakness in this tool was its linear or hierarchical search capabilities; that is, it was not a hypertext system whereby a document contains hidden links to other documents. This deficiency led to the development of the World Wide Web (WWW), with its hypertext capabilities. Because the Internet was not created as a research tool but as an information exchange tool, finding information can be an arduous task. Various navigation tools are available to help compensate for this. These tools have made the Internet a valuable tool for professional accountants.

Navigating the Internet

A major challenge after accessing the Internet is the attempt to understand where and how to search for information. The major techniques for accessing and searching (surfing) are briefly described below.

FTP. File transfer protocol (FTP) is a method of moving files from one computer to another. It is similar to moving files from a disk to the hard drive of a computer. With a standard protocol system, file transfers can take place regardless of the type of computer being used for file transfers. However, FTP allows transfer of text documents only.

Vast libraries of files exist on the hundreds of thousands of systems connected to the Internet. A user can obtain such varied information as free or low-cost shareware programs to copies of various documents, such as recent corporate filings with the SEC or a recent Supreme Court decision. The file transfer protocol system (FTP) is the basic way of obtaining these files.

A database system automatically and on a regular basis searches the Internet and indexes files into a single searchable database called *Archie*. This allows a user to access this database (Archie) and quickly search the index of files for the particular file needed to transfer.

USENET. On the Internet, news and opinions about the state of the world are freely disbursed. Currently, USENET consists of a collection of over 10,000 bulletin-board type discussion groups called newsgroups. All types of news appear on the Internet and USENET is the tool used to access this information.

The basic benefit of participating in a newsgroup is that you share ideas with others who have the same interests on a particular subject. These discussions of similar topics resulted in the creation of thousands of newsgroups on the Internet. A sample of accounting newsgroups was presented in Figure 4–1. A more comprehensive list of accounting, tax, and auditing newsgroups is at the authors' web site for this text.

World Wide Web (WWW)

The Web's structure allows the entire Internet's data to be considered a hypertext (http—hypertext transfer protocol) system. When you select a keyword in a document, the Web moves you to another document containing that keyword. This document could be on the same computer or a different computer in a foreign country. These links (keywords) allow you to search documents interactively, rather than just in a linear method.

Web Browsers. A web browser is the software that provides the user ready access to the different Internet sites located on the World Wide Web. Two of the most popular browsing tools in the WWW setting are Microsoft's Internet Explorer and Netscape's Communicator. These multimedia browsers can not only display documents, but also any embedded graphics, video, or sound. These tools have become so popular that some claim they are causing a minor traffic jam on the Internet. This is because their ease of use makes browsing related subjects quick and convenient, resulting in an increase in users.

URL. The Universal (or Uniform) Resource Locator (URL) is the address of the site you are attempting to access. Each page in a web site has its own unique address or URL. This unique address has three parts. The parts for Ernst & Young's careers home page are shown below.

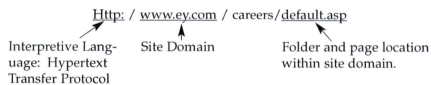

Http: / www.ey.com / careers/default.asp

| Interpretive Language: Hypertext Transfer Protocol | Site Domain | Folder and page location within site domain. |

For example, Ernst & Young's web page can be found at the URL of *http://www.ey.com*. The *http://* signifies the type of protocol the site is using. *Http://* is generally for web sites, *ftp://* for ftp sites, and *gopher://* for gopher sites. The rest is the domain and location for a particular page within a site. Ernst & Young's web site has a section on careers and employment at the firm. The first page of that section is located at *http://www.ey.com/careers/default.asp*. The *www.ey.com* is the domain of Ernst & Young's web site. The career sections home page is located in the folder "careers," and "default.asp" is the name of the current page. Today, most web browsers assume that you are looking for a web site, and will automatically add the *http://* to any address you type in. You will have to specify a protocol only if you are looking for ftp or gopher sites.

Searching the Web

A great wealth of information is available on the Internet. The problem is trying to find relevant information. Doing a search on keywords can bring up hundreds of sites, many of which may not have anything to do with the desired topic. A search on the name *Bill Gates* will bring up sites related to Microsoft's founder, gates that are found in a fence, legislative bills, bills found on a bird, and any other site with the words *bill* and/or *gates*. Performing an effective search on the Internet means choosing correct keywords, phrases, and operators, which include character and Boolean operators. The operators help to narrow and refine your searches. The following table contains common operators and their meanings.

Word/ Symbol	*Meaning*
+	Designates words that **must** be included in each document.
-	Designates words that **must not** be included in any document.
" "	Designates phrases that **must** be included in each document.
AND	Designates words that **must** be included in each document.
OR	Designates more than one word, either of which **may** be included.
NOT	Designates words that **must not** be included in any document.
( )	Designates groups of words using any of the above operators.

Types of Searches and Search Engines. Searches can be conducted in three basic ways: through search engines, directories, and search features found in some individual web sites.

First, you can use one of the many search engines available on the Web. A search engine is a software program located on a remote computer that provides keyword searches on the Internet. Search engines allow you to search for documents using keywords and operators. Each search engine conducts searches differently. Some search every word on a page for your keywords; others look only in the title of each document. Consequently, to do effective research on the Web, you should use at least two, if not three, different search engines and you should also search by multiple keywords, both separately and together.

Different search engines allow different operators. Some allow you to search using wildcard (* or $) searches which allow you to search for partial words. For example, if you want to search for an accounting term, but you are not sure of the correct spelling, you can search for part of the word along with the wildcard. If you want to search for amortization, but you don't know how to spell it, you could search for amort* or amort$. Every search engine has a help or search tips page, which will tell you what operators they use.

The second way to search the Web is through directories. Directory sites organize their links into categories, allowing you to narrow your search as you go along. One of the best directories on the Web is Yahoo!. Each directory organizes its links differently, and each link can be found through multiple routes. You could search for the web site of a Big Five accounting firm in Yahoo!'s directory by first choosing the Business & Economy category, then the companies category, then financial services, then firms. The path would look like this, with the carat (>) dividing each category: Home > <u>Business and Economy</u> > <u>Companies</u> > <u>Financial Services</u> > Accounting > Firms. You could also get to this site by first clicking the regional category, then U.S. States, then the state, then choosing the business & economy link, then companies, then financial services, then accounting, and so on until you find the company you are looking for. Directories make looking for information on the Web logical and easy, but an individual directory may contain only a portion of the number of sites that can be found using a search engine. Some search engines also contain directories. One of the most popular search engines that also has a directory is Yahoo!. Many times in a search through this type of dual engine, the category that link is listed under will also show. You can find related or similar sites to the one in your search results, even if the other sites do not appear in the original search.

The third way to do a search is to use the search capabilities that some sites have built into them. This lets you search their site for any relevant information you are looking for. These search features can be found in sites for newspapers, companies, and others. You can search individual sites for information that might not be readily available or in site archives.

Be aware that search engine directories can return links only to sites and documents registered with that particular engine. Results obtained through a search in one search engine may not be found on another engine, which again stresses the need to search on more than one engine. Since each search engine has a different retrieval scheme, find one that you are comfortable with and that meets your research needs.

Source Credibility. You should always be aware that when conducting searches on the Internet is that any information you find is only as credible as its source. Anybody can publish a web site on the Web and register it with a search engine. There is no regulation of web page content. Consequently, you must rely on your own judgment when evaluating a site for credibility. Some highly reliable sources include government sites such as the U.S. Treasury, academic institutions, and some established commercial sites. Also, if the information you find provided on the Internet can be found in other formats, such as legislative bills, you should be able to consider that source as credible. In other words, if you can verify the information you have found, it should be credible.

The Internet is a constantly changing entity. New sites are being added as more and more companies take their business online and more people post web pages. In addition, existing web sites are constantly changing and updated as needed. Many times, sites no longer exist because they are moved to new sites or are discarded completely. As a result, you may find broken links. These are links to web sites that no longer exist or have been moved. You can find these broken links in any kind of search you do. Don't get frustrated or discouraged by this. There is a huge amount of valid, credible information on the Web for you if you just keep trying. Refine your searches and try a variety of search methods to make your search as complete and effective as possible.

Search Engines. The following pages feature different search engines. The most popular engines, those which contain the variety of different features previously discussed, will be covered. You will utilize these search engines as you conduct professional research.

- **Yahoo!** (see Figure 4–3) has both a search engine and a directory. Its directory is one of the best and most comprehensive available on the Web. In addition to the previously mentioned operators, Yahoo! also allows you to do searches on URL and document titles only. You can do this by typing **t:** or **u:** in front of your keywords. For example, if you know that Arthur Andersen's web site address contains the firm's name, but are unsure of the exact address, you can do a URL search by typing in **u:+arthur +andersen**. This will return a link to Arthur Andersen's web site as the first link. You will see the category path it is listed under. Doing a title search for Arthur Andersen by typing in **t:+arthur +andersen** will yield the same results. Yahoo! is a great place to start your searches.

- One of the best features of **Infoseek** is its advanced search feature, shown in Figure 4–4. This feature allows you to do complex searches without needing to know any operators. You can reach this page by going to **www.infoseek.com** and then clicking on the Advanced Search link found

Figure 4–3 Yahoo! (www.yahoo.com) Home Page

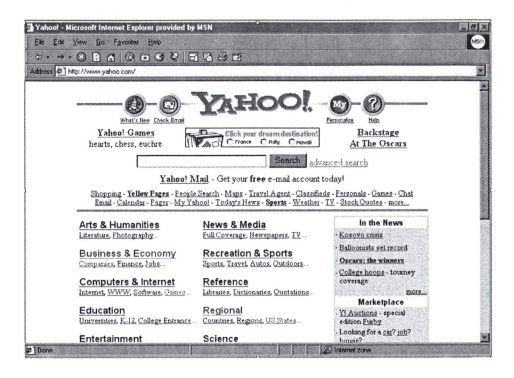

Figure 4–4 Infoseek (www.infoseek.com) Search Feature

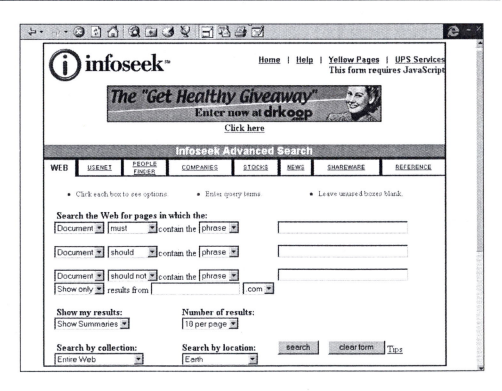

by the search text box. Infoseek searches over 50 million sites and updates its links regularly so you won't find any dead links. You can also do field searches with Infoseek. A field search can be performed on a link, site, URL, title, or ALT (pictures). The field name should be in lowercase and immediately followed by a colon with no spaces between the colon or the keyword. For example, **alt:"michael jordan"** will find links to pages with pictures of Michael Jordan.

- **MetaCrawler** (Figure 4–5) is a search engine that searches nine other search engines, such as Infoseek, Excite, Yahoo! and AltaVista. MetaCrawler queries the other search engines, organizes the results into a uniform format, and eliminates any duplicates. It then ranks them by relevance, and returns them to the user. This means that MetaCrawler is more likely to obtain accurate results for your search query. It also helps reduce the number of returns on your search, speeding up your research. Another advantage of Metacrawler is the standardization of query syntax, which improves the quality of your results.

- **AltaVista** (Figure 4–6) utilizes a ranking algorithm to determine the order in which matching documents are presented. Each document is first graded based on the number of search terms contained in the document. The Refine feature of the software dynamically sorts results into different topics, similar to a dynamic thesaurus, by giving you suggested keywords in order to refine your search. It also has a graphic version of the Refine feature. One of the items in its table of contents is the Usenet feature, which allows you to search through various Internet discussion or news groups on a wide variety of topics.

- **HotBot** (Figure 4–7) allows you to search the full text of more than 110 million documents in its database. It then sorts the documents in order of their relevance to your search keywords. Its advanced features utilize Boolean operators and Meta words, which are shortcuts that allow you to use HotBot's non-text search features. With similar features to AltaVista, it will serve as an alternative search engine.

- One of the best features of **Excite** (Figure 4–8) is that it ranks your search results by percentage, lists the best matches to your keyword(s) first, and

Figure 4–5 Metacrawler (www.go2net.com) Home Page

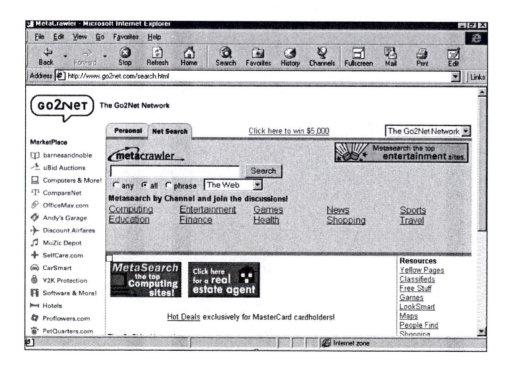

Figure 4–6 AltaVista (www.altavista.com) Home Page

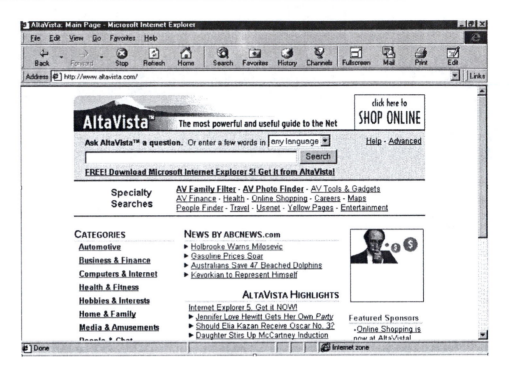

Figure 4–7 HotBot (www.hotbot.com) Home Page

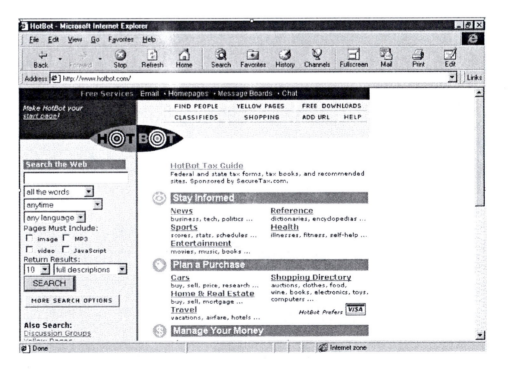

then lists additional matches by percentage. It is fairly easy to use, and allows you to set up a personalized start page. Search results are not limited to just web pages. A search on Excite can produce results on relevant information that includes stock quotes, sports scores, weather reports, and company information useful for investigation purposes, as well as headline news.

Figure 4–8 Excite (www.excite.com) Home Page

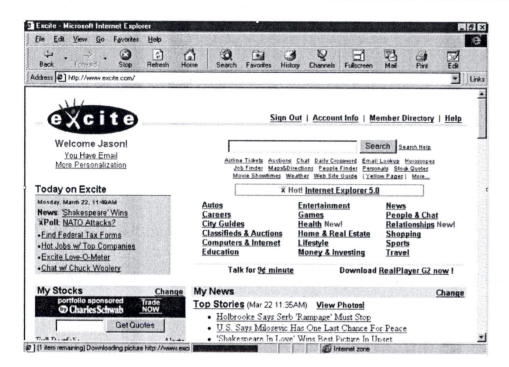

This software not only searches documents containing the exact words you entered into the Search box, but also searches for ideas closely related to the words in your query. For example, a search on "elderly individuals" would also yield a search for "senior citizens." For advanced searches, Excite uses many of the Boolean operators presented earlier in this chapter. It does have a limited directory, but some of the categories are good resources. Excite has many good city guides, allowing you to find all sorts of links and information on certain cities. Also, Excite has a very good mapping feature, enabling you to find maps to almost anywhere in the United States. and some places around the world. This feature would be of benefit to a fraud investigator, as discussed in Chapter 11, in attempting to find a location that supposedly contains stolen inventory belonging to the client.

SUMMARY

This chapter presented an overview of a major information technology tool (the Internet), which will have a significant impact on how the professional accountant gathers information. The authors' web site for this text provides a listing of some popular web sites for the professional accountant. Subsequent chapters will provide specific usage of the Internet and other computer tools to use for applications in conducting accounting, tax, or auditing research.

DISCUSSION QUESTIONS

1. What is the Internet? Briefly explain three ways the Internet can be utilized by the professional accountant.
2. What are the four basic ways of navigating the Internet?
3. Identify three Anet Discussion Groups available to the accountant/auditor.
4. What is a search engine?
5. When searching the Web utilizing a search engine, what would be the appropriate Boolean operator if you wanted the words Stock Options to be included in each document?
6. How would you configure your search if you were attempting to search for any form of the following words: depreciate, depreciation, depreciating, depreciated?
7. Access Yahoo's Web site. Under the *Business & Finance* feature, click on Finance. Obtain the names of two companies filing IPOs (Initial Public Offerings of securities) with the SEC. Why were the companies filing the IPO?
8. Access Infoseek's Web site. Click on the *Advanced Search* link. Obtain a listing of five hits that resulted from searching for a title that must contain the words "fraud detection." What is contained in these five listings?
9. Access Excite's Web site. You are conducting an investigation of a family member. Click on the *People & Chat* link and search for a personal relative. What did you find? If at first you do not succeed, enter another name of a relative until you get a hit.
10. Using Alta Vista's Usenet feature, find three newsgroups relating to accounting or auditing. Briefly report on the contents of each newsgroup.

The Environment of Accounting Research

LEARNING OBJECTIVES

After completing this chapter, you should understand:

- The environment of accounting research.
- The organizations that set accounting standards.
- The process of standard setting.
- The types of authoritative pronouncements.
- The meaning of GAAP.
- The hierarchy of GAAP.
- The hierarchy of SEC publications.
- The current status of international accounting and the need for a global set of accounting standards.

Research on an accounting issue is always conducted in a dynamic environment, since new professional standards are constantly being issued and existing standards updated or deleted. Of major significance is the fact that the researcher must be aware that in researching an issue, he or she needs to use the most recent authoritative pronouncement. The development of accounting standards in this dynamic environment is influenced by:

1. The requirements of federal, state, and local governments, and other regulatory bodies.
2. The influence of various tax laws on the financial reporting process.
3. The practices or problems of certain specialized industries, such as the motion picture or the oil and gas industries.
4. Inconsistencies in practice.
5. Disagreements among accountants, business executives, and others as to the objectives of financial statements.
6. The influence of professional organizations.
7. International differences among countries in setting international accounting standards.

Figure 5–1 illustrates the complex environment into which the accounting practitioner/researcher must venture in pursuing the solution to a problem. The acronyms shown will be explained as you proceed through this chapter. Within this setting are resources containing numerous accounting standards, rules, and recommended practices. Yet, with so many directions in which to turn for guidance and with the need to solve the dilemma efficiently, the accountant must have a basic understanding of when and how these resources

Figure 5–1 Accounting Research Environment

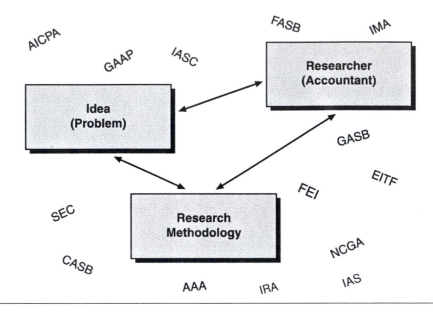

apply. The accountant must know not only where to find the generally accepted accounting principles and the established exceptions that are pertinent to the question at hand, but also who speaks with the greatest authority within that context.

This chapter concentrates on the standard-setting process in accounting, including the process conducted by the private sector (Financial Accounting Standards Board–FASB) and its predecessors, and the public sector (Governmental Accounting Standards Board–GASB, and the U.S. Securities and Exchange Commission–SEC), as well as international dimensions. It emphasizes three questions.

1. What constitutes generally accepted accounting principles (GAAP)?
2. What is the hierarchy of authoritative support? That is, which organizations speak with the loudest voices?
3. Where does one start the research process, and when can one stop the research process?

STANDARD-SETTING ENVIRONMENT

Accounting standards have emerged over time to meet the needs of financial statement users. The number of users—primarily investors, lenders, and governmental entities—has increased enormously over the past 75 years, and the complexity of the business enterprise has increased with it. The result has been greater demand by users for more uniformity in accounting procedures to allow easier comparison of financial statements. Government agencies, legislative bodies, and professional organizations have responded to this demand.

ACCOUNTING STANDARD-SETTING PROCESS

Currently, the Financial Accounting Standards Board (FASB) is responsible for setting accounting standards in the private sector, just as the Governmental Accounting Standards Board (GASB) is for the public sector. Before 1973, the

American Institute of Certified Public Accountants (AICPA) set standards for both sectors. Following is a brief historical perspective of the accounting standard-setting process. The researcher should focus on different pronouncements of these organizations and where such pronouncements fit in the hierarchy of GAAP as discussed in a subsequent section of this chapter.

American Institute of Certified Public Accountants

In 1887, 31 accountants formed the American Association of Public Accountants (AAPA), the ancestor of the AICPA and the first national organization of accountants in the United States. The chief purpose of the AAPA was to attest to the competency and integrity of its members. Until the turn of the century, U.S. audits were patterned after their British counterparts, with detailed scrutinizing of balance sheet audits. In 1917, at the request of the Federal Trade Commission, the transformed AAPA, under its new name, the American Institute of Accountants (AIA), prepared the first authoritative pronouncement, entitled *Balance-Sheet Audits*.

From 1939 to 1959 the AICPA and its predecessor, the AIA, through its Committee on Accounting Procedures (CAP), published 51 Accounting Research Bulletins (ARBs) dealing with a wide spectrum of accounting issues. In 1959, the newly created Accounting Principles Board (APB), which replaced the CAP, issued two major series of publications; the first, a set of 31 APB Opinions, is now binding on all CPAs. Then, in 1984, the Institute required that departures from APB Opinions (APBOs) be disclosed either in the notes to financial statements or in the audit reports of AICPA members in their capacity as independent auditors. CPAs could not give their approval to financial statements that deviated from APB Opinions unless they wanted to assume the considerable personal risk and burden of proof of defending the "unauthorized practices." Since few business enterprises or auditors were anxious to assume the burden of defending financial statements that differed from APB Opinions, this action gave new strength and authority to those Opinions. The APB also issued four nonauthoritative Statements (which addressed broad concepts rather than specific accounting principles) and several unofficial interpretations.

Before the establishment of the FASB in 1973, the AICPA was the recognized standard-setting body for the private sector. During that time the AICPA recognized the National Council on Governmental Accounting (NCGA, the standard-setting body of the Governmental Finance Officers Association) as an authoritative rule-making body for governmental entities. Other governmental organizations, including the Securities and Exchange Commission (SEC), the Internal Revenue Service (IRS), and the Cost Accounting Standards Board (CASB), also set certain accounting standards for entities in their domain.

Following the formation of the FASB, the AICPA created an Accounting Standards Division to influence the development of accounting standards. The Accounting Standards Executive Committee (AcSEC) of the Accounting Standards Division issues Statements of Position (SOPs) to propose revisions of AICPA-published Industry Audit and Accounting Guides. These SOPs do not establish enforceable accounting standards; however, members of the AICPA must justify departures from practices recommended in the SOPs. In addition, the Accounting Standards Division prepares Issues Papers to develop financial accounting and reporting issues that the division believes should be considered by the FASB.

Thus, AcSEC has become the spokesperson for the AICPA on financial accounting matters. It responds, for example, to FASB and SEC accounting pronouncements by issuing Comment Letters, Issue Letters, and SOPs, which the FASB may convert into Statements of Financial Accounting Standards (SFASs). It also often publishes brief notes and news releases in the AICPA's bi-weekly publication, *The CPA Letter*, which reaches more than 340,000 members.

Various committees of the AICPA also publish *Accounting Research Monographs*, *Accounting Trends and Techniques*, and other publications, which are discussed in Chapter 7. The annual *Accounting Trends and Techniques* publication summarizes the accounting practices of over 600 publicly owned companies. It presents tabulations of the numbers of surveyed companies that use particular practices; it also presents excerpts of actual reports issued by the surveyed companies.

The AICPA's Technical Information Service

The Technical Information Service (TIS), one of the Institute's most valuable services, provides answers to any accounting or auditing question (except legal matters) posed by members. The Institute receives some 14,000 queries a year and publishes the answers to the most frequently asked questions in *The Journal of Accountancy* and the Technical Practice Aids looseleaf services.

In addition to the AICPA's Technical Information Service, the Institute's library contains the largest collection of accounting information in the country. The library:

1. Makes bibliographies and articles available (except on tax or "in-depth" matters).
2. Charges only nominal copying and postage fees.
3. Provides information on almost any topic that appears in the *Accounting & Tax Index*.
4. Is available to AICPA members by phone, by mail, or in person.

Financial Accounting Standards Board

In 1972 the Wheat Committee (an AICPA committee) proposed that professional accounting standards be established outside the AICPA. The APB was replaced by a full-time, seven-member Financial Accounting Standards Board with a broadened membership: only four members may be drawn from among practicing CPAs; the other three represent government, law, financial statement preparers and users, and academe. But this description does not begin to portray the complex structure of the organization, as we shall see.

The FASB's authoritative pronouncements are labeled *Statements of Financial Accounting Standards* (SFASs). The FASB also issues *Interpretations of Financial Accounting Standards*, which interpret Accounting Research Bulletins and APB Opinions, as well as the FASB's own *Statements*.

As noted in Figure 5–2, the financial accounting standard-setting process involves several entities: the Financial Accounting Foundation (FAF), the board itself, the FASB staff, and the Emerging Issues Task Force. The GASB, also under the umbrella of the FAF, is discussed later in this chapter.

The FAF is the parent organization. Consisting of 15 trustees nominated from organizations with a special knowledge of and interest in financial reporting, it oversees the FASB's budget. These are the nominating organizations:

- American Accounting Association
- American Institute of Certified Public Accountants

Figure 5–2 Organization of FAF, FASB, and GASB

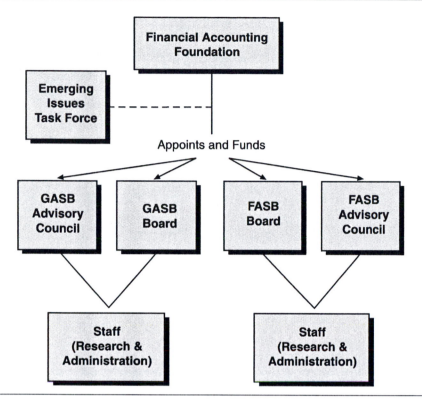

- Financial Analysts Federation
- Financial Executives Institute
- Government Finance Officers Association
- Institute of Management Accountants
- National Association of State Auditors, Comptrollers, and Treasurers
- Securities Industry Association

Three other trustees are elected at large, generally from the ranks of banking, law, and government.

In representing a broad spectrum of the financial community, the FASB membership typically consists of partners from large and small CPA firms, corporate executives, financial analysts, and an academic. The FASB pursues its investigative activities with a full-time research staff of approximately 50 professionals from various backgrounds. The Financial Accounting Standards Advisory Council (FASAC) advises the FASB on the priorities of its current and proposed projects, on selecting and organizing task forces, and on any other matters the FASB requests.

To help practitioners and their clients implement the provisions of FASB Standards, the FASB's staff periodically issues *Technical Bulletins* to provide timely guidance on implementation issues. These Bulletins allow conformity with FASB pronouncements without the need for the entire FASB Board to issue a new authoritative statement.

While *Technical Bulletins* help clarify conformance to a recently issued FASB authoritative pronouncement, financial statement preparers and users often have questions about issues not "clearly" covered by an existing set of authoritative pronouncements. To fill this void, the Emerging Issues Task Force (EITF) was established in 1984. Chaired by the FASB's Director of Research and

Technical Activities, the Task Force consists of individuals in a position to be aware of issues before they become widespread and before divergent practices regarding them become entrenched. The EITF normally address industry-specific issues, rather than those encompassing accounting and financial reporting as a whole. For example, EITF No. 93-5, "Accounting for Environmental Liabilities," applies mainly to those industries with exposure to environmental liabilities. Similarly, EITF No. 98-10, "Accounting for Energy Trading and Risk Management Activities," applies to the utility industry as to whether contracts for the purchase and sale of energy commodities should be marked to market.

If the EITF is unable to reach a consensus on an issue under consideration and it decides that the "problem" merits further action, it will forward the file to the FASB Board for further deliberation. Conversely, if the Task Force can reach a consensus on an issue, the FASB can usually infer that no Board action is necessary. The researchers need to be cognizant that the EITF's consensus positions are included in the hierarchy of GAAP, as identified later in this chapter in Figures 5–6 and 5–7.

Given the importance of FASB standards, the Board seeks to keep to due process, so much so that it has spent over eleven years deliberating on certain standards. The standard-setting process followed by the Board appears in Figure 5–3. Briefly, the FASB is held to a fixed procedure; before issuing a Statement of Financial Accounting Standards (SFAS), it must take the following steps:

1. Identify the problem or issue and take into account legal or SEC pressures.
2. Decide whether to consider the issue. At this point, the board generally seeks opinion from the FASAC and such professional organizations as Robert Morris Associates, the Institute of Management Accountants (IMA), and the Financial Executives Institute (FEI).
3. Establish a task force to study the problem; usually about 15 people are chosen.
4. Have its research staff investigate the issues.

Figure 5–3 FASB Standard-Setting Process

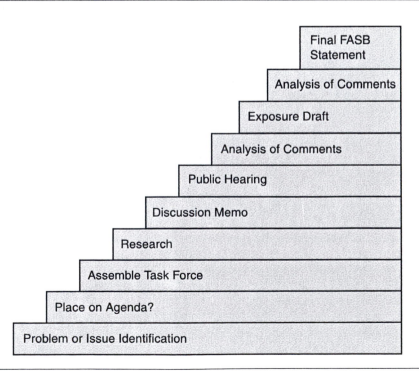

5. Issue a discussion memo to interested parties. Usually more than 30,000 copies of the discussion memorandum are issued to the public.
6. Hold public hearings and request written comments on the issue. Several hundred responses are usually received.
7. Analyze the results of the investigation, mail responses, and conduct public hearings.
8. If action is appropriate, issue an exposure draft, a preliminary SFAS. The normal exposure period is at least 60 days.
9. Request additional comments on the exposure draft and hold further public hearings.
10. After analyzing the public response, issue a final Statement of Financial Accounting Standards (SFAS).

Having gone through this due process procedure, the final pronouncement is placed in the highest level of authoritative support in the GAAP hierarchy. SFASs are issued in a standard format and reprinted in the *Official Release* section of the *Journal of Accountancy*. Most SFASs contain:

a. A summary.
b. Table of contents.
c. Introduction and other narrative.
d. The actual standard.
e. A list of the FASB members actually voting. (The FAF now requires a 5–to–2 majority to approve new standards.)
f. The basis for a qualifying or dissenting vote of a FASB member.
g. Appendices containing background information, a glossary of terms, numerical and other examples of applying the standard, and other ancillary information.

FASB's Conceptual Framework Project

In certain situations, an accounting issue may arise for which no precedent has been set and no authoritative pronouncement has been issued. In such cases, the researcher must develop a theoretically justifiable conclusion. A number of organizations and individuals have directed their efforts toward the development of accounting theory in order to provide a framework for resolving issues in a theoretically consistent manner.

The American Accounting Association (AAA), a national professional organization with a membership composed primarily of academicians, sponsors and conducts extensive research of a theoretical or conceptual nature. The AICPA also promotes research in accounting theory and has published a series of *Accounting Research Monographs*. As mentioned previously, the Accounting Principles Board of the AICPA issued four conceptual statements during its existence.

Despite these and other efforts, however, a widely accepted theoretical framework of accounting has not been fully developed. Recognizing the need for such a framework, the FASB has undertaken a comprehensive, long-range project called the Conceptual Framework Project. This project encompasses a series of pronouncements entitled *Statements of Financial Accounting Concepts* (SFACs), which describe concepts and relationships that underlie financial accounting standards. These pronouncements have addressed or will address such issues as elements of financial statements and their recognition, measurement, and display; capital maintenance; unit of measure; criteria for distinguishing information to be included in financial statements from that which should be provided by other means of financial reporting; and criteria for evaluating and selecting accounting information (qualitative characteristics).

Statements of Financial Accounting Concepts Nos. 1–6

The first six statements issued under the Conceptual Framework Project are as follows:

1. "Objectives of Financial Reporting of Business Enterprises." This statement sets forth the objectives of general purpose external financial reporting by business enterprises. For example, it states that financial reports should help society better allocate scarce economic resources.
2. "Qualitative Characteristics of Accounting Information." This statement examines the characteristics of accounting information that make the information useful.
3. "Elements of Financial Statements of Business Enterprises." This statement defines ten elements of financial statements of business enterprises: assets, liabilities, equity, investment by owners, distributions to owners, comprehensive income, revenues, expenses, gains, and losses. This SFAC was superseded by SFAC No. 6.
4. "Objectives of Financial Reporting of Nonbusiness Organizations." This statement establishes the objectives of general purpose external financial reporting by nonbusiness organizations.
5. "Recognition and Measurement in Financial Statements." This statement establishes recognition criteria and guidance regarding what information should be incorporated into financial statements. SFAC No. 5 also describes and defines the concept of earnings and what should be included in a full set of an entity's financial statements.
6. "Elements of Financial Statements." (Supersedes SFAC No. 3 and amends portions of SFAC No. 2). This statement redefines the ten interrelated elements of financial statements. It also defines three classes of net assets for not-for-profit organizations as well as accrual accounting and other related concepts.

The conceptual framework seeks to establish objectives and concepts to be used in the development of accounting standards and in the preparation of financial statements, especially where no published standards exist. The project's focus is to produce a constitution for accounting, resulting in a coherent set of accounting standards. However, since the FASB did not use full due process in this project, the SFACs are not authoritative; as with APB Statements, CPAs need not justify departures from their guidance. However, the researcher normally utilizes these pronouncements when no authoritative pronouncement is directly on point to the issue under consideration. In such cases, the researcher needs to develop a theoretical foundation for the solution to the problem.

U.S. Securities and Exchange Commission

The SEC is directed by five commissioners in Washington, D.C. The commissioners are assisted by a staff of professionals that includes accountants, lawyers, economists, and securities analysts. These professionals are assigned to the four Divisions in the SEC: Division of Corporation Finance, Division of Market Regulation, Division of Enforcement, and Division of Investment Management. The Commission receives its authoritative status from the public sector rather than the accounting profession. The Securities and Exchange Act of 1934 established the SEC and charged it with the duty of insuring full and fair disclosures of all material facts relating to publicly traded securities. Congress empowered the SEC to specify the form of documents filed with the Commission and prescribe the accounting principles used in generating the financial data presented in the reports.

The Commission publishes four basic documents delineating its reporting and disclosure requirements:

1. **Regulation S-X** describes the types of reports that must be filed and the forms that are to be used.
2. **Regulation S-K, Integrated Disclosure Rules** prescribes the filing requirements for information presented outside the financial statements required under **Regulation S-X**.
3. **Financial Reporting Releases (FRRs)** prescribe the accounting principles that must be followed in preparing reports filed with the Commission. These FRRs are analogous to the authoritative pronouncements of the APB or FASB.
4. **Accounting and Auditing Enforcement Releases** (AAERs) relate to enforcement of the Commission's reporting and disclosure requirements.

The FRRs and AAERs were first issued in 1982. These series of pronouncements replaced the SEC's *Accounting Series Releases* (ASRs), which were issued from 1937 to 1982. Nonenforcement-related ASRs that are still in effect have been codified by the SEC. The Commission has published a topical index to enforcement-related ASRs.

The SEC also publishes a series of *Staff Accounting Bulletins* (SABs), which are unofficial interpretations of the SEC's prescribed accounting principles. These bulletins are analogous to the FASB Technical Bulletins. The SEC has broad authority to prescribe accounting principles and informative disclosures to entities in its domain. Such corporations must file an annual Form 10-K report, quarterly Form 10-Q reports, and Form 8-K when significant accounting matters arise (e.g., a change in auditors).

The SEC has delegated the major responsibility for accounting standard setting to the FASB but has retained an oversight function. In essence, this is the recognition by the SEC of the authoritative support of accounting principles promulgated by the FASB. The Commission recognizes these principles as acceptable for use in filings with the Commission. In monitoring the FASB's activities, the SEC has from time to time overruled the FASB or APB, as in the issues of accounting for the investment tax credit, accounting for inflation, and accounting for oil and gas exploration.

SEC Rules and Regulations. Federal statutes give the SEC the authority to issue rules and regulations to administer the statutes. Those rules and regulations are formal SEC policy as approved by the five (SEC) commissioners (all other employees of the SEC are staff). The term "rules and regulations" refers to all rules and regulations adopted by the Commission, including the forms and instructions to the forms that are used to file registration statements or periodic reports.

Since the rules and regulations category serves a variety of purposes, many different captions are used. Some rules provide definitions of terms in certain statutes or regulations and are called general rules. Other rules are found in regulations, which are a compilation of rules related to a specific subject (e.g., Regulation 14A on solicitation of proxies). Still other rules relate to procedural matters, such as the steps to be followed in proceedings before the Commission, where to file documents, and what type size to use in materials filed with the SEC.

Commission's Published Views and Interpretations. The Codification of Financial Reporting (CFR) Policies is a compendium of the SEC's current published views and interpretations relating to financial reporting. It supplements the rules in regulations S-K and S-X by providing background and rationale for certain of those rules. Prior to its issuance, the Commission's views and interpretations relating to financial reporting were published in Accounting Series Releases (ASRs). ASRs were also used to publish Commission findings on enforcement actions relating to accountants. The Commission updates the Codification of Financial Reporting Policies and Regulations S-K and S-X by issuing Financial Reporting Releases. A typical Financial Reporting Release contains the following types of information:

- The background of the topic.
- An evaluation of the comments received on the proposed rules.
- A discussion of the final rules.
- A discussion of transition provisions.
- The text of new rules.

Generally the Codification of Financial Reporting Policies is updated for the discussion of final rules only. While that information is generally adequate in that it provides the important views of the Commission, accountants occasionally refer to the original release for more detailed background information.

AAERs announce enforcement actions involving accountants and other professionals. AAERs generally include a summary of the enforcement action, a discussion of the facts, the Commission's conclusions, and any orders issued (e.g., an order to restrict practice before the SEC by the accountant involved for a specific time period). Appendix A to AAER No. 1 contains a topical index to enforcement-related ASRs. It is updated when AAERs are issued. The index is intended to be a reference tool only.

SEC Staff Policy. SEC staff policy is followed by the SEC staff in administering rules, regulations, and statutes. It is not approved formally by the commissioners; therefore, it cannot be considered as official rules or interpretations of the Commission. SEC staff policy is published in no-action and interpretative letters, Staff Accounting Bulletins (SABs), correspondence about accountants' independence, and 1933 and 1934 Act Industry Guides.

No-action and interpretative letters are published SEC staff responses to inquiries for interpretations of the application of statutes or rules and regulations to a particular transaction contemplated by a registrant or to make a general interpretation of the statutes. The response may indicate that the staff will not recommend that the Commission take any action regarding the proposed transaction or that certain procedures must be followed regarding the transaction.

SABs are interpretations and practices followed by the SEC staff in the Chief Accountant's Office or the Division of Corporation Finance in administering the disclosure requirements of the federal securities laws. SABs relate to accounting and disclosure practices under the rules and regulations. Since the issuance of SAB No. 40 in January 1981, the SEC has maintained a codification of SABs to make staff accounting bulletins more useful to users.

Announcing SEC Policy. The SEC informs the public of proposed amendments of rules and regulations, final rules and regulations, the Commission's views and interpretations, and staff policy by using various releases. Proposed amendments of rules and regulations are exposed for a comment period of usually 90 days; however, the comment period can be shortened to 60 or 30 days for matters that are not complex. All releases are identified with "release numbers" that contain a prefix indicating the applicable statute or special type of release and a sequential number that is assigned in the order of issuance by category of prefix.

The prefix and following number are known as the release number. Some common prefixes and their applicable statute or special type of release are shown below.

Prefix	Applicable Statute or Special Type of Release
33	Securities Act of 1933
34	Securities Exchange Act of 1934
AS	Accounting Series Release
FR	Financial Reporting Release
ER	Accounting and Auditing Enforcement Release

In print, the number would be preceded by the words "Release No." or "Rel. No." Many reference sources exclude the prefix and print the applicable statute, special type of release, or some abbreviation of those. Normally a release contains more than one release number because it applies to more than one statute and possibly is a special type of release. For example, Release Nos. 33-6483, 34-20186 and FR-14 are the same release on an accounting matter that affects filings under the 1933 and 1934 Acts.

Given this vast literature regarding SEC pronouncements, Figure 5–4 summarizes in a hierarchical format the major SEC Authoritative Pronouncements and Publications.[1] Currently, many of the previously discussed items concerning the SEC are available on its Web site at *www.sec.gov*.

Cost Accounting Standards Board

The Cost Accounting Standards Board (CASB) was established by an Act of Congress in 1971 to increase the uniformity of cost allocations among companies holding large government contracts. Although Congress discontinued the CASB in 1980, it recreated the Board in 1989. The Board has exclusive authority to issue cost accounting standards that govern the measurement, assignment, and allocation of costs on federal government contracts over $500,000. Of the five CASB members, three are from federal agencies, one represents industry, and one represents the accounting profession.

---

1 Miller, Paul B. W., and Jack Robertson, "A Guide to SEC Regulations and Publications: Mastering the Maze," *Research in Accounting Regulation*, 1989, Vol. 3, 239–249.

Figure 5–4 A Hierarchy of SEC Authorities and Publications

LEVEL 1: **Statutes**
i.e., 1933 Securities Act
    1934 Securities Exchange Act

LEVEL 2: **Regulations and Forms**
i.e., Regulation S–X
    Regulation S–K

LEVEL 3: **Commission Releases**
i.e., Financial Reporting Releases
    Accounting and Auditing Enforcement Releases
    Securities Releases
    Exchange Act Releases

LEVEL 4: **Staff Advice**
i.e., Industry Guides
    Staff Accounting Bulletins

Internal Revenue Service

Income tax laws have significantly influenced the development and implementation of GAAP because of the willingness of the accounting profession to accept tax accounting requirements as GAAP. In order not to spend resources keeping two sets of books, many smaller businesses use tax-basis statements as their external financial statements. CPAs must recognize certain reporting problems when the two statements are not identical. The Internal Revenue Service's Interpretations, Private Letter Rulings, Regulations, and other tax accounting pronouncements also affect accounting practice. Researching a tax issue is discussed in Chapter 10.

Governmental Accounting Standards Board

Public sector (governmental) accounting is only now reaching the plateau of responsibility and credibility inhabited by private sector (proprietary) accounting, as the Governmental Accounting Standards Board (GASB) has developed in a fashion similar to that of the Financial Accounting Standards Board (FASB). Financial reports of local and state units of government have varied in quality and lacked uniformity for many years due to an absence of clearly defined principles. A body of generally accepted accounting principles (GAAP) for local units of government has evolved slowly. However, given the large value of assets that governmental entities "manage," as well as financial crises in municipal units such as New York, Cleveland, and Orange County, California, the financial community has paid increasing attention to governmental units' financial statements.

The first national organization to address government accounting standards was the National Committee on Government Accounting organized by the Municipal Finance Officers Association (MFOA) in 1934. The Committee issued two publications, *Municipal Accounting & Auditing* (1951) and *Classification of Municipal Accounts* (1953).

In 1968, the National Committee on Governmental Accounting published *Government Accounting, Auditing, and Financial Reporting*, known by the acronym GAAFR or simply as "The Blue Book." GAAFR brought together different governmental accounting practices and provided an authoritative source for such accounting; it became the basis for many state laws for uniform municipal accounting (e.g., Michigan Public Act 68-2). During 1973, the MFOA changed the name of the committee to the National Council on Governmental Accounting (NCGA). In 1974, when the AICPA published *Audits of State and Local Governmental Units* (ASLGU), the Audit Guide noted that GAAFR provided a significant source of GAAP for governmental entities.

In 1979, in an attempt to eliminate the accounting differences and to update, clarify, amplify, and reorder the principles of GAAFR, the National Council on Governmental Accounting (NCGA) issued *Statement 1, Governmental Accounting and Financial Reporting Principles*. Statement 1 contained significant modifications to the basic fund accounting and financial reporting philosophy of both GAAFR and the Audit Guide:

1. Eight generic funds were grouped into three categories.
2. Fiduciary funds were to be accounted for as governmental or proprietary funds.
3. Reporting was simplified with five overview financial statements.
4. A Comprehensive Annual Financial Report was developed. It was organized on a financial reporting pyramid.

5. A comparison report of budget and actual for those funds using budgetary accounts was required.
6. Various levels of acceptable scope of independent audits were redefined.

In addition, financial reporting was improved significantly through standardization of treatment of encumbrances, the use of "all-inclusive" operating statement formats, clarification of reporting of interfund transactions, and elimination of excessively detailed schedules. In 1980, the AICPA issued SOP 80-2, which brought Statement 1 into the Audit Guide by stating financial statements issued in accordance with Statement 1 were in conformity with GAAP. Also in 1980, the Government Finance Officers Association revised the 1968 version of *Governmental Accounting, Auditing, and Financial Reporting*. This work did not intend to establish or authoritatively interpret GAAP for governmental units, but instead provide for an effective application of Statement 1.

Finally, in 1984, after several years of consideration, the Financial Accounting Foundation (FAF) established the GASB (as the successor to the NCGA) to set financial accounting and reporting standards for the public sector (i.e., state and local governmental entities) as the FASB does for all private entities.

The formation of the GASB caused two government organizations (the Government Finance Officers Association (GFOA) and the National Association of State Auditors, Treasurers, and Controllers) to be added to the list of FAF sponsors. The former organization is composed primarily of local operating financial personnel (e.g., municipalities, counties, and port and transit authorities), while the latter consists primarily of state financial officers. Both organizations focus primarily on GASB standards—applicable in the public sector of the economy.

As the successor to the voluntary, part-time National Council on Governmental Accounting, whose standards remain effective until superseded or amended, the GASB received authoritative status for its standards under Rule 203 of the American Institute of Certified Public Accountants' Rules of Conduct and legislation in the various states.

The GASB is a five-member organization, currently consisting of a former state auditor, a former treasurer of a major city, a university professor, and two retired Big Five accounting firm partners.

The Board's ten-member professional staff works directly with the Board and its task forces, conducts research, participates in public hearings, analyzes oral and written comments received from the public on documents, and prepares drafts of documents for consideration by the Board.

Similar to its FASB counterpart, the GASB has established a practice of due process. Thus, for all major projects, the Board generally will:

- Research the subject to define the issues and to determine the scope of the projects.
- Appoint a task force to advise the Board on the issues and to aid in developing alternative solutions prior to issuance of a discussion document.
- Issue a discussion memorandum or invitation to comment, which will set forth the definition of the problem, scope of the project, and the issues involved; discuss relevant research; and include alternative solutions to the issues identified.
- Hold a public hearing, at which concerned individuals will be encouraged to state their views on the issues contained in the discussion document.
- Issue an exposure draft of a proposed Statement for public comment prior to adoption of a final standard.
- Issue a final Statement. A Statement may be issued by a majority vote of the Board members.

During all of these steps, the Board deliberates the issues in meetings open to public observations. The Board may issue a Statement following exposure for public comment without appointing a task force, issuing a discussion document, or holding a public hearing if, in the judgment of its members, the Board can make an informed decision based on available information. GASB pronouncements would be a beginning reference for the researcher in dealing with an issue associated with local or state governmental accounting. Also, since the GASB goes through the due process procedure, its pronouncements are in the highest level of governmental GAAP.

Similar to its FASB counterpart, the GASB has an advisory council. The Governmental Accounting Standards Advisory Council (GASAC) is responsible for consulting with the GASB as to major policy questions, technical issues on the Board's agenda, project priorities, matters likely to require the attention of the GASB, selection and organization of task forces, and such other matters as may be requested by the GASB or its chairperson. The GASAC also is responsible for helping develop the GASB's annual budget and aiding the Financial Accounting Foundation in raising funds for the Board. At present, the Council has 22 members who are broadly representative of preparers, attestors, and users of financial information.

Professional Organizations

Many professional organizations that do not set accounting standards nevertheless influence directly or indirectly the setting of those standards.

- The Institute of Management Accountants (IMA), through its Management Accounting Practices Committee, provides formal input to the FASB, although it does not establish standards.
- The National Association of State Auditors, Controllers, and Treasurers is an information clearinghouse and research base for state financial officials. Although it publishes no journal, the Association performs financial management projects for state fiscal officers, and it appoints members to the Financial Accounting Foundation.
- The Financial Executives Institute (FEI) influences accounting standards development through its Panel on Accounting Principles, which makes recommendations on discussion memoranda issued by the FASB. The FEI also conducts its own research through the Financial Executives Research Foundation.
- The Securities Industry Associates (SIA), which represents investment bankers and manages the portfolios of large institutional investors, and the Financial Analysts Federation are typical of the kind of organizations that influence the setting of standards and the shaping of GAAP because they help select members of the Financial Accounting Foundation, which in turn selects the members of the FASB and the GASB. Since these groups represent users of financial statements, they usually favor standards providing for additional disclosures, just as the IMA, representing preparers, protects the interests of its members.
- The academic arm of accounting, the American Accounting Association (AAA), emphasizes the need for a theoretical foundation for accounting and influences standard setting through the research and analysis of accounting concepts presented in committee reports and in its quarterly journal, *The Accounting Review*, and other publications.

Figure 5–5 summarizes the constituencies and the missions of organizations affecting standard setting and the shaping of GAAP.

Figure 5–5 The Role of Professional Accounting Organizations in Developing GAAP

Organization	Principal Membership	Principal Mission	Professional Journal
* 1. American Accounting Association (AAA)	Accounting academicians	Helps develop a logical, theoretical basis for accounting. Promotes research and education in accounting.	*The Accounting Review*
* 2. American Institute of Certified Public Accountants (AICPA)	Certified Public Accountants	Its various committees have issued authoritative pronouncements on accounting principles and auditing standards. Conducts programs of research, conducting education, surveillance of practice, jurisdiction consistency, and communications.	*Journal of Accountancy*
* 3. Association of Government Accountants (AGA)	Federal, state, and local government accountants	Professional society of accountants, auditors, comptrollers, and budget officers employed by federal, state, and local governments in management and administrative positions. Monitors the activities of and often provides input to the Government Accounting Standards Board (GASB).	*Government Accountants' Journal*
* 4. Financial Analysts Federation	Financial analysts and Chartered Financial Analysts	Promotes the development of improved standards of investment research and portfolio management. An organization of primary users of accounting information, it represents those who analyze information and provide professional advice on investment matters.	*Financial Analysts Journal*
* 5. Financial Executives Institute (FE)	Corporate financial executives	Professional organization of financial and management executives performing duties of a controller, treasurer, or VP-finance, primarily from large corporations. Sponsors research activities through its affiliated Financial Executives Research Foundation.	*FE: The Magazine for Financial Executives*
* 6. Governmental Finance Officers Association (GFOA)	State and local public finance officials	Provides technical service center and technical inquiry service for public finance officials. Monitors the activities of and often provides input to the GASB.	*Governmental Finance Review*
* 7. Institute of Internal Auditors (IIA)	Internal auditors and Certified Internal Auditors	Cultivates, promotes, and disseminates knowledge concerning internal auditors. Sponsors research on the internal auditor's role in promoting more reliable financial information.	*The Internal Auditor*
* 8. Institute of Management Accountants (IMA)	Corporate controllers and financial officers and Certified Management Accountants	Conducts research primarily on management accounting methods and procedures, and has recently increased its role in the development of financial accounting standards	*Management Accounting*

(continued)

Figure 5–5 The Role of Professional Accounting Organizations in Developing GAAP (continued)

Organization	Principal Membership	Principal Mission	Professional Journal
* 9. National Association of State Auditors, Controllers, and Treasurers	State financial officials	Serves as an information clearing-house and research base for state financial officials.	
10. Robert Morris Associates	Bank officers	Promotes studies on comparative industry practices to provide bench-marks against which to judge corporate performance.	*Journal of Commercial Bank Lending*
11. Securities Industry Association (SIA)	Broker dealers in securities	Monitors and provides input to stockbrokers regarding SEC, stock exchanges (e.g., NYSE and AMEX), and congressional actions.	*Securities Industry Trends*

* Also appoints members to the Financial Accounting Foundation.

GENERALLY ACCEPTED ACCOUNTING PRINCIPLES

According to APB Statement No.4, GAAP is "a technical accounting term which encompasses the conventions, rules, and procedures necessary to define accepted accounting practice at a particular time." This wide but wary definition implies two truths:

1. GAAP is not a static, well-defined set of accounting principles, but a fluid set of principles based on current accounting thought and practice. GAAP changes in response to change in the business environment. Therefore, the researcher needs to be cognizant that the most current authoritative support is being reviewed since older pronouncements may have been superceded or modified by more recent ones.
2. GAAP is not composed of mutually exclusive accounting principles. Alternative principles for similar transactions may be considered equally acceptable. The researcher does not quit, then, when one acceptable principle is found.

GAAP performs two major functions:

1. **Measurement.** GAAP requires that revenues of a given period should be recognized (i.e., matched) with all expenses that were incurred to generate those revenues (e.g., depreciating fixed assets and recognizing stock options and pension liabilities). Besides attempting to measure periodic income objectively, the measurement principle focuses on valuation of financial statement accounts (e.g., reporting inventories at the lower of cost or market valuations).
2. **Disclosure.** GAAP provides information necessary for the users' decision models (e.g., methods to group accounts and descriptive terminology, as in reporting lease obligations in the footnotes). However, GAAP does not require disclosure of certain macroeconomic factors (e.g., interest and unemployment rates) often of interest to the entity, bankers, and other financial statement users.

CPAs may not express an opinion that the financial statements are presented in conformity with GAAP if the statements depart materially from an accounting principle promulgated by an "authoritative body" (i.e., a senior technical committee) designated by the AICPA Council, such as the APB and the FASB.

While opinions from these bodies provide the "substantial authoritative support" necessary to create GAAP, other sources of GAAP are available. Most notable are standard industry practices that provide material for GAAP either when a practice addresses a principle that does not exist in GAAP or when a practice seems to conflict with GAAP. In either case, management must state the case for the practice, and the CPA must evaluate the case to ascertain whether the practice violates established GAAP. In addition, if "unusual circumstances" would make following the normal procedure misleading, management must disclose departures from authoritative guidelines and justify the alternative principle.

The FASB arrives at GAAP by relating principles to three objectives of financial reporting set out in Statement of Financial Accounting Concepts No. 1. Financial reporting should provide information that:

1. Is useful to present and potential investors and creditors and other users in making rational investment, credit, and similar decisions. The information should be comprehensible to those who have a reasonable understanding of business and economic activities and are willing to study the information with reasonable diligence.
2. Helps present and potential investors and creditors and other users in assessing the amounts, timing, and uncertainty of prospective cash receipts from dividends or interest and the proceeds from the sale, redemption, or maturity of securities or loans. Since investors' and creditors' cash flows are related to enterprise cash flows, financial reporting should provide information to help investors, creditors, and others assess the amounts, timing, and uncertainty of prospective net cash inflows to the related enterprise.
3. Clarifies the economic resources of an enterprise, the claims to those resources (obligations of the enterprise to transfer resources to other entities and owners' equity), and the effects of transactions, events, and circumstances that change its resources and claims to those resources.

To minimize the haphazard establishment of GAAP, standards emerge according to these objectives, which, in turn, provide standards necessary for measuring the effectiveness of existing and proposed conventions, rules, and procedures that define accepted accounting practice.

Authoritative Support

Unlike the natural scientist, the accounting practitioner does not search for natural laws but rather attempts to discover a consensus among users of financial information. Since the accounting process is an artificially created mathematical model of an entity, the accountant relies heavily on authoritative support in determining the principles and procedures used to implement the accounting model.

As stated earlier, CPAs may not attest to the validity of financial statements (i.e., may not express an opinion that the statements are presented in conformity with GAAP) if the statement departs materially from an accounting principle promulgated by an authoritative body (i.e., a senior technical committee) designated by the AICPA Council, such as the APB, the FASB, and the GASB. However, a CPA may justify an alternative principle if unusual circumstances would make following the normal principles misleading. That is, under Rule 203 of the AICPA's Code of Professional Conduct, if the entity's management feels the circumstances do not warrant compliance with the standard, an exception can be taken. Under these circumstances, the auditor's report must clearly disclose the nature of and the reason for the exception in the financial statements.

The Hierarchy of GAAP[2]

Accountants in general agree that a body of generally accepted accounting principles exists. The components of GAAP that currently exist can be depicted in a hierarchy. This hierarchy shows the researcher where to begin in a search for a solution to the problem or issue under review. Figures 5–6 and 5–7 present the basic components of the hierarchy for Financial Statement GAAP and Government GAAP, respectively, as five different levels. Those in level one have the highest level of authority.

---

2   Statement on Auditing Standards No. 69, "The Meaning of Present Fairly in Conformity with Generally Accepted Accounting Principles in the Independent Auditor's Report," AICPA, 1991.

Figure 5–6 Basic Principles and Assumptions Underlying Financial Reporting

Level	Components
1	Pronouncements of an authoritative Body designated by the AICPA Council in Rule 203 of the Code of Professional Conduct.
	a. FASB Statements and Interpretations
	b. APB Opinions
	c. AICPA Accounting Research Bulletins
	d. Rules and Interpretative Releases of the SEC for SEC registrants
2	Pronouncements of bodies composed of expert accountants who follow a due process procedure; such pronouncements have been cleared by a body referred to in Level 1.
	a. Cleared AICPA Industry Audit and Accounting Guides
	b. Cleared AICPA Statements of Position (SPOs)
	c. FASB Technical Bulletins
3	Pronouncements of bodies organized by the AICPA or FASB but that do not necessarily go through due process procedures.
	a. AcSEC Practice Bulletins having been cleared by the FASB
	b. Consensus Positions of the FASB Emerging Issues Task Force
4	Practices or pronouncements that are widely recognized as being generally accepted because they represent prevalent practice in a particular industry, or the knowledgeable application to specific circumstances of pronouncements that are generally accepted.
	a. AICPA Accounting Interpretations
	b. Implementation Guides by the FASB Staff (Questions and Answers series)
	c. Notable Industry Practices
	d. Uncleared SOPs, and audit and accounting guides
5	Other Accounting Literature
	a. APB Statements
	b. AICPA Issues Pagers
	c. FASB Concepts Statements
	d. International Accounting Standards Committee Statements
	e. AICPA Technical Practice Aids
	f. Textbooks
	g. Journal Articles and monographs

Figure 5–7 Basic Principles and Assumptions Underlying Government Reporting

Level	Components
1	Pronouncements of an Authoritative Body
	a. GASB Pronouncements acknowledged by the GASB
	b. NCGA Pronouncements acknowledged by the GASB
	c. GASB and AICPA Pronouncements
	NOTE: If the accounting treatment of a transaction or event is not specified by a pronouncement of either 1a or 1b, then 1c is presumed to apply.
2	Pronouncements of bodies composed of expert accountants who follow a due process procedure.
	a. GASB Technical Bulletins
	b. Cleared AICPA Industry Audit and Accounting Guides, such as:
	Audits of State and Local Governmental Units
	Audits of Certain Nonprofit Organizations
	Audits of Colleges and Universities
	c. Cleared AICPA Statements of Position
3	Consensus positions of the GASB, EITF, and cleared AcSEC practice bulletins for state and local government.
4	Practices or pronouncements that are widely recognized as being generally accepted because they represent prevalent practice in a particular industry, or the knowledgeable application to specific circumstances of pronouncements that are generally accepted.
	a. Uncleared SOPs and audit Accounting Guides
	b. Questions and Answers issued by GASB staff
	c. Industry practice
5	Other Accounting Literature
	a. GASB Statements of Financial Accounting Concepts
	b. Elements of the Financial Statement Hierarchy
	c. Textbooks
	d. Journal articles

The foundation for this hierarchy contains the basic assumption or concepts of financial or government accounting. This foundation includes basic assumptions and principles underlying financial reporting: e.g., the going-concern assumption, substance over form, neutrality, the accrual basis, conservatism, materiality, objectivity, consistency, and full disclosure.

Levels one through four contain the components of four groups of reference sources containing established accounting principles. Level five provides other accounting literature in the absence of an established authoritative accounting principle as authorized by Rule 203 of the Code of Professional Conduct.

The following additional information about the levels of Financial Statement GAAP should enhance the reader's understanding of the items within each level.

Level 1 This level includes pronouncements of an authoritative body designated by the AICPA that officially establish GAAP, including:

    a. FASB Statements of Financial Accounting Standards (SFASs) and Interpretations.

    b. Thirty-one Opinions of the AICPA's Accounting Principles Board (APBOs).

c. Fifty-one Accounting Research Bulletins (ARBs), which were issued by the Committee on Accounting Procedure (CAP) of the AICPA.

d. Rules and Interpretative Releases issued by the Securities and Exchange Commission. Since the SEC has the ultimate authority to establish GAAP for publicly listed entities, these pronouncements have the highest level of authority that applies specifically to SEC registrants.

In short, FASB statements supersede some APB opinions, which, in turn, supersede some ARB statements, but those unsuperseded APB opinions and ARB statements are still effective. More recently issued standards supersede earlier ones. A FASB interpretation clarifies, explains, or elaborates on prior FASB, APB, and ARB statements, and has the same authority they do.

Level 2 This level includes pronouncements of bodies of expert accountants who follow a "due process" of deliberating and issuing accounting statements.

a. AICPA Industry Audit and Accounting Guides, which normally are reviewed by the Institute's Accounting Standards Executive Committee (AcSEC) and cleared by the FASB.

b. AICPA Statements of Position (SOPs), which have been reviewed by AcSEC and cleared by the FASB.

c. FASB Technical Bulletins, which provide guidance in applying authoritative pronouncements.

Level 3 This level includes AcSEC Practice Bulletins that have been cleared by the FASB, and also includes consensus positions of the FASB Emerging Issues Task Force (EITF).

Level 4 Included in this level are the AICPA Interpretations as well as implementation guides (referred to as "Questions and Answers") issued by the FASB staff. Also included in this level are the uncleared AICPA Statements of Position and uncleared audit and accounting guides (cleared SOPs and guides appear in level 3) and practices widely recognized in a particular industry.

Level 5 This level provides other accounting literature that the researcher could reference in the absence of a higher-level authority.

While reference to an authoritative pronouncement usually provides adequate support for an accounting decision, accountants forced to rely on lower levels of support must often build a case involving multiple references. Figure 5–8 provides a division between primary, self-supporting references and secondary, non-self-supporting references.

In researching an issue, often this question arises: Where does the researcher start and when can he or she stop the research process? To begin, the researcher would focus on the primary authoritative support, which has the highest level of authority according to the hierarchy of GAAP. If no primary sources are cited, the researcher would then drop down and review the secondary support.

If the researcher determines that the answer to the question is located in a primary authoritative support, he or she can stop the research process since these sources are sufficient for a conclusion. However, if the researcher cited secondary support, additional research is needed since any secondary source individually is insufficient authority. The researcher must recognize that many research questions will not be clear cut and, therefore, professional judgment is a key element in deciding when to stop the research process.

Figure 5-8 Accounting Authoritative Support

Primary Authoritative Support

Sources that provide sufficient authoritative support for including a particular accounting principle within GAAP.

A. General Application to the Field of Accounting

1. FASB and GASB Statements of Financial and Governmental Accounting Standards
2. FASB and GASB Interpretations
3. Opinions of the Accounting Principles Board
4. Accounting Research Bulletins of the Committee on Accounting Procedures
5. Consensus Positions of EITF

B. Special Application to Certain Entities

1. AICPA Industry Accounting Guides
2. AICPA Statements of Position
3. Regulations of the Securities and Exchange Commission
4. Statements of the Cost Accounting Standards Board
5. Interpretations of the Cost Accounting Standards Board

Secondary Authoritative Support

Sources that support inclusion of particular accounting principles within GAAP, but individually are not sufficient authoritative support.

A. Official Publications of Authoritative Bodies

1. FASB Statements of Financial Accounting Concepts
2. GASB Concept Statements
3. FASB Technical Bulletins
4. APB Statements
5. Interpretations of APB Opinions

B. Other Sources of Information

1. Substantive industrial practices
2. Pronouncements of industry regulatory authorities
3. Published research studies of authoritative professional and industrial societies
4. Publications of recognized industry associations
5. Accounting research monographs of the AICPA
6. SEC Staff Accounting Bulletins
7. Pronouncements of the IFAC and other international accounting bodies
8. Accounting textbooks and reference books authored by recognized authorities in the field

---

Economic Consequences

Selecting among possible accounting alternatives often affects economic decisions. Debates as to the proper accounting for stock options and the use of market values for derivatives are a few examples that have major economic implications. Thus, the researcher must recognize macroeconomic factors in planning and selecting accounting principles.

Rappaport[3] reported that the promulgation of financial accounting standards can affect economic behavior and wealth distribution in three ways. The standards can influence intended external users (e.g., competitors and stockholders), unintended external users (e.g., competitors, labor unions, and special interest groups) and internal users (e.g., corporate management). For example, assume that the research suggests that a significant piece of equipment should

---

3 Rappaport, Alfred, "Economic Impact of Accounting Standards—Implications for the FASB," *The Journal of Accountancy*, Vol. 2 (May 1977): 89–97.

be expensed immediately rather than continue to be capitalized over several years, since its future value "seems" impaired. This reduction in income could adversely impact the company's earnings per share and, thus, stock price; it could reduce the union members' profit sharing payouts or make their competitors' financial statements look relatively stronger, enabling them to attract new investors; and it could reduce the bonuses available to corporate management, thereby causing them to relocate to their competitors' organizations. The previous examples demonstrate that the "Law of Unintended Consequences" often generates many unexpected ramifications from the researcher's decisions. Nonetheless, the researcher is ethically bound to follow GAAP to help report accurate financial information—regardless of future economic consequences.

INTERNATIONAL ACCOUNTING

International competition has forced many firms to look to new markets and investors to finance the expansion and modernization needed to keep pace and advance in world markets. This expansion of increasingly internationalized capital markets is resulting in a need for internationally comparable financial statements and related internationally comparable accounting standards. Accounting principles and reporting practices are forms of communication which, in theory, should move across national boundaries as freely as the business practices they are intended to reflect. In truth, however, these accounting principles mirror the disparate economic and social environments of their respective nations and regions. As businesses and trade barriers between nations become less restrictive (e.g., under the influence of the North American Free Trade Agreement), differences among national accounting and auditing standards become more troubling. The present condition of international accounting is characterized largely by a collection of authoritative pronouncements of each individual country. This makes the task of comparing companies across national boundaries cumbersome and potentially confusing. Moreover, the growth of international joint ventures and American subsidiaries abroad requires mastery of international accounting standards.

Efforts have increased in recent years to move toward international standards. The movement toward harmonization has included the work of individual scholars as well as the activities of supra-national groups. Included in the latter category are the International Federation of Accountants (IFAC), the International Accounting Standards Committee (IASC), the Organization for Economic Cooperation and Development (OECD), and the European Economic Community (EEC).

The International Accounting Standards Committee (IASC), formed in 1973, is an independent private sector body with the objective of achieving uniformity in the application of accounting principles for financial reporting worldwide. The activities of IASC are conducted by a board comprised of representatives of accounting bodies in twelve countries and one federation, which currently consists of:

Australia	Malaysia
Canada	Mexico
France	Netherlands
Germany	Nordic Federation of Public Accountants
India	United Kingdom
South Africa	United States of America
Japan	

The IASC, through a due process procedure, has currently issued 38 International Accounting Standards which are being used for the following purposes:

1. As a basis for national accounting requirements in many countries.
2. As international benchmarks by countries that develop their own requirements.
3. By stock exchanges and regulatory authorities which allow financial statements to be presented in accordance with IASs.
4. By supra-national bodies, such as the European Commission, to produce results that meet the needs of capital markets.
5. By companies themselves.[4]

While the IASC works closely with the IFAC and membership in one automatically includes membership in the other, the IASC independently issues standards for presenting audited financial information. IASC has received support from the International Organization of Securities Commissions (IOSCO) and the World Trade Organization to create acceptable accounting standards for multinational securities and other international offerings.

The IASC and IOSCO agreed to a list of necessary accounting issues to address in a "core" set of international accounting standards for use in cross-border offerings and multiple listings. Ideally, establishing a core set of international accounting standards should reduce the costs of doing business and raising capital across borders, streamline internal accounting and auditing functions for multi-nationals, increase the efficiency of market regulations, and decrease the costs of international financial statement analysis and investment. However, the SEC has offered three conditions for accepting international accounting standards:

1. IASC standards should include a core set of accounting pronouncements that constitute a comprehensive, generally accepted basis of accounting.
2. IASC standards should be of high quality; they must result in comparability and transparency, and they must provide for full disclosure.
3. IASC standards should be rigorously interpreted and applied.

Since local regulations govern the preparation and issuance of financial statements in most countries, differences of form and content persist among countries. One objective of IASC is to harmonize this diversity. Although the IASC does not have the authority to require compliance with International Accounting Standards, the success of international accounting harmonization will depend upon the recognition and support of interested groups.

SUMMARY

This chapter has presented an overview of the bodies that set standards in accounting, the process of standard setting, the types of authoritative pronouncements, the meaning of GAAP, the hierarchy of GAAP, and the current status of international accounting. Since GAAP is not a static, well-defined set of accounting principles, but, rather, is a fluid set of principles based on current accounting thought and practice, the researcher needs to be aware of changes in pronouncements. And, because GAAP is not composed of mutually exclusive accounting principles, research in accounting does not consist of searching for a single acceptable principle, but for alternative principles that must be judged in the light of their place in a hierarchy.

---

4   *AICPA Professional Standards*, Volume 2, Section AC 9000.19.

DISCUSSION QUESTIONS

1. Discuss the environmental factors that influence the standard-setting process.
2. Identify the authoritative accounting pronouncements of the AICPA, FASB, and GASB.
3. What appears to be an underlying reason for the establishment of accounting standards?
4. Describe the rule-making or due-process procedures of the FASB in the establishment of a standard.
5. What is the FASB's Conceptual Framework Project? Of what benefit is this Project to the practitioner?
6. Identify the authoritative publications of the SEC, CASB, and AICPA.
7. What constitutes generally accepted accounting principles?
8. What is the purpose for the establishment of the hierarchy of GAAP?
9. What is meant by the term authoritative support?
10. What are the implications of GAAP and authoritative support to the researcher?
11. To conduct efficient research, where should one start in reviewing the accounting literature in search of a solution to a problem?
12. Compare the FASB's Statements in the hierarchy of Financial Statement GAAP and Government GAAP.
13. How can the promulgation of an accounting standard impact economic behavior? Can you discuss a specific example?
14. Distinguish between primary authoritative support and secondary authoritative support.
15. What two governmental organizations were added to the list of sponsoring organizations of the Financial Accounting Foundation (FAF) due to the establishment of the GASB's authoritative status?
16. What standards did the IASC develop?
17. Why are accountants generally more concerned with Regulation S-X and, to a lesser extent, Regulation S-K and 14A than with most other regulations?
18. What information is usually contained in a Financial Reporting Release?
19. Utilizing Figure 2–3 (Universal Elements of Reasoning), develop the eight elements for the following issue: Damieler Auto Parts, Inc., headquartered in Munich, Germany, is attempting to register with the SEC in order to list its stock on the New York Stock Exchange. Damieler currently is capitalizing most of its research and development (R&D) costs. Management of Damieler has requested your advice in regards to the proper accounting for R&D as to conformity with U.S. GAAP and/or International Accounting Standards.

CHAPTER 6

Sources of Authoritative Literature

LEARNING OBJECTIVES

After completing this chapter, you should understand:

- The main sources of authoritative literature on accounting principles and auditing standards.
- How to gather evidence from the AICPA Professional Standards, the FASB Accounting Standards, and the AICPA Technical Practice Aids.
- The basic format of APB Opinions and FASB and GASB Statements.

A major component of the research process is the review of the pertinent accounting or auditing literature. This chapter outlines the overall structure of the authoritative literature, with an emphasis on developing the technical skills required to access the AICPA Professional Standards and the FASB Accounting Standards series, which are the most comprehensive sources of authoritative accounting and auditing literature. This chapter will stress accessing hard-copy materials and Chapter 7 will focus on accessing the materials via electronic means.

Many of the techniques used to access the AICPA or the FASB Standards series, such as the use of keywords, are also applicable to pronouncements of other rule-making bodies. These keywords, identified in your statement of the problem that you are researching, provide the starting point in searching through various indices for sources in developing a conclusion to the research issue. In addition to the AICPA and the FASB, the Cost Accounting Standards Board (CASB), the Governmental Accounting Standards Board (GASB), and the U.S. Securities and Exchange Commission (SEC) produce publications stating their official positions on various issues. These organizations also publish unofficial interpretations and descriptive surveys to help the practitioner implement required accounting principles. The identification and use of these unofficial publications are also discussed.

Many research sources are available to aid the researcher in the quest for a solution to a particular problem or issue. A summary of the various sources of authoritative literature on accounting principles and auditing standards is shown in Figure 6–1.

ACCESSING THE AUTHORITATIVE LITERATURE

There are many sources of authoritative accounting and auditing literature. The publications presented in Figure 6–2 are among the researcher's most

Figure 6–1 Sources of Authoritative Literature

1. **Pronouncements of authoritative bodies that prescribe accounting principles that must be followed in order for the financial statements to be considered in conformity with generally accepted accounting principles.**

   Authoritative Body/Title of Literature

   AICPA:

   - Committee on Accounting Procedures (CAP)/*Accounting Research Bulletins (ARBs)*
   - Committee on Terminology/*Accounting Terminology Bulletins*
   - Accounting Principles Board (APB)/*APB Opinions*

   Cost Accounting Standards Board (CASB)/*Cost Accounting Standards (CASs)/ Interpretations*

   Financial Accounting Federation (FAF):

   - Financial Accounting Standards Board (FASB)/*Statements of Financial Accounting Standards (SFASs)/Interpretations*
   - Consensus of Emerging Issues Task Force (EITF)
   - National Council on Governmental Accounting (NCGA)/*Statements/Interpretations*
   - Governmental Accounting Standards Board (GASB)/*Statements of Governmental Accounting Standards (GASs)*

   Securities and Exchange Commission (SEC)

   /Regulation S-K
   /Regulation S-X
   /Accounting Series Releases (ASRs)
   /Financial Reporting Release (FRRs)
   /Accounting and Auditing Enforcement Releases (AAERs)

2. **Authoritative literature that is considered descriptive of generally accepted accounting principles, but does not prescribe such principles.**

   Authoritative Body/Title of Literature

   AICPA:

   - Special Committees/*Industry Accounting Guides*
   - Accounting Standards Division/*Statements of Position*

3. **Literature that unofficially interprets pronouncements of authoritative bodies.**

   Authoritative Body/Title of Literature

   AICPA: Accounting Principles Board (APB)/*APB Interpretations*

   FAF: Financial Accounting Standards Board (FASB)/*Technical Bulletins*

   Securities and Exchange Commission (SEC)/*Staff Accounting Bulletins (SABs)*

4. **Authoritative literature that expresses views on accounting theory rather than specific elements of generally accepted accounting principles.**

   Authoritative Body/Title of Literature

   AICPA: Accounting Principles Board (APB)/*APB Statements*

   FAF: Financial Accounting Standards Board (FASB)/*Statements of Financial Accounting Concepts (SFACs)*

   - Special Committees/*Industry Accounting Guides*
   - Accounting Standards Division/*Statements of Position*

5. **Authoritative literature on auditing standards.**

   Authoritative Body/Title of Literature

   AICPA:

   - Auditing Standards Division
     /Statements on Auditing Standards (SASs)
     /Auditing Interpretations
     /Industry Audit Guides
     /Statements of Position
   - Professional Ethics Division/Code of Professional Conduct

valuable tools for identifying and locating authoritative literature in the specific area under investigation. These research services enable the practitioner to keep abreast of the pronouncements, interpretations, and guidelines that govern today's technical and professional activities. The publications and techniques for using them to conduct efficient research are discussed in the following sections.

Sound research techniques rest on these basic principles:

1. The order of search is important. Searches should begin with sources that encompass a broad range of pronouncements and only then move to sources with a narrower scope (those that contain specific pronouncements). Primary authoritative support should be consulted first, followed by secondary sources, if necessary. Otherwise, the researcher may overlook major material.

Figure 6–2 Primary Research Publications

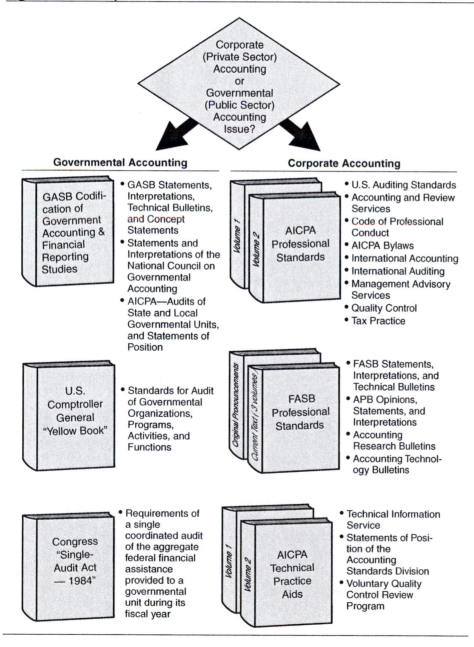

2. Sources are systems. That is, they are more than lists, and the researcher should seek their systematic aid. Many sources, for example, cross-reference items in order to guide the researcher to the most productive main terms (terms that may never have occurred to the researcher).

AICPA Professional Standards

The *Professional Standards* series is available in an annually updated paperback edition or in a two-volume looseleaf subscription service. The looseleaf service has the advantage of being continually updated. Volume 1 contains the U.S. Auditing Standards as well as Attestation Standards. Figure 6–3 shows the major divisions including the subdivisions of the Statement on Auditing Standards (SASs) section and the topics covered in the appendixes. The material within each subdivision is arranged by numbered section, and each paragraph within a section is decimally numbered. References to sections in Volume 1 are preceded by the citation AU. To illustrate the organization and referencing system of the *Professional Standards*, the table of contents of AU Section 200 is reproduced below:

AU Section 200—THE GENERAL STANDARDS

Section		Paragraph
201	Nature of the General Standards	.01
210	Training and Proficiency of the Independent Auditor	.01–.05
220	Independence	.01–.07
230	Due Care in the Performance of Work	.01–.13
	Professional Skepticism	.07–.09
	Reasonable Assurance	.10–.13

The numbering system facilitates references to specific sections or paragraphs within a section. For example, AU Section 210.03 refers to the third paragraph of Section 210.

Another major division in Volume 1 of the *Professional Standards* is Auditing Interpretations. As discussed previously, the Interpretations provide guidance on the application of SASs. Auditing Interpretations are numbered in the 9000 series, with the last three digits specifying the SAS section to which an Interpretation relates. For example, AU Section 9326 indicates that the Interpretation relates to AU Section 326.

Volume 2 contains ten major divisions, which are listed in Figure 6–3, along with the related citations. Within each major division are several subdivisions, which are too numerous to list here. The material within each division is organized by numbered sections and paragraphs in the same manner as in Volume 1.

A search for information on a particular subject may begin with the Master Topical Index, which identifies individual indexes containing detailed information. Alternatively, the researcher may go directly to the appropriate detailed index, and look up keywords identified in the problem or issue under investigation.

FASB Accounting Standards

Each year, the FASB compiles and publishes accounting standards in two complementary volumes. The first, *Original Pronouncements*, contains the complete

Figure 6-3 Organization of the AICPA *Professional Standards*

VOLUME 1	**Citation**
Statements on Auditing Standards	AU *Sec.*
Introduction	100
The General Standards	200
The Standards of Field Work	300
The First, Second, and Third Standards of Reporting	400
The Fourth Standard of Reporting	500
Other Types of Reports	600
Special Topics	700
Compliance Auditing	800
Special Reports of the Committee on Auditing Procedures	900
Auditing Interpretation	9000

Appendixes:

A. Historical Background
B. List of Statements on Auditing Procedure
C. Sources of Sections in Current Text
D. Cross-Reference Tables for Auditing Interpretations
E. AICPA Audit and Accounting Guides and Statements of Position

Statements on Standards for Attestation Engagements	AT *Sec.*
Attestation Standards	100
Attestation Standards Interpretations	9100
Financial Forecasts and Protections	200
Reporting on Pro Forma Financial Information	300
Reporting on an Entity's Internal Control Structure Over Financial Reporting	400
Compliance Attestation	500

VOLUME 2	**Citation**
Accounting and Review Services	AR
Code of Professional Conduct	ET
Bylaws of the AICPA	BL
International Accounting Standards	AC
International Standards on Auditing	AU
Consulting Services	CS
Quality Control	QC
Peer Review	PR
Tax Practice	TX
Personal Financial Planning	PFP

original text of APB Opinions, Statements, and Interpretations; AICPA Accounting Research Bulletins; and FASB Statements of Concepts, Statements of Standards, Interpretations, and Technical Bulletins. The pronouncements are arranged in chronological order. All superseded and amended material is printed in a lightly-colored panel to distinguish it from current material.

The other volume, *Current Text*, which is available in a paperback set or a three-volume looseleaf service, is organized alphabetically by subject. The material presented under each subject begins with an integrated presentation of all pronouncements covered under the AICPA's Code of Professional Conduct Rule 203: Accounting Principles. Pronouncements not covered by Rule 203 immediately follow the official text. The reader is advised to note that the *Current Text* does not include dissenting opinions of the board or committee members not in agreement with the original pronouncements. The dissenting opinions can often shed light on the scope and limitations of a pronouncement and can be located in the volume of *Original Pronouncements*.

The *Current Text* is divided into volumes 1 and 2—General Standards, which contain the standards that are applicable to all entities, and volume 3, Industry Standards, which contains the standards applicable only to entities in specific industries. The appendixes to these three volumes contain a cross-reference of the original pronouncements to the *Current Text* paragraphs, a schedule of amended and superseded accounting pronouncements, and the effective dates of the pronouncements.

Each section of the *Current Text* is identified by an alphanumeric code, and paragraphs within each section are decimally numbered. For example, the reference A06.110 refers to Section A06, "Accounting Changes," and paragraph 110. Each volume of the *Current Text* concludes with a comprehensive Topical Index. Exercises at the end of this chapter provide an opportunity to use the *Current Text*.

Technical Practice Aids

The AICPA publishes two volumes of non-authoritative examples and commentary under the title of Technical Practice Aids (see Figure 6–2).

Volume 1 contains the Technical Information Service (TIS), which consists of a series of questions and replies. The information is categorized under major headings: Financial Statement Presentation; Assets; Liabilities and Deferred Credits; Capital; Revenue and Expense; Special Industry Problems; Special Organizational Problems; Audit Field Work; and Audit Reports.

The TIS includes inquiries and replies based upon selected Technical Information Service correspondence dealing with various accounting or auditing issues. As a matter of policy, the TIS staff does not render opinions on tax or the legal aspects of questions submitted by practitioners. Additions to the Technical Information Service are initiated by practitioners' questions related to accounting or auditing problems. These questions are then answered by the TIS staff accountants. The responses are not authoritative pronouncements, but are expressions of an expert's professional opinion, supported by reference to authoritative literature if applicable. This service permits the practitioner to communicate directly with the AICPA in attempting to resolve an issue. By reading the questions posed to the TIS, and the TIS staff's previous responses, a researcher can gain insight into how other professionals have interpreted and implemented professional standards. If the particular area has not been presented to the TIS staff, the researcher can submit an inquiry. The information obtained from the TIS can be used by the researcher in forming conclusions and exercising professional judgment.

Each major section of the Technical Practice Aids is preceded by a table of contents indicating the main topics covered. There are two appendixes concluding Volume 1. The first appendix is a cross-reference index between official pronouncements cited in the volume and the section number where the pronouncement is cited. The second appendix is a keyword topical index to the volume.

Volume 2 contains the Statements of Position (SOPs) of the Accounting Standards Division and the Auditing Standards Division. These SOPs are arranged in chronological order as they are issued. The Accounting Division's SOPs are followed by a keyword topical index. Volume 2 concludes with a listing of the Accounting Standards Division's Practice Bulletins and Issues Papers.

GOVERNMENT ACCOUNTING PRONOUNCEMENTS

The researcher often must explore issues in the public area, in addition to those in the private sector. The not-for-profit arena's share of the country's gross national product has grown significantly, and this trend should continue into the foreseeable future. Thus, in addition to those for the financial arena, Figure 6–2 highlights the three major primary research publications in the governmental arena. First, the *GASB Codification of Government Accounting & Financial Reporting Studies* contains all GASB Statements, Interpretations, Technical Bulletins, and Concept Statements. It also codifies the National Council on Government Accounting's Statements and Interpretations, as well as the AICPA's Audit Guides of State and Local Governments and Statements of Position. The *GASB Codification* corresponds to the private sector's *FASB Accounting Standards*.

Second, the U.S. Comptroller General's "Yellow Book" contains a codification of audit standards for government organizations, programs, activities, and functions. This text operates much the same as the AICPA *Professional Standards*. Finally, the U.S. Congress's "Single Audit Act of 1984" requires all state and local government units receiving at least $100,000 of federal assistance per fiscal year to have an audit made in conformity with the standards of this Act. Government units receiving between $25,000–$100,000 of such annual assistance may also adhere to the audit requirement of this Act. These audits contain both financial and compliance components and are subject to oversight by federal agencies designated by the United States Office of Management and Budget.

READING AN APB OPINION, FASB STATEMENT, OR GASB STATEMENT

In researching an issue, the researcher may need to read a specific APB Opinion, FASB Statement, or GASB Statement. In such a case, the researcher should be aware that there is a basic format that is followed in the APB Opinions and FASB and GASB Statements. Depending upon the complexity of the pronouncement, the following elements may be included: an introduction to the accounting issues addressed by the pronouncement, the background of the business event and accounting issues, the basis of the Board's conclusions, the actual opinion or statement of accounting standard, the effective date to implement the standard, illustrations of application, and the disclosures required. These basic elements are not necessarily presented as separate sections of all Opinions or Statements. Those that are relatively short may combine the introduction and background information and eliminate the illustration of applications section if it is not a complicated principle. However, there is always a separate section designated as the Opinion or Standard of Accounting.

The introductory section defines the accounting issue that necessitated an authoritative pronouncement. This section gives the scope of the pronouncement; that is, it defines the type of entity affected. It can also limit the application of the pronouncement to companies of specific size (e.g., sales exceeding $250 million). The introduction also gives the effects of the new pronouncement on previously issued standards. It specifies which pronouncements or sections of prior pronouncements are superseded by the new standard. Generally, within the introduction, there is a summary of the standard so that the researcher sees quickly if the standard applies to the specific situation being investigated.

The background information section describes in more detail the business events and related accounting treatments presented in the pronouncement. This section develops the various arguments supporting alternative approaches to resolving the issue. The underlying assumptions for these alternatives are defined, and the different interpretations of the economic impact of the business event are presented. This section follows the introduction in the APB Opinions, while the FASB generally places the background information in an appendix to the official pronouncement.

The basis for conclusion of the authoritative standard is described in the Opinions and Statements. This section explains the rationale for the accounting principles prescribed in the pronouncement, indicating which arguments were accepted and which were rejected. (Generally, the APB incorporates the basis of conclusion within the Opinion section of the pronouncement. The FASB incorporates dissenting viewpoints at the end of its main section, Standards of Financial Accounting and Reporting, and positions the Basis for Conclusion in a separate appendix.) The background information and basis for conclusion provide the researcher with a description of the business events and transactions covered by the pronouncement. These sections can be helpful in determining if the pronouncement addresses the specific issue under investigation. If the researcher is in the early stages of investigation, these sections can be helpful in defining the business transactions, determining their economic impact, and relating them to the proper reporting format.

The opinion or standard section prescribes the accounting principles that must be applied to the business transactions described in the pronouncement. The length of this section will depend upon the complexity of the business events involved.

The standard section can be very short, as in the case of FASB Statement No. 73, "Reporting a Change in Accounting for Railroad Track Structures," which basically requires the change to depreciation accounting for railroad track structures be applied retroactively, or it can be very long and complicated, as in FASB Statement No. 13, "Accounting for Leases." In Statement No. 13, the board established specialized terminology; set up criteria for distinguishing various types of leases; and established accounting, reporting, and disclosure requirements for the various leases. All of these items are within the standard section. This section represents the heart of the official pronouncement and must be followed when the researcher concludes that the standard applies to the business transactions under investigation.

The effective date section states when the new pronouncement goes into effect. It also identifies any transition period that might be used by a company to implement a new standard. For example, FASB Statement No. 13 had a four-year transition period to permit companies to gather data for retroactive application of this complicated pronouncement on lease transactions. If the board prescribes the method of implementation, retroactive restatement, cumulative effect, or prospective application, the method will be indicated in this section of the pronouncement.

SUMMARY

A major task of the researcher is that of reviewing current professional literature in the search for authoritative support. This chapter focused on the sources of authoritative support and semiauthoritative literature, as well as efficient means of accessing the literature for a solution to the issue under investigation. The resources presented include the AICPA's Professional Standards and Technical Practice Aids, FASB Accounting Standards, and governmental accounting sources. These publications provide the most comprehensive, up-to-date coverage of the current standards in every major area of professional activity plus guidance in applying the standards in practice.

Appendix A to this chapter is a set of exercises that emphasizes the methodology of the literature search step in the research process. Chapter 7 presents additional research tools for your use and includes a discussion of computerized databases.

DISCUSSION QUESTIONS

1. Identify the major research tools (literature sources) that are discussed in this chapter. Also, briefly describe the basic contents of each source.
2. What primary research publication would the researcher use to locate:

   a. A FASB Technical Bulletin?
   b. A specific Rule of Conduct in the Code of Professional Conduct?
   c. A statement on auditing standards?
   d. An Accounting Research Bulletin?

3. Explain the purpose of the *keyword* concept in accounting and/or auditing research.
4. What is the purpose of the AICPA's Technical Information Service?
5. List the major elements or segments of a specific APB Opinion or FASB Statement.
6. Name four authoritative bodies that prescribe accounting principles that act as GAAP.
7. Name four publications that include prescribed accounting principles that act as GAAP.
8. a. Name two of the main divisions of Volume 1 of the *AICPA Professional Standards.*

   b. What is the relationship between the SASs and Section 9000?

9. What are the two complementary volumes published by the FASB annually, and how do they differ?
10. What are the elements of the basic format of APB Opinions and FASB Statements? Describe briefly what is contained in each element.
11. Briefly explain the contents of the "Yellow Book."

APPENDIX A

Exercises

The following exercises emphasize the use of the AICPA's *Professional Standards* and the FASB's *Accounting Standards Current Text.* Completion of the exercises should provide a working knowledge of these research tools. The ability to apply these tools will be tested in researching various comprehensive problems, throughout this text as well as cases at the authors' Web site for this text.

Exercises 1–3 relate to the use of the AICPA Professional Standards.

1. Identify the original pronouncement indicated by each of the following citations:

   a. AU Section 504
   b. AU Section 333A
   c. AU Section 9508.01
   d. AT Section 100.76

2. Give citations for authoritative literature covering the following topics:

   a. Confirmation of receivables
   b. Effects of illegal acts on auditor's report
   c. Custody of audit working papers
   d. Auditor's standard report

3. Using the *Professional Standards*, locate the authoritative literature addressing the problem presented in the following situation.

   The Press-Punch Corporation is a closely held company (ten major stockholders) that manufactures parts for the three major U.S. auto companies. Two of the major stockholders formed a partnership that owns the building occupied by Press-Punch. The leasing of the building to Press-Punch is the only business activity of the partnership. As the auditor for Press-Punch, you need to determine the financial statement disclosure requirements for this related-party transaction.

Exercises 4–7 relate to the use of the three volume set of FASB *Accounting Standards Current Text*.

4. Identify the source (original pronouncement) for each of the following citations:

   a. I73.125
   b. C51.109
   c. L10.116
   d. D22.509–.513

5. The Comet Powerboat Company manufactures one of the most popular speedboats in the United States. As an incentive to its dealers to keep an adequate stock in their showrooms, the company allows dealers to return any unsold boats at the end of the boating season. Locate authoritative literature in the *Current Text* that addresses the proper revenue recognition procedure for Comet Powerboat Company, taking into consideration the dealer's right to return.

6. Give the *Current Text* citations for the following keywords:

   a. Purchase method of accounting
   b. Dividend disclosure
   c. Patents
   d. Warranties-revenue recognition
   e. Personal property tax

7. Identify the authoritative literature indicated by the following citations:

   a. C11.101
   b. P16.147
   c. F80.101

Exercises 8–10 relate to the use of the *FASB Accounting Standards Original Pronouncements*.

8. What paragraphs of the original APB Opinion No. 11 have been superseded?

9. Referring to FASB Statement No. 5, "Accounting for Contingencies," identify the paragraph numbers for the following components of the Statement.

   a. Introduction
   b. Standard of accounting and reporting
   c. Effective date
   d. Examples or illustrations
   e. Background
   f. Basis for standard

10. Referring to APB Opinion No. 26, "Early Extinguishment of Debt," identify the paragraph numbers for the following components of the Opinion.

    a. Introduction
    b. Background
    c. Opinion
    d. Effective date
    e. Examples of illustrations

CHAPTER 7

Other Research Tools

LEARNING OBJECTIVES

After completing this chapter, you should understand:

- How the AICPA's *Accounting Trends and Techniques*, *Financial Report Surveys*, and *Audit and Accounting Manual* can assist the research effort.
- What is contained in the public files of the accounting and auditing authoritative bodies.
- The major trade directories, government publications, statistical sources, and business and international services available to the researcher.
- The characteristics of major, currently available accounting and auditing computerized research tools, including the Financial Accounting Standards Board's Financial Accounting Research System and LEXIS-NEXIS.

The previous chapters have presented practical guidance for conducting accounting and auditing research. Chapter 6 dealt with the search for authoritative support through the use of traditional manual research tools—the FASB's *Accounting Standards* and the AICPA's *Professional Standards*, and *Technical Practice Aids*. This chapter focuses on other manual research tools, but will emphasize computerized research tools currently available to the researcher.

Due to the recent increase in accounting and auditing pronouncements and the increase in financial reporting in general, more and more organizations use computerized research tools to gain rapid access to key information for decision making.

MANUAL RESEARCH TOOLS

In addition to those discussed in Chapter 6, other frequently used manual research tools include the *Accounting and Tax Index*; the AICPA's *Accounting Trends and Techniques*, *Financial Report Surveys*, and the *Audit and Accounting Manual*; research files of public accounting firms; and public files of the accounting and auditing authoritative bodies.

Accounting & Tax Index

The index, which is arranged in a dictionary format with full citations, covers virtually every English-language publication on accounting or accounting-related and taxation-related subjects, and also incorporates accounting firms, state and national legislation, compensation plans, consulting services, and corporate financial management. The index scans more than 1,000 publications for relevant citations. It is published in three quarterly issues, and a cumulative year-end volume provides quick access to a number of books, articles, pamphlets, speeches, and government documents. Figure 7–1 presents an excerpt from the index. An electronic version of this index is available through UMI's ProQuest Direct, or through the DIALOG database.

Figure 7–1 Excerpts from *Accounting & Tax Index*

PAYROLL TAXES

Social Security/Medicare. *Tax Management Financial Planning Journal*, v14n3, Mar 17, 1998 – p. 72–73

Social Security/Medicare. *Tax Management Financial Planning Journal*, v14n5, Mar 19, 1998 – p. 125–133

Social security saved: Reduce payroll taxes and return to pay-as-you-go system with optional personal accounts, by Daniel Patrick Moynihan. *Vital Speeches of the Day*, v64n13, Apr 15,1998 – p. 389–392

Structuring joint ventures betwen for-profit and nonprofit organizations, by Robert W Friz. *Journal of Taxation of Exempt Organizations*, v9n6, May/Jun 1998 – p. 259–270

A taxing problem, by Ken Phillips. *Charter*, v69n2, Mar 1998 – p. 26–27

PCB

Thermal treatment of PCB-contaminated soils, by William E Gallagher, Thomas C Ponder Jr. *Transactions of AACE International*, 1997 – p. 96–103

PEACHTREE SOFTWARE INC

Big changes in low-end accounting software, by Ted Needleman. *Accounting Today*, v12n10, Jun 8–Jun 21, 1998, – p. 28,34+

No Sweat Accounting Software, by Dave McClure, *Accounting Technology*, v14n4, May 1998 – p. 34–36+

Peachtree says MICA acquisition complete; announces Peachtree 2000. *Practical Accountant*, v31n4, Apr 1998 – p. 12

PEARCE, LINDA

Gymnastics in the swing, by Linda Pearce. *Australian CPA*, v68n5, Jun 1998 – p. 66–68

Oz Open shows upsets... and triumphs, by Linda Pearce. *Australian Accountant*, v68n2, Mar 1998 – p. 66–67

PEARL ASSURANCE PLC

Finance giants target firms, by Lawrie Holmes. *Accountancy Age*, Apr. 23, 1998 – p. 1

PEARSON, DAVID

Where are they now? by David Pearson. *CIO*, v11n15(Section 1), May 15, 1998 – p. 58–64

PEARSON, JOHN K

The new bankruptcy claim form, by John K Pearson. *Business Credit*, v100n4, Apr 1998 – p. 20–25

PEARSON, THOMAS C

A primer for internal auditors considering whistle blowing, by Thomas C Pearson, Terry Gregson, et al. *Internal Auditing*, v13n5, May/Jun 1998 – p. 9–19

Managing issues, by Stephen Harrison. *Charter*, v69n2, Mar 1998 – p. 6

What's up with peer review? by Michael G Stevens. *Practical Accountant*, v31n4, Apr 1998– p. 45–48

When the doctor calls: The Quality Assurance program, by Bernie Clancy. *Australian CPA*, v68n4, May 1998 – p. 32–34

PEHRSON, GORDON O JR

Product failure: Another adverse effect, by Gordon O Pehrson Jr. *Life Association News*, v93n3, Mar 1998 – p. 122

PELAEZ, ROLANDO F

Economically significant stock market forecasts, by Rolando F Pelaez. *Financial Review* v33n1, Feb 1998 – p. 65–76

PELLERVO, DUANE H

Tax consequences of corporate restructurings and acquisitions involving consolidated group members with intercompany obligations, by Duane H Pellervo. *Tax Management Memorandum*, v39n8, Apr 13, 1998 – p. 111–118

PENALTIES

see Fines & penalties

PENDLEBURY, MAURICE

Resource accounting and executive agencies, by Maurice Pendlebury, Yusuf Karbhari. *Public Money & Management*, v18n2, Apr–Jun 1998 – p. 29–33

PENNELL, JOHN S

When hypothetical transactions have real results – New Prop. Regs. for Subchapter K, by John S Pennell, Philip F Postlewaite. *Journal of Taxation*, v88n5, May 1998 – p. 262–271

PENNINGS, ENRICO

How to finance your investment opportunity internally: A note, by Enrico Pennings. *Journal of Futures Markets*, v18n5, Aug 1998 – p. 599–604

PENNY, MIKE

Are you managing your cashflow? by Mike Penny. *Director*, v51n11, Jun 1998 – p. 30–32

PENSION & WELFARE BENEFITS ADMINISTRATION

Department of Labor. *ACA News*, v41n3, Mar 1998 – p. 37

PENSION BENEFIT GUARANTY CORP

Pension distribution answer book: Forms and worksheets (208.9 G), by Joan Gucciardi, Melanie N Aska Knox. *Pension Distribution Answer Book (Panel, New York)*, 2nd ed, 1998 – p. 1 v. (various pagings)

Qualified retirement and other employee benefit plans (754.4 C), by Michael T Canan, *West's Employment Law Series* (West Goup, St Paul MN), 1997 – p.2 v. (1–1455: 1–522)

Source: Reprinted with permission from UMI, copyright 1998.

Accounting Trends & Techniques

For over 50 years, the AICPA has published an annual survey of accounting practices in *Accounting Trends & Techniques*. This publication provides comprehensive up-to-date excerpts of financial reporting practices and developments for about 600 publicly held companies. The findings illustrate the current reporting practices of such selected companies and chart significant trends in reporting practices. Approximately 90 percent of the surveyed companies are listed on the New York or American Stock Exchanges.

The survey enables the practitioner to determine how various-size companies in a wide range of industries have complied with professional standards for financial reporting. It also alerts the practitioner to emerging trends in reporting practices. Specific reporting requirements set forth in pronouncements of the APB, FASB, and SEC are cited wherever applicable. This survey is an appropriate source for the researcher to review in an attempt to determine current practice for a particular issue under investigation.

Each company surveyed in *Accounting Trends & Techniques* is assigned a reference number. As companies are removed from the survey because of an acquisition or merger, the identification number is retired. The appendix of this publication lists the companies in their reference number order. The survey contains a table of contents listing specific reporting and disclosure examples by the general categories of Balance Sheet, Income Statement, Stockholders Equity, Statement of Cash Flows, and Auditor's Report. A topical index is included at the end of the survey. An excerpt from *Accounting Trends & Techniques* is illustrated in Figure 7–2.

Financial Report Surveys

The AICPA's *Financial Report Surveys*, which supplement the overview that *Accounting Trends and Techniques* provides, are a continuing series of studies, which show in detail how companies in a wide range of industries disclose specific accounting and reporting questions in their financial reports. The surveys include numerous illustrations drawn from the National Automated Accounting Research System (NAARS), which stores data collected from thousands of published financial reports. NAARS is explained later in this chapter. The surveys also include the complete texts of official pronouncements and other pertinent material wherever applicable. For example, Survey No. 54 presents examples on how 53 corporate financial statements present certain provisions of FASB Statement No. 112, *Employers' Accounting for Postemployment Benefits*. To date, the AICPA has published 54 surveys, each focusing in depth on a specific issue of financial reporting

Audit and Accounting Manual

The *Audit and Accounting Manual*, prepared by the staff of the AICPA, provides a nonauthoritative guide for practitioners in the conduct of an audit. The manual explains and illustrates the actual procedures involved in major aspects of an audit engagement. Extensive examples of such items as engagement letters, audit programs, working papers, and various other forms and documents are provided. The contents of the manual include the following:

- Introduction
- Compilation and Review
- Engagement Planning and Administration
- Internal Control Structure

Figure 7–2 Excerpt from *Accounting Trends & Techniques*

TREASURY STOCK

APB Opinion No. 6 discusses the balance sheet presentation of treasury stock. As shown in Table 2-37, the prevalent balance sheet presentation of treasury stock is to show the cost of treasury stock as a reduction of stockholders' equity.

Examples of treasury stock presentations follow.

TABLE 2-37: TREASURY STOCK—BALANCE SHEET PRESENTATION

	1997	1996	1995	1994
Common Stock				
Cost of treasury stock shown as stockholders' equity deduction ...	360	350	349	342
Par of stated value of treasury stock deducted from issued stock of the same class	19	19	27	23
Cost of treasury stock deducted from stock of the same class	5	4	6	2
Other	3	1	3	6
Total Presentations	**387**	**374**	**385**	**373**
Preferred Stock				
Cost of treasury stock shown as stockholders' equity deduction ...	2	4	3	2
Par or stated value of treasury stock deducted from issued stock of the same class	2	1	—	2
Other	—	—	1	2
Total Presentations	**4**	**5**	**4**	**6**
Number of Companies				
Disclosing treasury stock	384	373	384	373
Not disclosing treasury stock	216	227	216	227
Total Companies	**600**	**600**	**600**	**600**

Cost of Treasury Stock Shown as Reduction of Stockholders' Equity

ALUMAX INC. (DEC)

(In millions of dollars, except per share amounts)	1997	1996
Stockholders' Equity:		
Preferred stock of $1.00 par value— authorized 50,000,000 shares	—	—
Common stock of $.01 par value— authorized 200,000,000 shares; issued and outstanding 53,390,250 shares in 1997 and 54,692,057 shares in 1996	$ .6	$ .5
Paid-in capital	935.8	920.2
Retained earnings	758.0	724.3
Cumulative foreign currency translation adjustment	(13.6)	(4.2)
Common stock in treasury, at cost—1,812,900 shares in 1997	(59.1)	—
Total stockholders' equity	1,621.7	1,640.8

NOTES TO FINANCIAL STATEMENTS

Note 10 (In Part): Stockholders' Equity

Treasury Stock. In the fourth quarter of 1997, the Company began acquiring shares of its common stock in connection with a stock repurchase program announced in July 1996. That program authorizes the Company to purchase up to 2.5 million common shares from time to time on the open market or pursuant to negotiated transactions at price levels the Company deems attractive. The Company purchased 1.8 million shares of common stock in 1997 at an aggregate cost of $59.1. The purpose of the stock repurchase program is to help the Company achieve its long-term goal of enhancing stockholder value. In February 1998, the Board of Directors amended the program to provide that purchases reported to, and ratified by, the Board of Directors or by the Executive Committee of the Board shall not be counted in determining compliance with the 2.5 million share limitation.

Sales Of Receivables With Recourse

DATA GENERAL CORPORATION (SEP)

NOTES TO CONSOLIDATED FINANCIAL STATEMENTS

Note 7 (In Part): Financial Instruments, Commitments, and Contingencies

Financial Instruments. The Company enters into various types of financial instruments in the normal course of business. Fair values for certain financial instruments are based on quoted market prices. For other financial instruments, fair values are estimated based on assumptions concerning the amount and timing of estimated future case flows and assumed discount rates reflecting varying degrees of perceived risk. Accordingly, the fair values may not represent actual values of the financial instruments that could have been realized as of year end or that will be realized in the future.

•   •   •   •   •   •

In the normal course of business, the Company enters into certain sales-type lease arrangements with customers. These leases are generally sold to third-party financing institutions. A portion of these arrangements contains certain recourse provisions under which the Company remains liable. The Company's maximum exposure under the recourse provisions was approximately $13.6 million, net of related allowances. A portion of this contingent obligation is collateralized by security interests in the related equipment. The fair value of the recourse obligation at September 27, 1997 was not determinable as no market exists for these obligations.

MCKESSON CORPORATION (MAR)

NOTES TO CONSOLIDATED FINANCIAL STATEMENTS

Note 5: Off-Balance Sheet Risk and Concentrations of Credit Risk

Trade receivables subject the Company to a concentration of credit risk with customers in the retail sector. This risk is spread over a large number of geographically dispersed customers.

At March 31, 1997, the Company sold $154.6 million of trade receivables at amounts approximating their fair value

Figure 7–2 Excerpt from *Accounting Trends & Techniques (continued)*

to a bank in accordance with SFAS No. 125, "Accounting for Transfers and Servicing of Financial Assets and Extinguishments of Liabilities."

Proceeds received by the Company on sales of accounts receivable with recourse to the Company for certain uncollectible amounts totaled $105 million and $47 million in 1996 and 1995, respectively.

WEYERHAEUSER COMPANY (DEC)

NOTES TO CONSOLIDATED FINANCIAL STATEMENTS

Note 15 (In Part): Legal Proceedings, Commitments and Contingencies

Other Items
The company's 1997 capital expenditures, excluding acquisitions, were $656 million and are expected to approximate $750 million in 1998; however, the 1998 expenditure level could be increased or decreased as a consequence of future economic conditions.

During the normal course of business, the company's subsidiaries included in its real estate and related assets segment have entered into certain financial commitments comprised primarily of guarantees made on $42 million of partnership borrowings and limited recourse obligations associated with $162 million of sold mortgage loans. The fair value of the recourse on these loans is estimated to be $3 million, which is based upon market spreads for sales of similar loans without recourse or estimates of the credit risk of the associated recourse obligation.

Source: Reprinted with permission from the American Institute of CPAs, Copyright © 1998.

- Audit Approach and Programs
- Working Papers
- Correspondence, Confirmations, and Representations
- Audit Risk Alerts
- Supervision, Review, and Report Processing
- Accountants' Reports
- Quality Control Forms and Aids

Examples and exhibits in the manual are presented for illustrative purposes only. Many sections, however, provide references to authoritative pronouncements in the AICPA *Professional Standards*. The *Audit and Accounting Manual* is available in an annual paperback edition or as a looseleaf subscription service.

Research Files of Public Accounting Firms

Many public accounting firms maintain research files on various accounting and auditing issues documented from the firm's own practice. The primary purpose of such a file is to provide firm personnel with access to previously researched issues and the firm's conclusions. The research file's design can be as simple or advanced as necessary to meet the firm's needs.

When confronted with a research issue, the practitioner searches the file index to determine if the issue has been previously researched and, if so, where to locate the details of the research. The index is typically an alphanumeric listing by subject matter of topics that are stored in the research files. The details of the research are often filed electronically for easy retrieval.

FASB, AcSEC, EITF, and ASB Files

The public files of the FASB, AcSEC, EITF, and ASB contain useful information for the researcher. The public files include all exposure drafts, letters of comment in response to the drafts, minutes of meetings, agenda items, and other correspondence related to the development of professional standards and other pronouncements, such as interpretations. The information contained in these files provides valuable insight in determining the rationale of the various boards or committees in developing standards.

GENERAL BUSINESS RESEARCH TOOLS

Some of the major business research tools that are available to the researcher in gathering business or statistical information include those listed in the following paragraphs.

Trade Directories

A trade directory often contains important information about an individual business and the products it makes, buys, or sells. Many comprehensive directories are indispensable in general business research. The main directories include *The Million Dollar Directory*, which provides a listing of U.S. companies; *Thomas Register of American Manufacturers*; and *America's Corporate Families* and *Who Owns Whom*, which provide information on linkages between parent companies and their subsidiaries.

Government Publications

The U.S. government is the world's largest publisher. Similarly, many state and local governments publish information useful in business research. A sample of the major publications of this type includes *Census of Retail Trade*, *Census of Manufacturers*, *Census of Services Industries*, *Census of Transportation*, *Survey of Current Business*, and the *Federal Reserve Bulletin*.

Statistical Sources

To help the researcher collect statistical information, the U.S. Government developed the Standard Industrial Classification Code (SIC). This classification system consists of a four-digit code for all manufacturers and nonmanufacturing industries. Some of the major statistical sources that use this SIC code system are the *Handbook of Basic Economic Statistics*, the *Statistical Abstract of the United States*, and *Standard and Poor's Statistical Service*.

Business Services

Many private organizations provide business services that supply summarized financial information on all major American companies. *Moody's Investors Service*, one of the better known services, publishes a weekly *Manual* in each of six business areas: transportation, industrials, OTC (over-the-counter) industrials, public relations, banks and finance, and municipals and governments. Other business services include *Corporate Records*, published by Standard and Poor's Corporation, along with their services *Value Line* and *Investment Service*.

International Services

Information for the international business researcher is available in a number of documents. *Principal International Businesses* lists basic information on major companies located around the world. For statistical information, one can use such services as the *Index to International Statistics*, *Statistical Yearbook*, or *Worldcasts*.

COMPUTERIZED RESEARCH TOOLS

Computerized document retrieval systems are now a commercial reality. They are used extensively in the medical and legal professions and have gained wide acceptance in the accounting profession. Such retrieval systems help the researcher search quickly through large masses of data for words that are pertinent to his or her inquiry, which, in turn, refer to authoritative pronouncements or other topical sources of information. Computerized retrieval systems are designed to retrieve from a vast library or collection of data (database) those documents that contain a specified pattern of words, phrases, numbers, or combinations of these that are likely to occur in accounting materials. To use these, the researcher formulates the specified pattern as a document search request, selecting a pattern of words that will list all relevant documents in the database that contain that pattern. The apparent useful features of such a retrieval system are the readily accessible location of the research materials as well as the time savings when compared to a manual search. Examples of the basic applications of these databases by accountants or auditors include the following:

- Using analytical procedures to compare a client to other companies in its industry.
- Obtaining a more in-depth understanding of current developments in the client's industry.
- Obtaining timely notice to any pending changes to the tax laws, forms, or regulations.
- Inquiring into executive backgrounds of new potential clients.

A potential problem the practitioner faces is the basic risk of missing an authoritative document or other piece of information if the document does not contain the exact word pattern called for in the document search request. Careful selection of word patterns becomes important; therefore, the researcher might need either to expand in some cases or reduce the word selection pattern in the search for specific information on a particular database. The remaining portion of this chapter, therefore, will highlight the capabilities of the major computerized retrieval systems as well as the research tasks that can be carried out with each database. Following is a summary of these databases. Other tax databases are highlighted in Chapter 10.

LEXIS-NEXIS

LEXIS-NEXIS maintains dozens of authoritative and semi-authoritative professional accounting publications in its databases. It contains a large set of databases consisting of the full text of all articles carried in more than 200 newspapers, magazines, and wire services, including the *New York Times*, *American Banker*, *Dun's Review*, *U.S. News and World Report*, *Washington Post*, and *P.R. Newswire*, as well as other publications and wire services. Searches on this database, for example, could help

- Locate earnings reports for a particular company. Various publications contained in this library regularly report the earnings of many public companies.
- Find background information on the president of a new client or the company itself.
- Monitor an issue with international dimensions, such as the Mideast oil cartel and the resulting impact on oil prices that has a direct impact on a client.
- Determine which public companies have recently gone through reorganization.

The *Directory of Online Services*, published annually by LEXIS-NEXIS, contains information from about 200 libraries, including Attorney General Opinions, Department of Treasury rulings, Public Service Commission

Decisions, Public Utility Reports, and court rulings from all 50 states—as well as a similar set of comprehensive databases for Canada, the United Kingdom and most industrialized countries. This *Directory* also contains ethics rulings and information about other administrative matters for such organizations as the American Bar Association, the Arbitration Association, and other providers of alternative dispute resolution. In the tax area, its databases contain information from the Bureau of National Affairs (BNA), Inc., Commerce Clearing House, (CCH) Inc., Matthew Bender, International Bureau of Fiscal Documentation (INFD), and Research Institute of America's Tax Analysts. However, two of its most important tools for accounting researchers are its *Accounting, Tax & Financial Library* (ACCTG) and National Automated Accounting Research System (NAARS) databases.

The ACCTG database contains such extensive case law, agency, and regulatory materials as IRS Bulletins, Private Letter Rulings and other key information from the Internal Revenue Service; authoritative and non-authoritative pronouncements from the AICPA; thousands of corporate annual reports from 1973 through the present; federal tax, bankruptcy, securities law and other relevant court rulings and federal regulations; pronouncements from the FASB, AICPA, SEC, Accounting Principles Board, Cost Accounting Standards Board, and International Accounting Standards Committee (IASC); secondary source materials from Harcourt Brace, Matthew Bender, Faulkner and Gray, Warren, Gorham and Lamont, and other leading publishers; and EDGAR data base filings from the SEC (e.g., 10-K, 10-Q, and proxy filings).

National Automated Accounting Research System

NAARS, an acronym for National Automated Accounting Research System, is a computerized information retrieval system developed by the AICPA and LEXIS-NEXIS. This research system has revolutionized the research function that supports the accounting profession and is a primary research system currently being utilized by accountants. Through the use of a terminal linked to the LEXIS-NEXIS computer system, a researcher can access the financial statements, footnotes, and auditors' reports of over 20,000 listed and over-the-counter companies, selected proxy statement information, and all authoritative pronouncements, both current and superseded, of the AICPA, FASB, and SEC that relate to financial reporting. This database provides up-to-date as well as immediate information to help locate the issues and answers to present-day practical problems. However, the LEXIS-NEXIS file generally subsumes the contents of the NAARS databases.

Presently, the NAARS library consists of the active files listed in the following paragraphs.

Annual Report File. This file includes reports of corporations whose stock is traded on the New York or American Stock Exchanges, or those companies traded over-the-counter. Information included consists of financial statements; *Fortune* rankings; auditors' reports; balance sheet data, including current assets, equity, and net income; interim data; and foreign currency exchange gains and losses.

Literature File. All current and superseded authoritative and semi-authoritative accounting literature is readily available through NAARS. Information included in this file contains the SEC regulations and accounting releases; Statements and Interpretations of the FASB, CASB, GASB, and the International Accounting Standards Committee; APB Opinions; and Accounting Research Bulletins and the Statements on Auditing Standards.

Proxy File. This file contains selected information from proxy statements of *Fortune*-ranked companies. This information includes non-audit accounting fees, legal proceedings and related-party transactions, and corporate board structure.

NAARS has the following characteristics that make it a unique retrieval system. First, it is a "full-text" system, rather than a system that simply provides abstracts of documents. The system provides a comprehensive version of documents that are stored in the computer and readily displayed for review. Each word of every document on file is recorded in the database and each word of the text is treated as an index term. Therefore, the researcher can retrieve a document based upon the words in the document. The research display could include the full text of the document, a specific segment, or a search word surrounded by a small amount of the text to help determine the context of the search word. Thus, the system is considered a "free text" searchable system.

Second, NAARS is a real-time system that enables the researcher to use a terminal or a portable computer (PC) to communicate directly with the database via telephone from his or her office. Costly delays are greatly reduced through this direct communication with the computer.

Third, the system operates in an interactive mode, which permits the researcher to carry on a dialogue with the computer, providing the opportunity to broaden or narrow the research to retrieve the precise information needed.

Typical applications of the LEXIS-NEXIS and/or NAARS system(s) would include answers to the following types of questions or issues:

- What consolidation policies do companies use to account for less than 100 percent-owned subsidiaries?
- The balance sheet presentation of unfunded pension liabilities.
- Which CPA firm audited which companies?
- Examples of dual-dated audit reports.
- The *Fortune* 500 ranking of a company.
- The disclosure of pending government investigations.
- Footnote disclosure requirements for leases.

LEXIS-NEXIS Academic Universe. This Web-based product is developed and marketed by Congressional Information Services, Inc. (CIS), a wholly owned subsidiary of LEXIS-NEXIS. Academic Universe provides access to a subset of the vast amount of information found on the commercial LEXIS-NEXIS database. This service, only available to the academic community, provides the researcher the use of the powerful LEXIS-NEXIS search engine and Boolean search logic which is made available with a standard Web browser at your university.

Currently, one can search over 5,000 sources on the system. These sources are classified into five general areas as identified in Figure 7–3, which is the opening screen for Academic Universe. Clicking on the **Business** classification provides access to U.S. authoritative accounting and auditing literature, accounting journals, tax sources, as well as other various business sources. The CD accompanying this text provides a tutorial as to the use of Academic Universe. Please review this tutorial as selected end of chapter questions and cases will require the use of this powerful product for research purposes.

Such comprehensive searches provide the researcher with more confidence in the thoroughness of the search. If no authoritative pronouncement is identified, the accountant might turn to the FASB's conceptual framework project to develop a solution or to review other firms' approaches as precedents.

Figure 7–3 LEXIS-NEXIS Academic Universe—Main Menu

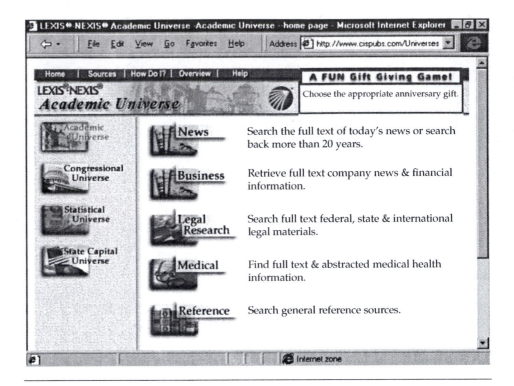

FASB's Financial Accounting Research System (FARS) for Windows

The Financial Accounting Standards Board, in conjunction with FolioViews, Inc., have created a financial accounting research system that is given the acronym of FARS—Financial Accounting Research System. Researchers can easily access this database, which is available on a CD-ROM at many college libraries or computer labs, at many organizations' networks or by subscription from the FASB. The database, which is easily accessible and user-friendly, contains such information as

1. **Original Pronouncements.** Contains the verbiage—in chronological order—of all standards from the Committee on Accounting Procedure (including *Accounting Research Bulletins* and *Accounting Terminology Bulletins*), Accounting Principles Board (including *APB Statements* and *Opinions*), Financial Accounting Standards Board (including FASB *Statements, Interpretations, Implementation Guides, Concepts Statements, Technical Bulletins*, and Appendices), and AICPA Accounting Pronouncements and Interpretations. Materials superseded or amended are denoted (i.e., shaded) in different colors.

2. **Current text.** Contains the verbiage—in alphabetical order—matching the three volumes of the FASB's Accounting Standards (as illustrated in Figure 6–2), plus a listing of superseded and not yet implemented pronouncements, and a schedule of AICPA *Practice Bulletins, Accounting and Audit Guides*, and *Statements of Position*. Volumes I and II of the *Current Text* compiles this information for the general standards, and Volume III does so for industry standards. The *Current Text Section* also includes the authoritative sources (e.g., APB Opinion Numbers) for each listed topic.

3. **Emerging Issues Task Force (EITF) Statements.** Contains the full text of EITF Abstracts (including the date discussed, related authoritative citations,

and the issue's current status), a list of task force members, general and administrative matters, other technical matters, a topical index, and a topical table of contents.

4. **(Staff) Implementation Guides.** Contains Questions and Answers for certain Statements from the FASB (e.g., Can a company voluntarily apply the provisions of SFAS No. 80 to future contracts on foreign currencies?).

5. **Topical Index.** Contains an alphabetical listing of all topics which is identical to the one found in Volume I of the *Current Text of Accounting Standards*.

6. **About FARS.** Contains a brief introduction of the above five "infobases" that constitute FARS, including some tips on how to search more efficiently and methods to get help on using this software.

The FARS database should enable researchers to obtain authoritative evidence to help solve their research questions much more efficiently than they could using manual tools. The following provides a brief tutorial with screen shots of using FARS for a research project.

Brief Tutorial for Using FARS

The following examples provide cases demonstrating some of the power of FARS. Start by assuming that the researcher first wants to ascertain whether certain costs should be considered as research and development (R&D) costs, and, if so, whether to capitalize them or to write them off. The researcher should first double-click the (Topical) **Index** button in the opening screen, as shown in Figure 7–4 to derive the Topical Index as shown in Figure 7–5. The researcher would then double-click the **R** button and scroll down to Research and Development—Elements of Costs to Be Identified with, and Examples of Activities Typically Excluded (Included) as shown in Figure 7–6.

Figure 7–4 Financial Accounting Research System Opening Screen

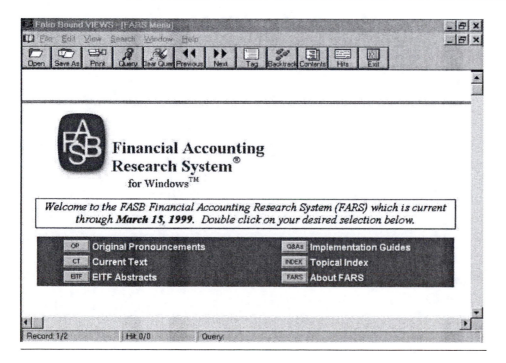

Figure 7–5 Financial Accounting Research System Topical Index

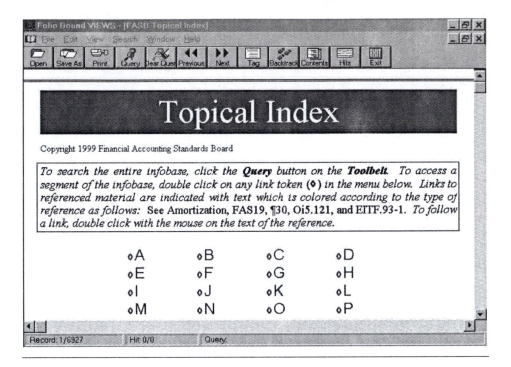

The "hot links" shown would then refer to FASB Statement No. 2 (paragraphs 9–11) *Original Pronouncements*, and to the FASB's *Current Text—* Section R50.107–112. Figure 7–7 shows that per Section 10.i. of this authoritative pronouncement the company should exclude legal fees, but include outside contract services as part of R&D costs. A researcher wanting

Figure 7–6 Research and Development Section of Topical Index

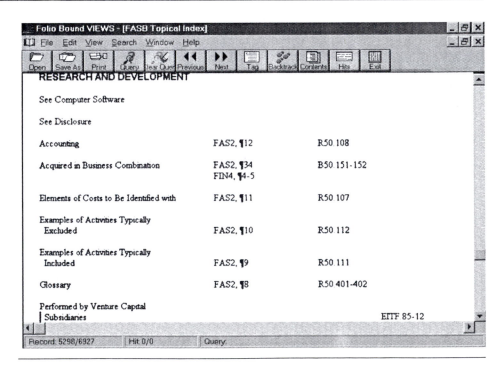

Figure 7–7 Section 10 of FASB Statement No. 2

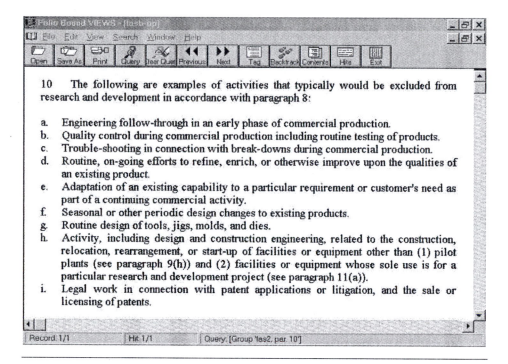

to see further authoritative information on R&D could click on the **(CT)** Current Text button as shown in Figure 7–4 to derive the Table of Contents shown in Figure 7–8, and then click to Section R50 to derive the verbiage shown in Figure 7–9 (page 96).

Section R50 shows that *FASB Statement Nos. 2* and *86* and *Interpretation No. 6* form the basis for such authoritative standards on R&D. It also summarizes

Figure 7–8 Table of Contents for Financial Accounting Research System

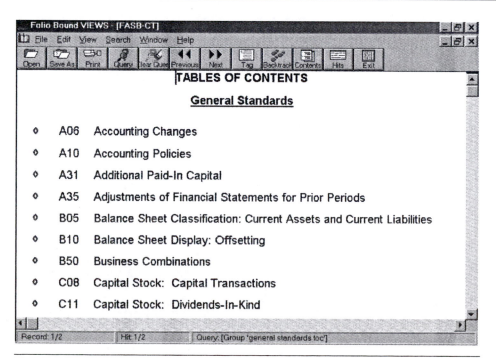

Figure 7–9 Section R50

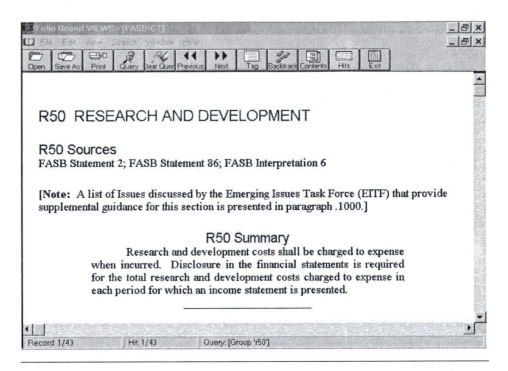

these provisions, and notes (in paragraph .1000) that EITF No. 86–14 discusses Purchased R&D Projects in a Business Combination. The researcher may well click on this hot link to find (as shown in Figure 7–10) that no official consensus exists on whether an acquiring company should capitalize or expense the acquired company's "incomplete" R&D costs (i.e., it should first examine the technological feasibility of the projects under investigation).

Figure 7–10 Purchased R&D Projects in a Business Combination

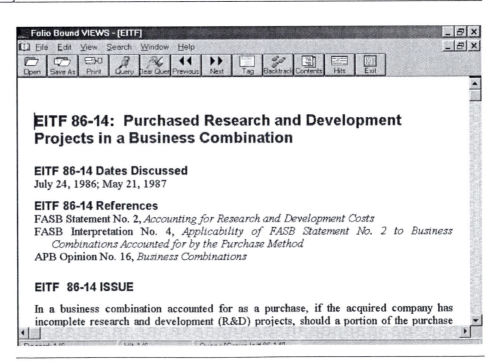

Next, assume that the accounting researcher wants to ascertain if the company should capitalize or expense the software that it issues with the final R&D product. Using the FARS database, the researcher ascertains that the Staff Implementation Guides (under the **Q&As** button of the opening screen) provides a hot link to "Computer Software: Guidance on Applying Statement 86," (see Figure 7–11). As shown in Figure 7–12, Paragraph Nos. 1–2, the company should consider as a product cost only software that is "linked" or otherwise indispensable to selling another product or service.

Further examples and diagrams of using the FARS system appear in Chapter 8 of this text.

Edgarscan

An Internet-based product developed by PricewaterhouseCoopers' Global Technology Centre, Edgarscan is a tool for the practitioner/researcher in gathering financial data about companies that have filed with the SEC. Edgarscan serves as an interface to the SEC's public filings and prepares financial tables and other normalized financial information into common format for comparison purposes. A sub-part of Edgarscan is a Java applet called "Benchmarking Assistant" that can perform graphical financial benchmarking or performance measurement tasks interactively. This tool is an invaluable tool for the practitioner in providing assurance services to clients as well as improving the efficiency of the audit function as described in Chapter 9.

PricewaterhouseCoopers has provided a tutorial of Edgarscan that is included on the CD that accompanies this text. It is suggested that you review this demo in order to gain familiarity with the tool for the end of chapter questions. The actual Web site for Edgarscan is http://edgarscan.tc.pw.com.

In addition to the primary databases previously highlighted, other databases available with features appropriate for accounting and auditing research are briefly described below.

Figure 7–11 Link to Guidance on Applying Statement 86

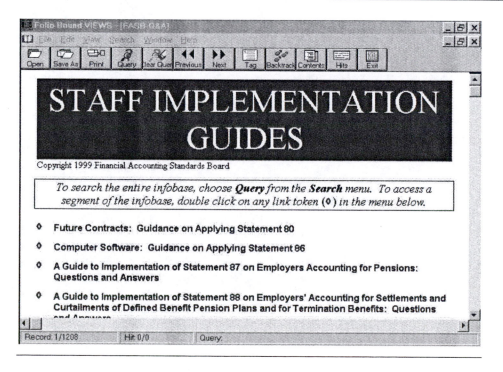

Figure 7–12 Guidance on Applying Statement 86

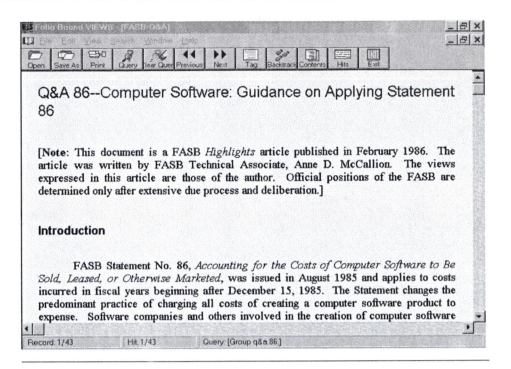

ABI/INFORM

This system contains citations with abstracts to articles appearing in approximately 1,800 international periodicals, newspapers, and other key industry publications. The ABI database covers business and management topics and related functional areas such as accounting, auditing and taxation.

Disclosure

Disclosure, Inc. offers several software packages and databases for commercial use, including balance sheets, income statements, cash flow statements, listing of corporate officers, and many other types of information from annual and quarterly reports on about 12,000 publicly traded companies. Disclosure's related Worldscope GLOBAL database contains similar information on about 14,000 worldwide corporations. Both Disclosure databases are updated weekly.

DIALOG

DIALOG, prepared by DIALOG Information Services, Inc., is an online service that incorporates the full-text or abstracts of many journal articles relating to accounting and tax issues. The service provides databases that extract information on a variety of subjects. Such topics include agriculture, energy, business, economics, governmental publications, chemistry, law, medicine, science, and engineering. Also available on DIALOG is PREDICASTS, which provides extensive industry information, including market data, product design, resource use, and technology information. Another DIALOG database is the Marquis Who's Who file, which contains detailed biographies of thousands of top professionals. This file would be useful to the auditor in the investigation of management of a potential new audit client.

Standard & Poor's Database Services

These computerized databases contain information from nine of Standard & Poor's most popular publications, including its *Stock Reports, Industry Surveys, Corporation Records,* and *Dividend Record.* Its up-to-date information in the databases includes interim earnings, dividends, contract awards, management changes, bond descriptions, and mergers, all available through DIALOG.

BNA

The Bureau of National Affairs, Inc. (BNA) provides a number of databases of importance for the accounting and auditing researcher. The major databases include:

- BNA Antitrust & Trade Regulation Daily
- BNA Bankruptcy Law Daily
- BNA Daily News from Washington
- BNA Environmental Law
- BNA Financial Service
- BNA International Business & Finance Daily

Predicasts PROMPT

PROMPT's database provides summary and full-text data from about 1,000 business and trade journals, industry newsletters, newspapers, market research studies, news releases, and investment and brokerage firm reports from 1996 to the present. Researchers can have the results from using this database reformatted and printed to their browsers, retrieved and printed from an Acrobat Reader, or forwarded to their e-mail address.

Newsletters ASAP

Newsletters ASAP provides summary and full-text information from specialized business, industry, and technology newsletters that various news services and watchers issue, from 1994 to the present. This concise reporting of timely, concise data on leading edge business news and market trends can help the researcher obtain information on emerging companies and events.

Information Access Company Online Databases

Information Access Company is one of the world's leading suppliers of periodical indexes. Founded and staffed by professional librarians and information specialists, Information Access Company provides access to over three million articles from over 2,500 journals, tabloids, newsletters, and newspapers. Major databases of value to the accounting/auditing researcher include the following, which are also available through the DIALOG service:

1. **Magazine Index.** A general research tool that covers current affairs, business, education, consumer information, home and leisure activities, performing arts, science, and travel.
2. **Trade and Industry Index.** An invaluable source of information on business and technological developments for all major industries. The Index provides information on new products, company mergers, personnel, management, technological innovations, the regulatory environment, industry trends, forecasts, and statistics.

3. **National Newspaper Index.** A leading source for news from five of the most important nationally distributed newspapers. Business information includes contracts, mergers, products, companies, current affairs, people, social conditions, scientific developments, and consumer issues.
4. **Annual Report Abstracts.** This database contains more than 250,000 records of annual report summaries for publicly held U.S. corporations and selected international companies whose securities are traded on U.S. stock exchanges.
5. **Management Contents.** Current information provided by Management Contents includes a wide variety of business and management topics. Researchers will find pertinent information on marketing, accounting, organizational behavior, public administration, and more.

AICPA'S ELECTRONIC BODY OF KNOWLEDGE

In order to enhance the research process in the review of the volumes of authoritative literature that exists, the AICPA has developed, utilizing the powerful Folio search engine, a series of its publications in electronic format. To date, the AICPA has developed a powerful yet convenient CD-ROM called *reSOURSE* that contains the AICPA's professional literature. A user can customize his or her professional library by selecting any of the following to include on the CD-ROM from the AICPA:

- AICPA Professional Standards
- AICPA Audit and Accounting Guides
- AICPA Technical Practice Aids
- AICPA Audit Risk Alerts

In addition to the above-named research sources, the AICPA currently provides other electronically formatted publications and software as computerized aids for the practitioner. Many of their self-study programs are now available in a CD-ROM format. The AICPA has also established an online service for members called the *Accountants' Forum*. This service allows members to have electronic access to the Institute's professional literature, exposure drafts, legislative alerts, newsletters, and other information sources. Through the forum, members can communicate better with each other on the forum's bulletin boards and e-mail system.

SUMMARY

Many research tools are available to the accountant/auditor in conducting practical research—primarily manual or computerized retrieval systems. As business information in general expands, and with the availability of massive amounts of information through such computerized databases as LEXIS-NEXIS and FARS, computerized research has undoubtedly become the primary research methodology. In addition to these major databases, the use of the Internet has become critical in order to conduct effective and efficient accounting and auditing research. Since information is accessible within seconds, the professional will have more time for the more important role of decision maker.

DISCUSSION QUESTIONS

1. Describe the contents of the following manual research tools: *Accounting & Tax Index, Accounting Trends and Techniques, Financial Report Surveys*, and *Audit and Accounting Manual.*
2. What is the purpose of a public accounting firm's research file?
3. List some advantages of computerized document retrieval systems over manual research.
4. What is the basic risk of utilizing a computerized retrieval system?
5. What data files are currently available in the NAARS library?
6. Identify the four major characteristics of NAARS.
7. Identify three possible applications of the NAARS system.
8. What information is included in the AICPA's Electronic Body of Knowledge?
9. What are the contents of the LEXIS-NEXIS library?
10. Describe briefly the contents of the following databases: Information Access Company Online, DIALOG, ABI/INFORM, and Standard & Poor's Database Services.
11. What five major databases comprise the FASB's Financial Accounting Retrieval System?
12. Which FARS database contains:
    a. FASB Concepts Statements?
    b. AICPA Practice Bulletins?
    c. A topical index of EITF Statements?
13. What is the AICPA's "Accountants' Forum?" Suggest two ways that practitioners can use it.
14. Access LEXIS-NEXIS Academic Universe. Click on the Accounting, Auditing & Tax link and search on the keyword "derivatives" for the previous year. What documents were displayed?
15. Access LEXIS-NEXIS Academic Universe. Click on the Accounting, Auditing & Tax link and search on the keyword "derivatives" in accounting journals. What journals were displayed?
16. Access Edgarscan to obtain and review the most current quarterly report and 10-K filings for Dow Chemical Co. What was the operating income for the most current quarter reported by Dow Chemical, and what legal proceedings were reported?
17. a. Utilizing Edgarscan, obtain the most recent 10-K filing for Waste Management Inc. and provide a summary of their properties (Item 2 of the 10-K).
    b. Access the "Benchmarking Assistant" applet of Edgarscan and compare Waste Management to three peers using four different financial statement ratios.
18. Utilizing Edgarscan, what were the two initial public offerings (IPOs) most recently filed with the SEC?

CHAPTER 8

Refining the Research Process

LEARNING OBJECTIVES

After completing this chapter, you should understand:

- How to execute the five basic steps in the research process introduced in Chapter 1.
- The three stages in identifying the issue or problem to research.
- How to review related accounting or auditing literature (using both manual and computerized tools, including Internet "hot links") and then collect the evidence.
- The preparation of keyword/citation diagrams and reference matrix.
- The importance of professional judgment in evaluating the results of your research.
- How a research memorandum documents the results of your research process.
- How to prepare a research summary worksheet.
- How to "keep current" with the ever-expanding body of accounting and auditing pronouncements.

The preceding chapters have laid the foundation for conducting efficient and effective applied accounting and auditing research. At this point in the text, you should be familiar with the various manual and computerized research tools and should have a clear understanding of the basic five-step research process introduced in Chapter 1.

This chapter expands upon the application of these steps by applying them to a comprehensive problem that illustrates the research process in detail. Specific steps and procedures for conducting and documenting the research process are summarized in Figure 8–1, which presents a flow chart depicting an overview of the complete research process. Each step should be executed and documented for every research project.

METHOD OF CONDUCTING RESEARCH

The foundation for practical accounting and auditing research has now been set. The practitioner will generally be confronted with problems relating to proper accounting treatment for given transactions or the proper financial presentation of accounting data and disclosures. The focus of the research will be to determine the appropriate alternative principles, locate authoritative sup-

Figure 8–1 Overview of the Research Process

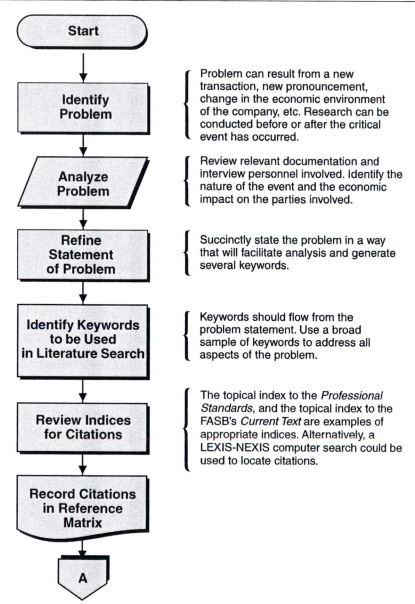

Problem can result from a new transaction, new pronouncement, change in the economic environment of the company, etc. Research can be conducted before or after the critical event has occurred.

Review relevant documentation and interview personnel involved. Identify the nature of the event and the economic impact on the parties involved.

Succinctly state the problem in a way that will facilitate analysis and generate several keywords.

Keywords should flow from the problem statement. Use a broad sample of keywords to address all aspects of the problem.

The topical index to the *Professional Standards*, and the topical index to the FASB's *Current Text* are examples of appropriate indices. Alternatively, a LEXIS-NEXIS computer search could be used to locate citations.

port for those alternatives, and apply professional judgment in selecting one principle from the list of alternatives. What the researcher now needs is a systematic method for conducting research.

Following is an illustrative problem used to demonstrate the application of the research methodology depicted in Figure 8–1. You should follow the problem and research steps carefully in order to comprehend the complete research process.

> *Keller Realty, Inc., is a national real estate firm. The firm was incorporated fifteen years ago, and Alex Keller, the founder and president, is the majority stockholder. Recently, Keller decided to expand his successful regional real estate firm into a national operation. He established offices in major cities across the country. The corporation leased all of the office space. The standard*

Figure 8–1 Overview of the Research Process (continued)

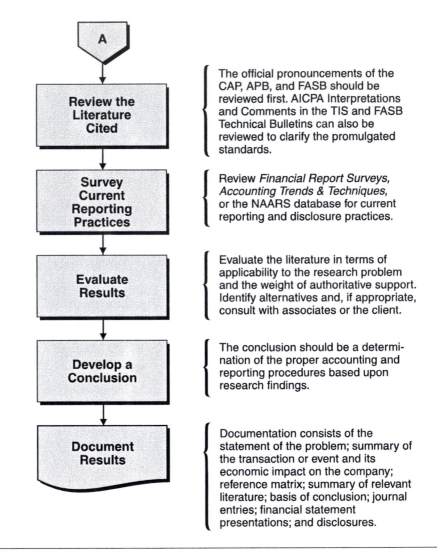

Review the Literature Cited — The official pronouncements of the CAP, APB, and FASB should be reviewed first. AICPA Interpretations and Comments in the TIS and FASB Technical Bulletins can also be reviewed to clarify the promulgated standards.

Survey Current Reporting Practices — Review *Financial Report Surveys*, *Accounting Trends & Techniques*, or the NAARS database for current reporting and disclosure practices.

Evaluate Results — Evaluate the literature in terms of applicability to the research problem and the weight of authoritative support. Identify alternatives and, if appropriate, consult with associates or the client.

Develop a Conclusion — The conclusion should be a determination of the proper accounting and reporting procedures based upon research findings.

Document Results — Documentation consists of the statement of the problem; summary of the transaction or event and its economic impact on the company; reference matrix; summary of relevant literature; basis of conclusion; journal entries; financial statement presentations; and disclosures.

lease agreement included a ten-year, noncancelable term and a five-year option renewable at the discretion of the lessee.

During the next two years of operations, the residential home market became severely depressed due to tight monetary policies and high interest rates. Because of the depressed market, Keller decided to eliminate 25 offices located in depressed economic areas that he believed would not experience a recovery in the housing market in the succeeding five years. This year, Keller Realty, Inc. did close the 25 offices. The realty company, however, was bound by the lease agreements on all these offices. The company was able to sublease 10 of the offices but continued to make lease payments on the 15 remaining vacated ones.

The lease commitments have been properly classified as operating leases. The controller for the company, Elaine Wise, has expressed concern to Keller about the proper accounting for the lease commitments on the 15 offices that have not been subleased. Wise feels that the future lease commitments should be recognized as a loss for the current period. However, Keller disagrees and believes that the rental payments are period costs that should be *recognized as expense in the year paid. Keller is confident that the vacant offices can be subleased within the next year, and there is no need to book a loss and corresponding liability in this accounting period. He has, however, given the controller the task of researching this problem and making a recommendation supported by current authoritative pronouncements. Elaine has asked your firm, Arthur & Young, CPAs, to help in the development of the recommendation.*

Step 1—Identify the Issue or Problem

Identification of the issue or problem, a critical step in the research process, is too often given the least attention. A clear and concise statement of the issue is important to begin the research process. This step can be subdivided into three stages:

1. Preliminary problem identification.
2. Problem analysis.
3. Refined statement of the problem.

Preliminary Problem Identification. This simply means that a potential problem must be recognized before any action will be taken to solve it. The initial step in the research process, therefore, is identification of a potential problem. In this example, the controller has recognized a potential problem in the accounting and reporting treatment of lease commitments on vacated offices. It should be noted that the president, Alex Keller, does not agree that a problem exists. He believes the fact that the offices are vacant does not change the nature of the lease commitment, and that there is no need for changing the established accounting and reporting procedures. It is the problem recognition by the controller that initiates the entire research process.

The initial statement of the problem could be written as follows: "Should a loss be recognized in the current period from lease commitments on vacant offices?"

Problem Analysis. The controller examines the lease agreements and finds the following information:
1. Karen Roth, attorney for Keller Realty, Inc., prepared the lease agreements. All the leases were standardized, and the details were filled in for specific locations.
2. The terms of the lease require the lessee to make all the monthly payments over the noncancelable term or find a sublessee suitable to the lessor.
3. The controller prepared a summary of the lease commitments as follows:

Number of Leases	Monthly Rental Rate	Remaining Noncancelable Terms in Months	Total Commitment
10	$1,500	60	$900,000
5	$2,500	60	$750,000

4. In discussing the lease agreements with the lawyer, the controller learned that Keller Realty, Inc. is bound by the terms of the leases and would probably be sued by the lessors and forced to make the lease payments if the company dishonored its commitment.
5. Ken Riley, the general manager at the company headquarters, is responsible for subleasing the vacated offices. In a discussion with the controller, he

indicated that it is highly unlikely that all of the vacant offices would be subleased. He explained that the ten offices that had been subleased are in areas that have not been severely depressed. The remaining fifteen offices will be more difficult to sublease. He feels confident that he can sublease five offices by the middle of the next fiscal year, but doubts that the remaining properties can be subleased. Under the terms of existing subleases, the monthly rent paid by the sublessees equals the rent expense that the realty company was obligated to pay under the original leases. Riley indicated that each of the five additional offices that he expects to sublease could be rented for the $1,500 per month currently paid by the realty company.

6. The company's incremental borrowing rate is currently 12%.

After considering the information gathered through a review of the lease documents and discussions with the lawyer and the office manager, the controller concludes that the economic impact is contingent upon the ability of the company to sublease the vacant offices. It is clear that the costs incurred to make lease payments on the vacant offices represent a loss to the company, since no revenues are being generated from these units. The controller feels that she can rely upon the office manager's ability to estimate the number of offices that will not be subleased.

Refined Statement of Problem. After the analysis, the controller restates the research problem as follows:

> *Should a contingent loss be recognized currently on future rental commitments on vacant offices, and, if so, what amounts should be recognized?*

Step 2—Collect Evidence

The collection of evidence generally involves (1) a review of related accounting or auditing literature and (2) a survey of present practice.

Review of Accounting Literature (Using Manual Techniques). The review of the literature should begin with the pronouncements of official standard-setting bodies—generally the FASB and AICPA or, in certain cases, the SEC, CASB, or the GASB. It is important to note the scope of any pronouncements reviewed. Time should not be spent in a detailed review of pronouncements that are not applicable to the transaction under investigation. However, pronouncements that do not specifically address the research problem, but are related to it, should not be completely ignored. They can be reviewed for possible references to other appropriate sources; discussions within these pronouncements may add insights into the problem at hand. If these primary sources do not provide the needed accounting information, the search must extend to secondary authoritative sources such as industrial practices, published research studies, and other sources. The researcher should begin the review of primary sources and those that have the highest level of authority as indicated by the hierarchy of GAAP. Once the researcher has exhausted the primary sources, then he/she should proceed to secondary sources.

A list of keywords is essential to locating relevant authoritative literature. The reader should note that a good problem statement would generate the initial keywords necessary to access the appropriate sections of the professional literature. After the search has begun, additional keywords may be identified. From the analysis and statement of the problem stated previously, the controller can identify the following keywords to be used in the literature search:

Losses	Contingent Loss
Loss Recognition	Leases
Commitments	Rent Expense

Using keywords to locate citations is akin to traveling through a maze, with the researcher encountering cross references that circle back to original starting points and keywords that prove to be dead ends. The literature search must be conducted carefully and systematically; otherwise, the process can be frustrating and inefficient. One approach for the researcher is to use the FASB's current text to systematically conduct the literature search.

Figure 8–2 diagrams one path that could be taken through the *text*. The diagram aids the researcher in conducting and documenting an efficient literature search. The starting point of the search is the list of keywords identified from the statement of the problem. As these terms are reviewed for relevant citations, cross-references to other terms—broader, narrower, or related—are found in the *text*. These additional terms are then examined for potential citations. The *text* citations are listed alphabetically by authoritative source. The reader can determine the authoritative weight of each citation directly from the hierarchy of GAAP presented in Chapter 5. The researcher would want to start with the highest level of primary authoritative literature. If the researcher finds the answer in a primary authoritative pronouncement, he or she can stop the research process. Otherwise, the researcher must continue the review of secondary sources.

After believing that he or she has identified all relevant citations, the researcher would next locate and review the authoritative literature. All the citations in Figure 8–2 reference sections of the *FASB Accounting Standards—Current Text*.

Section C59, "Contingencies," includes two relevant authoritative pronouncements—FASB Statement No. 5 and FASB Interpretation No. 14. The Topical Index of the *Current Text* can be used to locate specific paragraphs within this section. The paragraph references are located in the Topical Index under the keyword "Contingencies." A reference matrix similar to that shown in Figure 8–3 can be constructed to facilitate identification of section references and original pronouncements.

Following is a summary of the relevant portions of the literature:

> *A loss contingency as defined in FASB Statement No. 5, paragraph 1, is "an existing condition, situation, or set of circumstances involving uncertainty as to possible . . . loss . . . to an enterprise that will ultimately be resolved when one or more future events occur or fail to occur."*

FASB Statement No. 5, paragraph 8, states that "[an] estimated loss from a loss contingency . . . should be accrued by a charge to income if both of the following conditions are met:

a. . . . it is probable that . . . [a loss has] been incurred . . . [i.e., it is probable that] future events will occur confirming the fact of the loss.
b. The amount of loss can be reasonably estimated."

FASB Interpretation No. 14 clarifies the point that a loss should be accrued even if no single amount for the loss can be estimated. If only a range of potential loss can be estimated, the minimum amount should be accrued.

After reviewing relevant sections in the *Current Text*, the researcher could read the original pronouncements—FASB Statement No. 5 and Interpretation No. 14—to obtain additional insight into the background and rationale underlying the standards.

Figure 8–2 Keyword/Citation Diagram

Keyword	Reference Descriptions	Citation
Losses ⟶	No Relevant Citations	
Loss Recognition (See: Deferring Gain and Loss Recognition) ⟶	Recognition Criteria, Guidance In Application . . . Loss or Lack of Future Benefit	CON5*, par. 85–87
Commitments ⟶	No Relevant Citations	
Contingencies ⟶	Loss Contingencies	FAS5**, par. 2, 4, 8, 21–45; FAS113, par. 30; FAS114, par. 21; FIN14***, par. 4–7
Contingencies . . . Loss ⟶	No Relevant Citations	
Leases ⟶	Classifying; Financing; Operating (i.e., Accounting & Reporting)	FAS13
Leases . . . Subleases ⟶	Accounting by Original Lessee	FAS13, par. 38–39; FIN27, par. 2–3
⟶	Recognition of Gain or Loss	FTB79–15****, par. 1–3
Rent Expense ⟶	No Relevant Citations	

Note: *CON = FASB Concepts Statement; **FAS = FASB Statement; ***FIN = FASB Interpretation; ****FTB = FASB Technical Bulletin

Figure 8–3 Reference Matrix

| Keyword | Reference | | |
	Current Text Section	FASB Statement No. 5	FASB Interpretation No. 14
Contingencies Loss Contingencies	C59.105–.107 C59.109–.110 C59.124–.127	par. 8 par. 9–10	par. 2–3 par. 4–7
Description of Term	C59.101	par. 1	
Range of Loss	C59.109 C59.124–.127	par. 10	par. 4–7
Loss Contingency Classification	C59.104	par. 3	

Review of Accounting Literature (Using Computer Database Techniques). While the above method of reviewing the accounting literature will undoubtedly uncover relevant citations to investigate further, more efficient means are available. Specifically, as discussed in Chapter 7, the researcher can use the FASB's Financial Accounting Research System (FARS) to electronically find relevant, authoritative citations to help solve research dilemmas. Naturally, using the speed and power of electronic databases and the Internet is faster than using manual tools. An alternative to the FARS system would be LEXIS-NEXIS Academic Universe.

For example, the researcher first logging on to FARS would see a menu similar to that found in Figure 8–4, which allows the selection of Original Pronouncements, *Current Text*, EITF Abstracts, (Questions and Answers to) *Implementation Guides*, Topical Index, and Information about FARS. Researchers unfamiliar with FARS may wish to start the process by "clicking on" to the "About FARS" icon. After becoming familiar with the FARS process, the researcher should then click on to the Topical Index icon and find an alphabetical listing of "links" to relevant topics, as shown in Figure 8–5. If the researcher then clicks on the **L** icon to find *Loss Contingencies*, the FARS program would direct him or her to check under *Contingencies—Loss*. Doing so would derive a Topical Index (shown in Figure 8–6).

Next, just as with a "manual" search, the researcher would focus on "Loss Contingency Classifications" by scrolling down in Figure 8–6 and click on to Section C59.104 of the *Current Text*. This process would derive the authoritative verbiage found in Figure 8–7. Alternatively, the researcher could have clicked directly on the icon under the *Current Text* Section of FARS "C59 Contingencies" (Figure 8–8 on page 111) or under the Original Pronouncements Section of FARS "FAS 5" (Figures 8–9 and 8–10 on page 112). The researcher could have clicked directly on the "General Standards" icon in the Current Text Section and by scrolling down to C59 Contingencies and clicking on it, would have produced Figure 8–8.

Figure 8–4 FARS Initial Menu

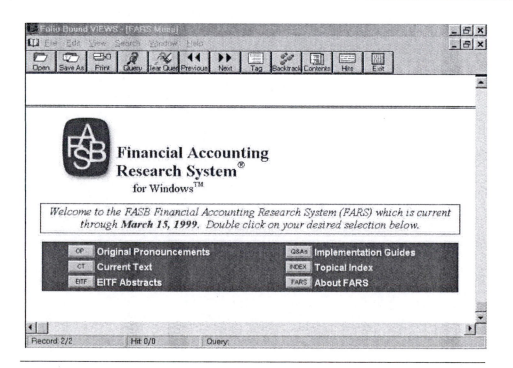

Figure 8–5 FARS Links to Relevant Topics

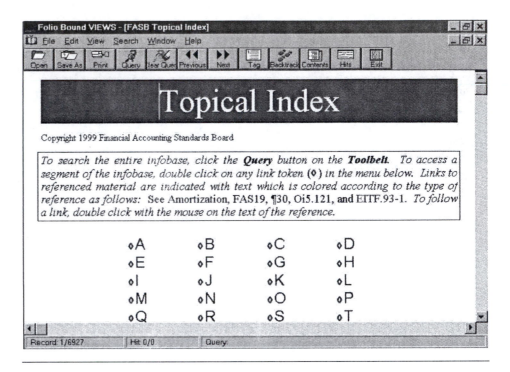

Figure 8–6 FARS Topical Index

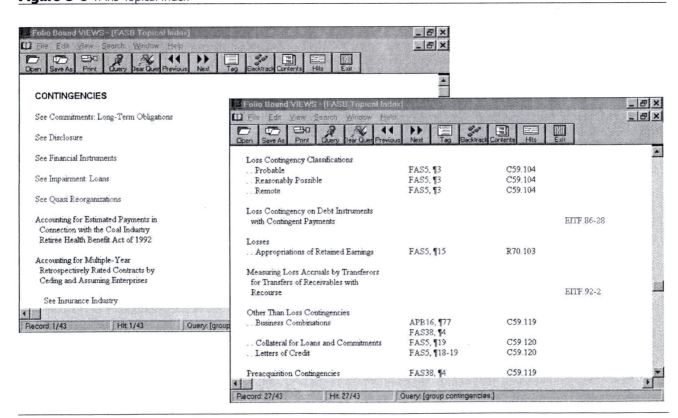

Figure 8–7 Section C59.104 of the *Current Text*

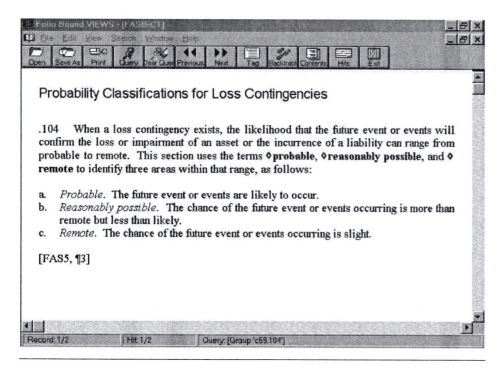

Survey of Present Practice. In addition to the review of authoritative literature, Step 2 involves determining how other companies with similar circumstances or transactions have handled the accounting and reporting procedures. This survey could include a review of *Accounting Trends & Techniques* or *Financial Reporting Surveys* as well as a discussion of the issue with colleagues via the Internet.

Figure 8–8 FARS "C59 Contingencies"

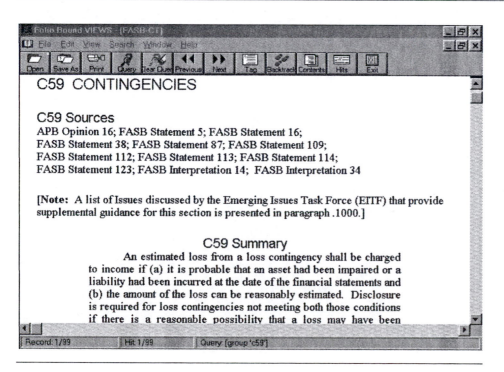

Figure 8–9 FASB Original Pronouncements Menu

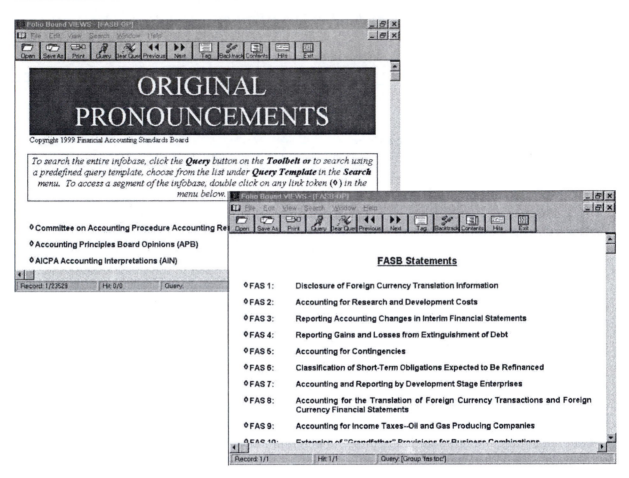

Figure 8–10 Original Pronouncements "FAS5"

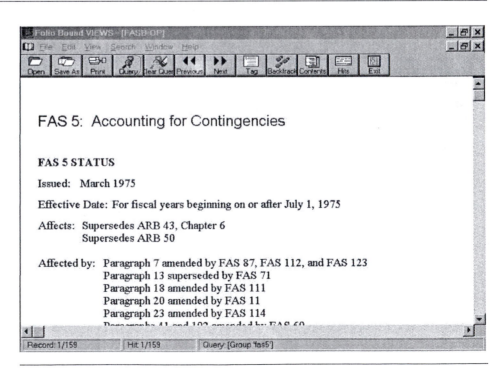

The researcher may well also take advantage of the many available Web sites and other accounting resources available on the Internet. Researchers can make use of "hot links" to Web sites of larger public accounting firms, professional organizations (e.g., the AICPA and Institute of Management Accountants), government agencies (e.g., the EDGAR database available from the SEC), financial markets and services (e.g., the New York and American Stock Exchanges), and search tools and engines (e.g., Yahoo! and Infoseek). Reviewing these sites can help the researcher quickly find the latest information on the topic in question. For example, searching the Infoseek search engine (or clicking on the attached "hot link") and searching for the topic "loss contingencies" derives a total of 373 hits, as shown in Figure 8–11. Clicking on the first available link derives a summary of FASB Statement No. 5 as shown in Figure 8–12. The researcher could easily perform similar, efficient searches for many of the Internet data base links discussed previously.

Step 3—Evaluate Results and Identify Alternatives

This step requires the exercise of professional judgment. The evidence should be carefully reviewed and one or more tentative conclusions identified. The quality and amount of authoritative support for each alternative should be evaluated. In addition, the evidence may be reviewed with other accountants knowledgeable in the field.

The initial concern on the real estate problem was whether to recognize any loss currently on the lease commitments on vacant offices. Through the examination of related documents and discussions with persons involved with the transactions, the following facts were identified:

1. The realty company has an enforceable obligation to make the lease payments on the vacant offices.

Figure 8–11 Infoseek "Loss Contingencies" Search

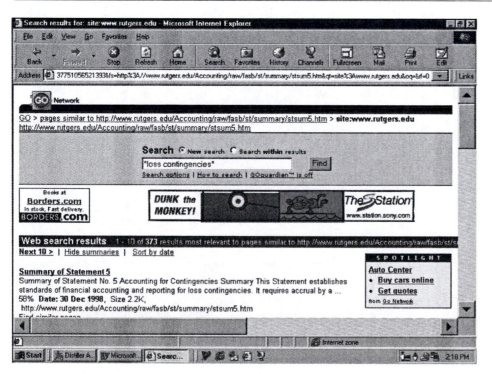

Figure 8–12 Summary of FASB Statement No. 5

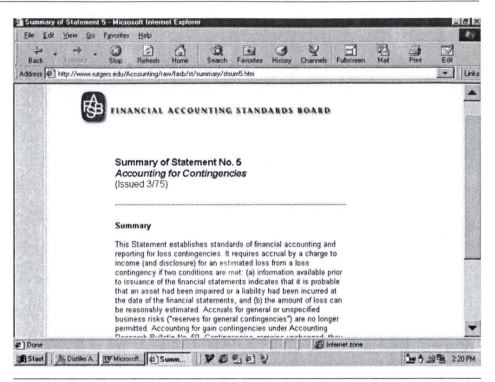

2. The payments will represent a loss to the company because no revenues will be generated by the costs incurred.
3. The amount of the loss is contingent upon the ability of the realty company to sublease the offices. A reasonable estimate is that a maximum of five buildings could be subleased, and it is possible that none will be subleased.

The literature search has provided authoritative support for recognizing a contingent loss. The amount of the loss is to be measured by the minimum amount for the range of the estimated loss. There was no support in the literature for considering the rental payments as period costs to be recognized as expense when paid. FASB Technical Bulletin 79–15, which is an unofficial interpretation of FASB Statement No. 13, addresses the loss on a sublease not involved in a disposal of a business segment. It states that a loss should be recognized in a sublease in order to follow the general principle of providing for losses when it is reasonable to assume they have occurred. This same reasoning can be extended to the problem at hand where there will be no sublease payments to reduce the amount of the loss.

Step 4—Develop Conclusion

If the evaluation process is properly performed, the researcher should be able to develop a well-reasoned, well-supported conclusion as to the appropriate resolution of the issue. In the illustrative problem, the authoritative literature found through the research process supports accrual of the loss on the lease agreements. The amount of the loss should be the minimum of the range of the contingent loss. The financial statements should disclose the nature of the contingent loss and the amount of potential loss above the amount accrued in the financial statements.

Step 5—Communicate Results

Once the researcher has determined a solution to the research problem, the conclusion should be presented concisely and clearly to the client. Generally, a research memorandum serves as this communication medium, as shown in Figure 8–13 on the following page.

DOCUMENTATION OF THE RESEARCH PROCESS

Thorough documentation is a crucial part of the entire research process. The documentation should include:

1. A statement of the problem and relevant facts.
2. References to authoritative literature used.
3. A description of alternative procedures considered and the authoritative support for each alternative.
4. An explanation of why certain alternatives were discarded and why the recommended principle or procedure was selected.

Figure 8–14 contains an example of a documentation worksheet that the accounting firm might use to organize the pertinent research information for its records.

KEEPING CURRENT

In concluding this text, the authors would like to emphasize the importance of keeping current with the ever-expanding accounting and auditing pronouncements and to share with the reader some techniques that have been used successfully by various practitioners. Adopting one or a combination of the following techniques may save valuable time—to spend possibly on the golf course—rather than reading volume upon volume of materials in an attempt to stay current.

1. **Checklists**—Some practitioners develop a checklist for keeping current. They prepare listings of new pronouncements and update them periodically with indications as to which clients a pronouncement may affect. Pronouncements having no direct immediate impact on any client are placed in a "rainy day" reading file.
2. **Pronouncement summaries**—In some firms, in-house staff memos are prepared at specific intervals and distributed to all staff members. Such memos identify new pronouncements and provide a brief summary write-up of each new pronouncement.
3. **Reading of periodicals**—Many business and accounting periodicals report summaries or the full text of new pronouncements. The practice of reading certain periodicals, such as the *Journal of Accountancy*, *Management Accounting*, and *The Wall Street Journal*, will aid the practitioner attempting to keep current.
4. **Accounting newsletters**—Many organizations publish accounting newsletters to update practitioners on current events. Major newsletters available include the following:

   - **The CPA Letter.** This newsletter, published by the AICPA, contains current information concerning the profession. Such topics include AICPA board business, new pronouncements on accounting and auditing, disciplinary actions against members, upcoming events, and briefs on events in Washington.

Figure 8–13 Research Memorandum of Conclusion

To: Alex Keller, President

From: Elaine Wise, Controller and Arthur & Young, CPAs

At your request, we have researched the following matter to determine the impact on Keller Realty. The specific issue researched concerns whether a loss should be recognized currently on the rental commitments on the vacant offices. If recognition is required, what amount should be accrued?

In researching the authoritative literature, the following keywords were utilized: Losses, Loss Recognition, Commitments, Contingent Loss, Leases, and Rent Expense. FASB Statement No. 5, "Accounting for Contingencies," states that a loss contingency should be accrued by a charge to income if (1) it is probable that a loss has been incurred and (2) the amount of the loss can be reasonably estimated. FASB Interpretation No. 14, "Reasonable Estimate of the Amount of Loss," states that when no single amount for the loss can be estimated, the minimum amount of loss should be accrued.

Keller Realty, Inc. has an enforceable obligation to make the lease payments on the vacant offices, and no revenues will be generated by the costs incurred. We can reasonably estimate that from zero to five buildings could be subleased. The authoritative literature supports the accrual of a loss for the vacant lease offices. The amount of the loss will be the minimum estimate of the range of potential loss. Since the lease obligations extend over more than one accounting period, the accrual will be at the present value of the lease payments discounted at the Realty Company's marginal borrowing rate.

	Number of Leases	Monthly Rate	Months	P.V. Factor of Annuity Due at 1%	P.V. Amount*
Additional units:					
Subleased	5	$1500	3 **	2.9704	$ 22,278
Not subleased	5	1500	60	45.4046	340,534
Not subleased	5	2500	60	45.4046	567,557
Loss accrual					$ 930,369
Potential additional loss	5	$1500	57	43.720	327,900
. . . .					$1,258,269
Current portion	5	$1500	3	2.9704	$ 22,278
of loss	5	1500	12	11.3676	85,257
recognized	5	2500	12	11.3676	142,095
. . . .					$ 249,630

* P.V. Amount = (Number of Leases x Monthly Rate x P.V. Factor).
**Since 5 units are expected to be subleased within 6 months, the vacancy period on these units is averaged at 3 months.

The financial statement presentation and proper footnote disclosure should appear as follows:

<u>Financial Statement Presentation and Disclosure</u>

Income statement:
Revenues   XXXXX
Operating expenses
  Loss on lease commitments $930,369
Balance sheet:
Current liabilities:
  Current portion of lease commitments $249,630
  Long-term portion of lease commitments   680,739

<u>Notes</u>

Contingent Liabilities—The company has entered into certain lease agreements that have 5-year noncancelable terms remaining. Some of these offices are currently neither used nor subleased. The present value of the potential rental liability above the amount accrued is $327,900.

Figure 8-14 Documentation Worksheet of Accounting/Auditing Research

| Client Information
Name: Keller Realty, Inc.
Address: 1300 W 5th St.
New York, NY

Client Code # K143

I. Problem Identification

Scope or Statement of Problem:

Should a contingent loss be recognized currently on future rental commitments on vacant offices?

Contact Person (Client):

Elaine Wise—Controller | II. Research Evidence

Keywords Utilized:

Losses (No Cites noted)
Contingent Loss
Loss Recognition
Leases
Commitments
Rent Expense

References (Citations):

FASB No. 5, par. 8–10
FASB Interp. No 14, par. 2–7
FASB Tech Bulletin No. 79–15.
FASB No. 13

Database (Library Resources) Utilized:

FARS Database
FASB Stds—Current Text
Accounting Trends & Techniques
Internet sites | III. Alternatives Available

No other alternatives are permissible

IV. Brief Summary of Conclusions

The authoritative literature requires the accrual of its loss on the lease agreements. The amount should be the minimum of the range of the contingent loss. |

- **FASB Status Report.** This monthly publication, issued by the Financial Accounting Standards Board, covers FASB official actions and releases. It periodically reports the agenda of the FASB in addition to summary comments on recently issued statements, exposure drafts, or technical bulletins.
- **Action Alert.** This is a weekly publication of the FASB on actions and future meetings.
- **GASB Action Report.** Similar in content to the FASB newsletter, this publication of the Governmental Accounting Standards Board issues quarterly reports of the GASB comments on GASB statements, exposure drafts, interpretations, or technical bulletins.

5. **Internet**—Utilizing the newsgroups on the Internet can keep you abreast of topics of interest to you and your clients. Some practitioners have developed personal Web pages that capture information designated by the practitioner on a timely basis which is then review by the practitioner.

Keeping up to date on the details of all new pronouncements is an impossibility. However, every practitioner must develop and consistently use a technique to keep as current as possible, especially with pronouncements that directly affect clients.

SUMMARY

The professional accountant who attempts to keep current and has developed skills in researching accounting and auditing issues will be well rewarded by having obtained the confidence and respect of management and colleagues. Such respect is generally reserved for the truly professional accountant or auditor. This text attempts to aid the practitioner in fulfilling his or her professional role, which includes that of a competent researcher in accounting and auditing matters.

DISCUSSION QUESTIONS

1. What is the focus of accounting and auditing research?
2. What are the three components used to identify the problem or issue?
3. Explain two ways to collect evidence.
4. How are keywords used to evaluate and collect evidence?
5. What is the purpose of a research memorandum?
6. What are two common causes of accounting problems?
7. What should be included in the documentation of the research process?
8. What are some basic ways of keeping current with the authoritative literature?

APPENDIX A

Abbreviations Used in Citations

Abbreviation	Title of Pronouncement
AAG-APC	Audit and Accounting Guide, Audits of Agricultural Producers and Agricultural Cooperatives
AAG-BRD	Audit and Accounting Guide: Audits of Brokers and Dealers in Securities
AAG-BNK	Audit and Accounting Guide: Audits of Banks and Savings Institutions
AAG-CAS	Audit and Accounting Guide: Audits of Casinos
AAG-CIR	Audit and Accounting Guide: Common Interest Realty Organization
AAG-CON	Audit and Accounting Guide: Construction Contractors
AAG-CRU	Audit and Accounting Guide: Audits of Credit Unions
AAG-EBP	Audit and Accounting Guide: Audits of Employee Benefit Plans
AAG-FGC	Audit and Accounting Guide: Audits of Federal Government Contractors
AAG-FIN	Audit and Accounting Guide: Audits of Financial Companies (Including Independent and Captive Financing Activities of Other Companies)
AAG-HCD	Audit and Accounting Guide: Audits of Health Care Organizations
AAG-INT	Audit and Accounting Guide: Consideration of Internal Control in a Financial Statement Audit
AAG-INV	Audit and Accounting Guide: Audits of Investment Companies
AAG-NPO	Audit and Accounting Guide: Audits of Certain Not-for-Profit Organizations
AAG-NPR	Audit and Accounting Guide: Audits of Certain Nonprofit Organizations
AAG-OGP	Audit and Accounting Guide: Audits of Entities with Oil and Gas Producing Activities
AAG-PLI	Audit and Accounting Guide: Audits of Property and Liability Insurance Companies
AAG-PRO	Audit and Accounting Guide: Guide for Prospective Financial Information

AAG-RLE	Audit and Accounting Guide: Guide for the Use of Real Estate Appraisal Information
AAG-SAM	Audit and Accounting Guide: Audit Sampling
AAG-SLG	Audit and Accounting Guide: Audits of State and Local Governmental Units
ACC-PB	Accounting Standards Division Practice Bulletins
ACC-SOP	Accounting Standards Division Statements of Position
ACIJ	AICPA Accounting Interpretations
APB	Accounting Principles Board Opinions
APBS	Accounting Principles Board Statements
ARB	Accounting Research Bulletins
ATB	Accounting Terminology Bulletins
AUD-SOP	Auditing Standards Division Statements of Position
AUG-AIR	Industry Audit Guide: Audits of Airlines
AUG-COL	Industry Audit Guide: Audits of Colleges and Universities
AUG-SLI	Industry Audit Guide: Audits of Stock Life Insurance Companies
AUG-VHW	Industry Audit Guide: Audits of Voluntary Health and Welfare Organizations
AUIJ	AICPA Auditing Interpretations
CASB	Cost Accounting Standards Board Standards
CASB-I	Cost Accounting Standards Board Interpretations
EPS	Computing Earnings
ET-INT	Ethics Interpretations of Rules of Conduct
ET-RLNG	Ethics Rulings
ET-RULE	Code of Professional Conduct—Rules
FAC	Financial Accounting Standards Board Statements of Financial Accounting Concepts
FAS	Financial Accounting Standards Board Statements of Financial Accounting Standards
FASEITF	Financial Accounting Standards Board Emerging Issues Task Force Consensus
FASI	Financial Accounting Standards Board Interpretations
FAST	Financial Accounting Standards Board Technical Bulletins
GAC	Governmental Accounting Standards Board Statement of Financial Accounting Concepts
GAS	Governmental Accounting Standards Board Statements on Governmental Accounting Standards
GASI	Governmental Accounting Standards Board Interpretations
GAST	Governmental Accounting Standards Board Technical Bulletins
GUD-PFS	Personal Financial Statements Guide
IAS	International Accounting Standards
IAU	International Statements on Auditing
IAU/RS	International Statements on Auditing/Related Services

NCGA	National Council on Governmental Accounting Statements
NCGAI	National Council on Governmental Accounting Interpretations
PFP	Statements on Responsibilities in Personal Financial Planning Practice
QC	Statements on Quality Control Standards
QCI	Quality Control Standards Interpretations
QR	Standards for Performing and Reporting on Quality Reviews
QRI	Quality Review Interpretations
SAR	Statements on Standards for Accounting and Review Services
SARI	Accounting and Review Services Interpretations
SAS	Statements on Auditing Standards
SEC-AAER	Accounting and Auditing Enforcement Releases
SEC-FRR	Financial Reporting Releases
SEC-SAB	Staff Accounting Bulletins
SECSK	Regulation S-K
SECSX	Regulation S-X
SSAE	Statement on Standards for Attestation Engagements
SSAEI	AICPA Attestation Engagements Interpretations
SSCS	Statements on Standards for Consulting Services

CHAPTER 9

Assurance Services Standards-Setting Environment and Professional Judgment

LEARNING OBJECTIVES

After completing this chapter, you should understand:

- The types of assurance services offered by the practitioner, and the applicable standards.
- The environment of the assurance services standard-setting process.
- Authoritative auditing support.
- The role of auditing in the public sector.
- The hierarchy of the Code of Professional Conduct.
- The role of professional judgment in the research process.
- The international dimensions of auditing.

Since information technology has had a significant impact on the accounting profession and society in general, the public accounting profession has focused on its willingness and ability to design and offer additional "value-added" services in addition to such traditional services as tax preparation and auditing. The accounting professional is being transformed from a "number cruncher and certifier of information," to a "decision support specialist and enhancer of information." Many professionals are keeping abreast of the major changes in the profession and transforming their practices and market orientation to these new "value-added" services referred to under the umbrella of "assurance services." As a result, the practitioner/researcher needs to be cognizant of these new services and any related standards that apply in offering these services.

ASSURANCE SERVICES

The AICPA formed the "Special Committee on Assurance Services (SCAS) to focus on the current and changing needs of users of decision-making information in order to determine how best to improve the related services, or new services, that could be provided to these users. The Committee conducted research that consisted of assessing customer needs, external factors, information technology, and needed competencies to offer these new 'value-added services.' The umbrella term selected by the Committee of existing and new services is referred to as 'assurance services.' This term is defined by the Committee as follows:

> *Assurance Services are independent professional services that improve the quality of information, or its context, for decision makers.*

Notice that this definition implies that the service itself will be of value to the user, not necessarily just the report, such as an audit report, the user receives. Additionally, the services should be offered by an independent professional in order to improve the quality of the information or its context.

In reviewing this definition of assurance services, one can conclude that the concepts contained in the definition are familiar and that certain current services fall under the umbrella of assurance services. Figure 9–1 presents an overview of assurance services with specific details provided in the following sections of this chapter. As depicted, the traditional audit service is an attestation function that falls under the broader term of assurance services.

Consulting Services & Standards

Historically, consulting services offered to clients (two party contracts) by CPAs have often been referred to as management consulting services or management advisory services. These services have generally evolved from accounting-related matters in connection with audits or tax engagements. In a consulting engagement, the CPA develops findings and conclusions which are followed with recommendations for the benefit of the client. This is in contrast to an attest engagement (three party contracts) whereby the CPA reports on the reliability of a written assertion that is the responsibility of a third party. Examples of consulting engagements include operational audits, systems reliability studies, and Eldercare (a new assurance service).

The typical consulting engagement is quite similar to the research process presented in this text. The consulting engagement would normally include:

- The determination of the client's objective.
- Fact-finding.

Figure 9–1 Assurance Services Umbrella

ASSURANCE SERVICES

Attestation Services

i.e.,

Audits

Reviews of Financial Statements

Agreed-upon Procedures Engagement

Web Trust

Consulting Services

i.e.,

Operational Audits

Eldercare

Systems Reliability

Computer Installations

Market Studies

- Definition of the problem.
- Evaluation of alternatives.
- Formulation of a proposed action.
- Communication of the results.
- Implementation and follow-up.[1]

In researching the professional standards for consulting services, the practitioner will be directed to general standards and specific consulting standards. In rendering professional services (including consulting) the general standards of the profession are contained in Rule 201 of the Code of Professional Conduct as discussed in a following section of this chapter. Additionally, the AICPA issues Statements on Standards for Consulting Services (SSCS), which provide standards for the practitioner rendering consulting services.

Attestation Services and Standards

Attestation services (a subset of assurance services) are increasingly being demanded of the accounting profession by society. In the past, attest services were normally limited to audit opinions on historical financial statements based upon audits that followed Generally Accepted Auditing Standards (GAAS). However, in more recent times, professional accountants have been requested to render opinions on representations other than historical financial statements. The concern of the practitioner, therefore, was that there did not exist standards or guidelines to meet the demands of society. As a result, the AICPA developed attest standards and related interpretations to provide a general framework for attest engagements.[2]

The term *attest* means to provide assurance as to the reliability of information. The AICPA has defined an attest engagement as follows:

> *An attest engagement is one in which a practitioner is engaged to issue or does issue a written communication that expresses a conclusion about the reliability of a written assertion that is the responsibility of another party.*[3]

Whether the attest service is for the traditional financial statements audit or reporting on an entity's internal control or prospective financial information, the professional accountant must follow certain guidelines and standards in rendering these services. In conducting an attest engagement, the professional accountant reviews and conducts tests of the accounting records deemed necessary to obtain sufficient evidence to render an opinion. Choosing the accounting records and other information to review and deciding upon the extent to which they should be examined are strictly matters of professional judgment, as many authoritative pronouncements emphasize.

Figure 9–2 presents the major elements of the attest environment that face the accountant in conducting attest research. Figure 9–3 presents an overview of attest engagements and guidelines the researcher should be familiar with. The following sections of this chapter will focus on an overview of this attest standard-setting environment, the auditing standard-setting process, authoritative auditing pronouncements, and the role of professional judgment in the research process. The chapter also includes a summary of the attestation standards and compilation and review standards, as well as an overview of auditing in the public sector and the international dimensions of auditing.

---

1   AICPA, *Professional Standards*, Vol. 2, Section CS–100.05.
2   AICPA, *Professional Standards*, Vol. 1, Section AT–Introduction.
3   AICPA, *Professional Standards*, Vol. 1, Section AT 100.01.

Figure 9–2 Attest Research Environment

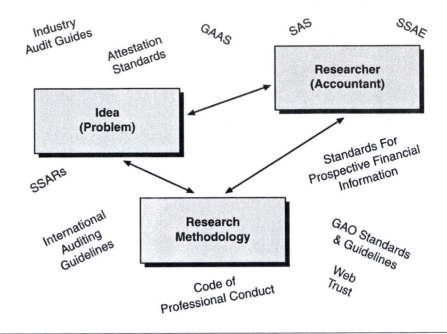

Recently, as the range of attest services has expanded, many CPAs have found it difficult to apply the basic concepts underlying Generally Accepted Auditing Standards (GAAS) to these attest services. These services have included the following examples: reporting on descriptions of the client's system of internal controls; reporting to the client on which computer system is the cheapest or has the most capabilities; reporting on insurance claims data; reporting on compliance with regulatory requirements; or reporting on prospective financial statements. (In one instance, Wilson Sporting Goods requested an accounting firm to attest to the statement that Wilson's Ultra golf ball outdistanced its competitors!) Consequently, the AICPA has issued *Statements on Standards for Attestation Engagements, Statements on Standards for*

Figure 9–3 Attest Engagements and Guidelines

Attest Engagement:	Guidelines:	Issued by:
Audit	Generally Accepted Audit Standards (GAAS)	Auditing Standards Board (ASB)
	Statements on Auditing Standards (SASs)	
Accounting and Review Services	Statements on Standards for Accounting and Review Services (SSARs)	Accounting and Review Services Committee (ARSC)
Accountant's Services on Prospective Financial Information	Statements on Standards for Accountants' Services on Prospective Financial Information	Auditing Standards Board
Other Attest Services	Statements on Standards for Attestation Engagement	ASB, ARSC, and the Management Consulting Services Executive Committee

Accounting and Review Services, and *Statements on Standards for Accountants' Services on Prospective Financial Information* to provide a general framework and set reasonable guidelines for an attest function and the audit function in order to be responsive to the changing environment and demands of society.

The broad guidelines for an attest engagement have been issued by the Auditing Standards Board (ASB) in conjunction with the Accounting and Review Services Committee and the Management Consulting Services Executive Committee of the AICPA. As listed in Figure 9–4, these attestation standards do not supersede any existing standards but are considered a natural extension of the ten generally accepted auditing standards. The design of these attestation standards is such that they provide guidance to the professional to enhance both consistency and quality in the performance of attest services.

AUDITING STANDARD-SETTING ENVIRONMENT

In a society where credit is extended widely and business failures occur daily, and where investors wish to study the financial statements of many enterprises, auditing is indispensable. The purpose of the audit report is to add credibility

Figure 9–4 Attestation Standards

General Standards

1. The engagement shall be performed by a practitioner or practitioners having adequate technical training and proficiency in the attest function.
2. The engagement shall be performed by a practitioner or practitioners having adequate knowledge in the subject matter of the assertion.
3. The practitioner shall perform an engagement only if he or she has reason to believe that the following two conditions exist:
   • The assertion is capable of evaluation against reasonable criteria that either have been established by a recognized body or are stated in the presentation of the assertion in a sufficiently clear and comprehensive manner for a knowledgeable reader to be able to understand them.
   • The assertion is capable of reasonably consistent estimation or measurement using such criteria.
4. In all matters relating to the engagement, an independence in mental attitude shall be maintained by the practitioner or practitioners.
5. Due professional care shall be exercised in the performance of the engagement.

Standards of Field Work

1. The work shall be adequately planned, and assistants, if any, shall be properly supervised.
2. Sufficient evidence shall be obtained to provide a reasonable basis for the conclusion that is expressed in the report.

Standards of Reporting

1. The report on an engagement shall identify the assertion being reported on and state the character of the engagement.
2. The report shall state the practitioner's conclusion about whether the assertion is presented in conformity with the established or stated criteria against which it was measured.
3. The report shall state all of the practitioner's significant reservations about the engagement and the presentation of the assertion.
4. The report on the engagement to evaluate an assertion that has been prepared in conformity with agreed-upon criteria or on an engagement to apply agreed-upon procedures should contain a statement limiting its use to the parties who have agreed upon such criteria or procedures.

Source: AICPA *Professional Standards,* Vol. 1, AT Section 100.

to the financial information. The early development of auditing standards and procedures in the United States arose from significant economic upheavals. In 1917 the Federal Reserve Board issued the first audit guideline, entitled "A Memorandum on Balance Sheet Audits," a result of the credit crises during the early 1900s. Later, the stock market crash and the ensuing depression led to the creation of the Securities and Exchange Commission and prompted the New York Stock Exchange to require that listed companies be audited. Throughout these years, the AICPA has been actively involved in the development of auditing standards and procedures. The general environment within which any given audit is conducted is a very dynamic one and is constantly evolving as the various factors impact the audit process.

The independent auditor's role can be described as a secondary communication function, wherein an opinion is expressed on financial information reported by management. A primary concern of the auditor, therefore, is whether the client's financial statements are presented in accordance with generally accepted accounting principles. The auditor must also conduct audits in a manner that conforms to auditing standards and procedures and take actions that are guided by professional ethical standards. Additionally, in non-audit engagements the accountant must be aware of attestation standards and statements dealing with compilation and review services, as well as standards for accountants' services on prospective financial information, (i.e., forecasts and projections).

Auditing Standards

Auditing standards differ from auditing procedures in that standards provide measures of the quality of performance, whereas audit procedures refer to the acts or steps to be performed in an engagement. Auditing standards do not vary. They remain identical for all audits. Auditing procedures change, depending on the nature and type of entity under audit and the complexity of the audit.

In contrast to generally accepted accounting principles, which cannot be identified with exactness, the AICPA has formally adopted ten broad requirements for auditors to follow in examining financial statements. These ten requirements, referred to as the *Generally Accepted Auditing Standards* (GAAS), are listed in Figure 9–5. In addition to the issuance of the generally accepted auditing standards, the AICPA publishes a series of *Statements on Auditing Standards* (SASs). These statements supplement and interpret the ten generally accepted standards by clarifying audit procedures or prescribing the form and content of the auditor's report. These SASs serve as the primary auditor support in conducting an examination and are a major source of authoritative information when conducting auditing research.

Various forms of the generally accepted auditing standards are also recognized by governmental and internal auditors. The General Accounting Office (GAO), through the comptroller general of the United States, has issued *Governmental Auditing Standards*. The Institute of Internal Auditors has issued *Standards for the Professional Practice of Internal Auditing* under which internal auditors operate.

AUDITING STANDARD-SETTING PROCESS

Concern has always existed as to who should set auditing standards for the independent auditor. Prior to establishment of the SEC, Congress debated having audits conducted by a corps of governmental auditors. However, federal

Figure 9–5 Generally Accepted Auditing Standards

General Standards

1. The examination is to be performed by a person or persons having adequate technical training and proficiency as an auditor.
2. In all matters relating to the assignment, an independence in mental attitude is to be maintained by the auditor or auditors.
3. Due professional care shall be exercised in the performance of the audit and the preparation of the report.

Standards of Field Work

1. The work is to be adequately planned, and assistants, if any, are to be properly supervised.
2. A sufficient understanding of the internal control structure is to be obtained to plan the audit and to determine the nature, timing, and extent of the tests to be performed.
3. Sufficient competent evident matter is to be obtained through inspection, observation, inquiries, and confirmations to afford a reasonable basis for an opinion regarding the financial statements under audit.

Standards of Reporting

1. The report shall state whether the financial statements are presented in accordance with generally accepted accounting principles.
2. The report shall identify those circumstances in which such principles have not been consistently observed in the current period in relation to the preceding period.
3. Informative disclosures in the financial statements are to be regarded as reasonably adequate unless otherwise stated in the report.
4. The report shall contain either an expression of opinion regarding the financial statements, taken as a whole, or an assertion to the effect that an opinion cannot be expressed. When an overall opinion cannot be expressed, the reasons therefor should be stated. In all cases where an auditor's name is associated with financial statements, the report should contain a clear-cut indication of the character of the auditor's work and the degree of responsibility the auditor is taking.

Source: AICPA *Professional Standards*, Vol. 1, AU Section 150.

chartering of auditors did not take place, and to this day the auditing standard-setting process for independent audits remains in the private sector under the auspices of the AICPA's present senior technical committee on auditing standards—the Auditing Standards Board (ASB).

The establishment and issuance of auditing standards has traditionally been the responsibility of the AICPA. Its Committee on Auditing Procedure (CAP) was formed on January 30, 1939, and functioned until 1972, issuing a series of 54 *Statements on Auditing Procedure*, which were to serve as guidelines for the independent auditor in the exercise of professional judgment on the application of auditing procedures.

In November 1972, the Statements on Auditing Procedure were codified in *Statement on Auditing Standards No. 1*, "Codification of Auditing Standards and Procedures." At this time, the AICPA reorganized its auditing section and changed the name of the committee to the Auditing Standards Executive Committee (AudSEC) and created the Auditing Standards Division within the AICPA. AudSEC served as the AICPA's senior technical committee with the charge of interpreting generally accepted auditing standards and responsibility for issuing Statements on Auditing Standards (SASs). These statements have been incorporated into the AICPA's looseleaf service, *Professional Standards*, which provides a continuous codification of Statements on Auditing Standards.

As a result of the recommendations of the Commission on Auditors' Responsibilities, an independent study group appointed by the AICPA in 1974 to study the structure of the auditing standard-setting process, the AICPA restructured its auditing committee in May, 1978. In October, 1978, a 15-member Auditing Standards Board (ASB) was formed as the successor to AudSEC on all auditing matters and is the present body authorized to issue Statements on Auditing Standards. The Board was given the following charge:

> *The AICPA Auditing Standards Board shall be responsible for the promulgation of auditing standards and procedures to be observed by members of the AICPA in accordance with the Institute's rules of conduct.*
>
> *The board shall be alert to new opportunities for auditors to serve the public, both by the assumption of new responsibilities and by improved ways of meeting old ones, and shall as expeditiously as possible develop standards and procedures that will enable the auditor to assume those responsibilities.*
>
> *Auditing standards and procedures promulgated by the board shall:*
>
> a. *Define the nature and extent of the auditor's responsibilities.*
> b. *Provide guidance to the auditor in carrying out his duties, enabling him to express an opinion on the reliability of the representations on which he is reporting.*
> c. *Make special provisions, where appropriate, to meet the needs of small enterprises.*
> d. *Have regard to the costs which they impose on society in relation to the benefits reasonably expected to be derived from the audit function.*
>
> *The Auditing Standards Board shall provide auditors with all possible guidance in the implementation of its pronouncements, by means of interpretations of its statements, by the issuance of guidelines, and by other means available to it.*[4]

In addition, the staff of the Auditing Standards Division of the AICPA has been authorized to issue auditing interpretations on the application of pronouncements (SASs) of the Auditing Standards Board. The interpretations are not to be considered as authoritative as a Statement on Auditing Standards. However, members need to be aware that they may have to justify any departure from an interpretation issued by the Auditing Standards Division of the AICPA. Other publications of the Auditing Standards Division include a number of Industry Audit Guides and Statements of Position. Figure 9–6 presents an overview of the current hierarchy of authoritative auditing support. The auditor should be aware of each of the sources listed, particularly the Statements on Auditing Standards. Figure 9–7 presents a listing of the current existing Audit and Accounting Guides.

The current standard-setting process of the ASB is somewhat similar to that of the FASB:

1. A specific auditing problem or issue is identified.
2. A task force may be established to conduct research on the problem or issue.
3. Public meetings are held to discuss the auditing issue.
4. An exposure draft of a proposed Statement on Auditing Standards may be issued for public comment.
5. A final pronouncement, or Statement on Auditing Standards, is issued.

4　AICPA *Professional Standards*, Vol. 1, Section AU–Appendix A.

Figure 9–6 Auditing Authoritative Support

Primary Authoritative Support

A. General Application
    1.   Generally Accepted Auditing Standards
    2.   Statements on Auditing Standards
    3.   Auditing Interpretations
    4.   AICPA Code of Conduct
    5.   International Auditing Guidelines
B. Special Application to Certain Entities
    1.   Industry Audit Guides
    2.   Statements of Position of the Auditing Standards Division
    3.   GAO-Government Auditing Standards

Secondary Authoritative Support

A. Audit Research Monographs
B. AICPA Audit and Accounting Manual
C. Journal articles and textbooks

Due to changing economic conditions, the AICPA's Auditing Standards Division currently issues *Audit Risk Alerts* on a periodic basis. These statements provide auditors with an overview of recent economic conditions as well as new professional developments that may affect the audits they perform. Although these documents have not been approved, disapproved, or other- wise acted upon by the ASB, they provide valuable audit guidance for the auditor.

Unlike an audit that expresses whether the financial statements are in con- formity with GAAP, the accountant's examination of prospective financial statements provides assurance only as to whether (1) the prospective financial statements conform to the AICPA's guidelines, and (2) the assumptions used

Figure 9–7 AICPA Audit and Accounting Guides

Audit Sampling
Agriculture Producers and Agriculture Cooperatives
Airlines
Banks & Savings Institutions
Brokers and Dealers in Securities
Casinos
Not-for-Profit Organizations
Credit Unions
Employee Benefit Plans
Entities with Oil and Gas Producing Activities
Federal Government Contractors
Finance Companies
Investment Companies
Property and Liability Insurance Companies
State and Local Governmental Units
Health Care Organizations
Common Interest Realty Associations
Consideration of Internal Control Structures in a Financial Statement Audit
Construction Contractors
Prospective Financial Statements
Use of Real Estate Appraisal Information
Personal Financial Statements

in the projections provide a reasonable basis for a forecast or projection. The accountant must keep in mind that any type of attest service provided must be accompanied by a report as described in the various attestation and auditing standards.

Benchmarking (Performance Measurement)

Since the audit engagement today is often considered as a commodity, audit practitioners attempt to "add value" to the engagement. A typical extension of the audit is providing the assurance service of "benchmarking" whereby the practitioner provides quality information as to management's strategies and performance in relation to other similar companies. This service (benchmarking) is a performance measurement tool used in conjunction with improvement initiatives to measure comparative operating performance and identify best practices. Benchmarking issues have studied such areas as accounting and financial systems, acquisitions, business facilities management, corporate downsizing, foreign currency, as well as a host of other topics. Various Internet sites currently provide benchmarking surveys (i.e., *www.Benchnet.com*).

Not only has this assurance service of benchmarking been beneficial to clients, for many accounting firms the service has also improved the audit function. As corporations have reengineered their processes, accounting firms are involved in a continuous process of reengineering their audit methodologies in order to become more efficient. This reengineered audit methodology includes in some form the following three basic components: Strategies and Business Process Analysis, Risk Assessment, and Business Measurement.

The first component, Strategies and Business Process Analysis, includes a thorough understanding of the client—the client's strategies, objectives, and management processes to maintain its competitive advantage; the client's business risks associated with these elements; and how the client is responding to these risks. The output from this first component of the audit methodology is to compare the client's elements to industry standards or best practices in order to assess the client's effectiveness in these areas. Such an in-depth analysis has a significant impact on the scope of the audit. PricewaterhouseCoppers' Internet applet called Edgarscan is an excellent tool for performance measurement or benchmarking activities. If you have not done so yet, please view the demo of Edgarscan that is on the CD included with this text.

The second component of the audit methodology is risk assessment. Based on the auditor's understanding of the client's strategies, objectives, processes, and related business risks, the auditor must determine whether the client has appropriate controls to mitigate the risks. This detailed assessment of the client's risk profile has a major impact on the audit plan for the client. More audit effort will be assigned to the high risk areas within the client's operations.

The third major component of the audit methodology is business measurement. Here the auditor not only focuses on the financial statement numbers, but also the client's accounting recognition practices, the quality of earnings, and financial and non-financial performance measures. Again, benchmarking aids in this component of the audit process. The end result of this audit methodology is not only a report on the fairness of the entity's financial statements, but also constructive advice for improvement in the client's operations and performance. This assurance service of benchmarking with related tools, such as Edgarscan, is having a significant impact on improvements in client operations and also improving the business audit methodology of accounting firms. The accounting practitioner needs to be aware of the research tools available in order to conduct benchmarking activities.

CODE OF PROFESSIONAL CONDUCT

A distinguishing mark of any profession is the establishment and acceptance of a code of professional conduct. This code, which a profession imposes upon its membership, outlines a minimum level of conduct that is mandatory and enforceable. Such a code of ethics emphasizes the profession's responsibility to the public as well as to colleagues. Every CPA in the practice of public accounting should be familiar with the code and its applicability to audit, tax, and consulting services. The AICPA Code of Professional Conduct consists of two main sections, Principles and Rules.

The Principles serve as the basic framework for the Rules, which are mandatory and enforceable. Periodically, the Executive Committee of the Professional Ethics Division of the AICPA issues ethics rulings and interpretations for the purpose of clarifying the Code. The Interpretations render guidance to the accountant as to the scope and applicability of the rules. The Rulings help to clarify specific situations confronted by the accountant. Figure 9–8 depicts the hierarchy of these components.

Departure from the Rules may result in disciplinary action unless the departure can be justified in the circumstances. Disciplinary action may lead to suspension or termination of AICPA membership. Furthermore, a violation of professional conduct may result in revocation of a CPA certificate or license to practice by a state board of accountancy; in many cases, the revocation is sanctioned by the Securities and Exchange Commission. The AICPA's Code of Professional Conduct applies to all members. Certain rules, however, are specifically applicable to the independent auditor. Rule 202 requires compliance with the standards and is stated as follows:

> *Rule 202—Compliance with standards. A member who performs auditing, review, compilation, management consulting, tax, or other professional services shall comply with standards promulgated by bodies designated by Council.*[5]

---

5   AICPA *Professional Standards*, Vol. 2, Section ET–202.

Figure 9–8 Hierarchy of the AICPA's Code of Professional Conduct

Level 1	**Principles**—The Principles provide the framework for the development of the Rules.	
Level 2	**Rules**—The Rules serve as the enforceable part of the Code that governs the professional services of the AICPA members.	Official Section of the Code
Level 3	**Interpretations of the Rules of Conduct**—Interpretations are those that have been adopted by the professional ethics division's executive committee to provide guidelines as to the scope and application of the Rules.	
Level 4	**Ethics Rulings**—The Ethics Rulings consist of formal rulings made by the professional ethics division's executive committee. Their rulings summarize the application of the Rules and Interpretations to particular factual circumstances.	Members who depart from interpretation of rulings must justify such departures.

Rule 203 generally prohibits the auditor from expressing an opinion that financial statements are in conformity with generally accepted accounting principles if the statements contain any departure from the official pronouncements of the Financial Accounting Standards Board, its predecessors, or the Governmental Accounting Standards Board. Rule 203 is stated as follows:

> *Rule 203—Accounting principles. A member shall not (1) express an opinion or state affirmatively that the financial statements or other financial data of any entity are presented in conformity with generally accepted accounting principles or (2) state that he or she is not aware of any material modifications that should be made to such statements or data in order for them to be in conformity with generally accepted accounting principles, if such statements contain any departure from an accounting principle promulgated by bodies designated by Council to establish such principles that has a material effect on the statements taken as a whole. If, however, the statements or data contain such a departure and the member can demonstrate that due to unusual circumstances the financial statements would otherwise have been misleading, the member can comply with the rule by describing the departure, its approximate effects, if practicable, and the reasons why compliance with the principle would result in a misleading statement.*[6]

As noted in the above two rules, it is important to emphasize that the CPA must comply with generally accepted auditing standards and also be familiar with generally accepted accounting principles when expressing an opinion. Therefore, the practitioner should master a research methodology in order to determine if the audit is in compliance with GAAS and the entity is following GAAP.

Rule 203 was clarified with the issuance of the following two Interpretations:

> *Interpretations under Rule 203—Accounting principles:*
>
> *203-1—Departures from established accounting principles. Rule 203 was adopted to require compliance with accounting principles promulgated by the body designated by Council to establish such principles. There is a strong presumption that adherence to officially established accounting principles would in nearly all instances result in financial statements that are not misleading.*
>
> *However, in the establishment of accounting principles it is difficult to anticipate all of the circumstances to which such principles might be applied. This rule therefore recognizes that upon occasion there may be unusual circumstances where the literal application of pronouncements on accounting principles would have the effect of rendering financial statements misleading. In such cases, the proper accounting treatment is that which will render the financial statements not misleading.*
>
> *The question of what constitutes unusual circumstances as referred to in Rule 203 is a matter of professional judgment involving the ability to support the position that adherence to a promulgated principle would be regarded generally by reasonable men as producing a misleading result.*
>
> *Examples of events which may justify departures from a principle are new legislation or the evolution of a new form of business transaction. An unusual degree of materiality or the existence of conflicting industry practices are examples of circumstances which would not ordinarily be regarded as unusual in the context of Rule 203.*

---

6   AICPA *Professional Standards*, Vol. 2, Section ET–203.

203-2—Status of FASB and GASB interpretations. Council is authorized under Rule 203 to designate bodies to establish accounting principles. Council has designated the Financial Accounting Standards Board (FASB) as such a body and has resolved that FASB Statements of Financial Accounting Standards, together with those Accounting Research Bulletins and APB Opinions which are not superseded by action of the FASB, constitute accounting principles as contemplated in Rule 203. Council has also designated the Governmental Accounting Standards Board (GASB), with respect to Statements of Governmental Accounting Standards issued in July 1984 and thereafter, as the body to establish financial accounting principles for state and local governmental entities pursuant to rule 203.

In determining the existence of a departure from an accounting principle established by a Statement of Financial Accounting Standards, Accounting Research Bulletin or APB Opinion encompassed by Rule 203, or the existence of a departure from an accounting principle established by a Statement of Governmental Accounting Standards encompassed by Rule 203, the division of professional ethics will construe such Statements, Bulletin or Opinion in the light of any interpretations thereof issued by the FASB or the GASB.[7]

As a result, the recognition of the FASB, its predecessors, and the GASB as the designated bodies in setting GAAP, and the due process these organizations conduct, their pronouncements are placed in Level One in the Hierarchy of GAAP as identified in Chapter 5.

AUDITING IN THE PUBLIC SECTOR

Until the early 1970s, there was little interest in whether governmental auditors adhered to auditing standards in auditing a governmental entity. However, as public sector spending accelerated, legislators, government officials, and the general public became increasingly concerned about how their money was spent and whether government was achieving its goals funded by public dollars. Associated with these concerns was the desire to establish standards for governmental auditing as guidelines for the governmental auditor. To a large degree, the standards and guidelines used in a governmental audit are similar to auditing requirements in the corporate sector. Federal, state, and local governments have placed substantial reliance on the auditing requirements of the AICPA's Auditing Standards Division. However, specific governmental audit concerns have been addressed by various governmental regulatory bodies.

In 1972, the Comptroller General of the United States issued the first major governmental auditing publication, entitled *Standards for Audit of Governmental Organizations, Programs, Activities and Functions* (revised in 1981). These standards, applicable to all governmental organizations, programs, activities, and functions, have the objective of improving the quality of governmental audits at the federal, state, and local levels. These governmental standards were founded on the premise that governmental accountability should focus not only on which funds have been spent, but also the manner and effectiveness of the expenditures. Therefore, these standards provide for an audit scope to include financial and compliance auditing as well as auditing for economy, efficiency, and effectiveness of program results. In 1994, the GAO revised and reissued its auditing publication entitled *Government Auditing Standards*, commonly referred to as the "Yellow Book."

---

7   AICPA *Professional Standards*, Vol. 2, Section ET–203.

Federal legislation requires that these GAO auditing standards be followed by federal inspector generals. Also, these standards are audit criteria for federal executive departments and agencies.

Other major audit guidelines for nonprofit organizations issued since 1972 are listed in Figure 9–9. Of major importance has been the issuance of The Single Audit Act of 1984 (Public Law 98–502), which incorporated the concept of an entity-wide financial and compliance "single audit." This Act requires an annual audit of any state or local government unit that receives federal financial assistance. The single audit concept thus eliminates the need for separate financial and compliance audits conducted by the various federal agencies from whom the entity has received funding. By Congressional directive, the Director of the Office of Management and Budget has been given the authority to establish policy and guidelines and the mechanisms to implement single, coordinated financial and compliance audits of grant recipients on a government-wide basis.

ACCOUNTING SERVICES

In response to the needs of nonpublic clients,[8] regulatory agencies, and the investing public, the public accounting profession offers compilation or review services to clients rather than conducting an audit examination in accordance with GAAS. Compilation and review of financial statements are defined as follows:

> *Compilation—a service presenting, in the form of financial statements, information that is the representation of management without undertaking to express any assurance on the statements.*
>
> *Review—a service performing inquiry and analytical procedures that provide the accountant with a reasonable basis for expressing limited assurance that there are no material modifications that should be made to the statements in order for them to be in conformity with generally accepted accounting principles or, if applicable, with another comprehensive basis of accounting.[9]*

---

8 The distinction between a public versus nonpublic client is based on whether the entity's securities are traded publicly on a stock exchange or in the over-the-counter market.

9 Accounting and Review Services Committee, *Statement on Standards for Accounting and Review Services No. 1*, "Compilation and Review of Financial Statements," AICPA, 1978

Figure 9–9 Major Guidelines for Public Sector Auditing

GAO (General Accounting Office)
Government Auditing Standards ("Yellow Book")

OMB (Office of Management and Budget)
"Single Audit Act"

AICPA (American Institute of CPAs)
Attestation Standards
Generally Accepted Auditing Standards (GAAS)
Audit Guides: Audits of Not-for-Profit Organizations
Audits of Federal Government Contractors
Audits of State and Local Governmental Units
Audits of Health Care Organizations

Statements of Position

Therefore, the basic distinction between these two services is that a review service provides limited assurance about the reliability of unaudited financial data presented by management, whereas a compilation engagement provides no assurance as to the reliability of the data since the CPA prepares financial statements only from information supplied by management in order to obtain more accurate and reliable statements. The CPA need not verify this information furnished by the client and therefore provides no assurance regarding the validity of this information.

Guidance for the public accountant for these services has been established by the Accounting and Review Services Committee of the AICPA with the issuance of Statements on Standards for Accounting and Review Services (SSARS). To date, the committee has issued seven statements:

1. "Compilation and Review of Financial Statements," Dec. 1978.
2. "Reporting on Comparative Financial Statements," Oct. 1979.
3. "Compilation Reports on Financial Statements Included in Certain Prescribed Forms," Dec. 1981.
4. "Communication Between Predecessor and Successor Accountants," Dec. 1981.
5. "Reporting on Compiled Financial Statements," July 1982.
6. "Reporting on Personal Financial Statements Included in Written Financial Plans," Sept. 1986.
7. "Omnibus Statement on Standards for Accounting and Review Services," Nov. 1992.

INTERNATIONAL AUDITING

In October, 1977, the International Federation of Accountants (IFAC) was organized through an agreement signed by 63 accounting bodies representing 49 countries. The IFAC stated that its broad objective was to develop a worldwide accounting profession with harmonized standards. To meet part of the objective relating to auditing standards, the IFAC established the International Auditing Practices Committee (IAPC) to develop and issue International Standards on Auditing (ISAs) on the form and content of audit reports. The purpose of the Standards is to improve the uniformity of auditing practices throughout the world. In addition to the Standards, the IAPC also issues International Auditing Practice Statements (IAPSs) that provide practical assistance in implementing the Standards, but do not have the authority of Standards.

The International Standards on Auditing apply to every independent audit of financial information regardless of the type or size of the entity under audit. However, within each country, local regulations govern. To the extent that the ISAs conform to the specific country's regulation, the audit will be considered in accordance with the Standards. In the event that they differ, the members of the IFAC will work towards the implementation of the Standard, if practicable, within the specific country.

The ASB has specifically addressed the concern of reporting on financial statements prepared for use in other countries through the issuance of Statement on Auditing Standards No. 51, *Reporting on Financial Statements for Use in Other Countries*. This statement provides guidance to the independent auditor practicing in the United States and reporting on financial statements of an American entity that have been prepared in conformity with accounting principles of another country for use outside the United States. If the financial statements are for use outside of the United States only, the auditor may use either of the following:

1. An American-style report modified to report on the accounting principles of the particular country, including:

   a. Identity of the financial statements (F/S).
   b. Reference to the note that describes the basis of presentation, including the nationality of GAAP.
   c. Examination made in accordance with U.S. GAAS (and of the other country, if appropriate).
   d. Opinion as to conformity with basis of presentation and consistency.

2. The report form of the other country, provided that:

   a. Such a report would be used by auditors in the other country in similar circumstances.
   b. The auditor understands and can make such attestations.

Since GAAP reports from other countries are generally not useful to U.S. readers, the auditor should consider issuing two reports—one using U.S. GAAP and the other using GAAP from the other country. Such financial statements may receive limited distribution in the United States (i.e., the parties have the opportunity to directly discuss the F/S with the entity). However, such financial statements may not receive a general distribution unless:

1. They are accompanied by statements prepared in conformity with U.S. GAAP.
2. The auditor uses a U.S.-type report, qualified for departures from U.S. GAAP.

Subcommittees of the IAPC have been established for the preparation and drafting of audit guidelines on specific subjects determined by the IAPC. After initial preparation, an exposure draft is balloted by the IAPC. If approved by three-quarters of the total voting, the exposure draft is disseminated for review. After the comments and suggestions are reviewed, the IAPC then votes on the issuance of a definitive International Standard on Auditing.

ROLE OF JUDGMENT IN ACCOUNTING AND AUDITING RESEARCH

The accountant or auditor exercises professional judgment in considering whether the substance of business transactions differs from the form, in evaluating the adequacy of disclosure, in assessing the probable impact of future events, and in determining materiality limits. This informed judgment on the part of the practitioner is the foundation of the accounting profession. In providing an attest engagement, the result is often the rendering of a considered opinion or principled judgment. In effect, the independent accountant gathers relevant and reliable information, evaluates and judges its contents, and then formalizes an opinion on the financial information or statements.

A review of current authoritative literature reveals that certain pronouncements on generally accepted accounting principles disclose specifically which accounting principle is applicable for a given business transaction. Other pronouncements provide only general guidelines and in some cases suggest acceptable alternative principles. The process of applying professional judgment in choosing among alternatives is not carried out in isolation, but through consultation with other professionals knowledgeable in the area. In rendering his/her professional judgment, the accountant/ auditor should exercise critical-thinking skills in the development of a solution or opinion.

Statement on Auditing Standards No. 5 makes the following point on the use of professional judgment in determining conformity with GAAP:

> .04 *The auditor's opinion that financial statements present fairly an entity's financial position, results of operations, and changes in financial position in conformity with generally accepted accounting principles* should be based on his judgment *as to whether*
>
> (a) *the accounting principles selected and applied have general acceptance;*
> (b) *the accounting principles are appropriate in the circumstances;*
> (c) *the financial statements, including the related notes, are informative of matters that may affect their use, understanding, and interpretation;*
> (d) *the information presented in the financial statements is classified and summarized in a reasonable manner; that is, neither too detailed nor too condensed; and*
> (e) *the financial statements reflect the underlying events and transactions in a manner that presents the financial position, results of operations, and changes in financial position stated within a range of acceptable limits; that is, limits that are reasonable and practicable to attain in financial statements. (Emphasis added)*[10]

In order to render an opinion based upon professional judgment, the auditor often considers the opinions of other professionals. In such cases, the practitioner can use several published sources to determine how others have dealt with specific accounting and reporting applications of GAAP. The AICPA publishes *Technical Practice Aids*, which contains the "Technical Information Service." This service consists of inquiries and replies that describe an actual problem that was encountered in practice and the interpretation and recommendations that were provided along with relevant standards and other authoritative sources. Chapter 6 included a discussion of *Technical Practice Aids*.

ECONOMIC CONSEQUENCES

Since time is a scarce commodity, the auditor should weigh the cost/benefit tradeoffs in extending the research process. The researcher should address the problem until all reasonable doubt relating to the issue has been eliminated, recognizing the hidden costs of making an improper audit decision. Besides the legal damages from an association with a negligent audit, the auditor can face criminal penalties; FTC, SEC, and other government sanctions; loss of reputation among the auditor's peers; and a significant loss of existing clients in a competitive environment.

OTHER REFERENCE SOURCES

The AICPA also provides other reference sources for the practitioner to use in determining how to apply accounting principles. *Accounting Trends & Techniques* is an annual publication designed to illustrate current reporting practices and chart significant trends in these practices. *Financial Reporting Surveys* consist of a continuing series of studies designed to show in detail how specific accounting and reporting questions are actually being handled. The National Automated

---

10 AICPA *Professional Standards*, Vol. 1, Section AU–411.04.

Accounting Research System (NAARS) is a full-text, computer-based information retrieval system. Among the information stored by this system are the annual reports of over 4,000 publicly traded corporations. These research tools and others were discussed in detail in Chapter 7. The practitioner can use these references to determine current accounting and reporting practices. With the use of information gathered, and through consultation with other accountants, a decision may be reached on the appropriate accounting principle to be used for the transaction being researched or the auditing issue under investigation.

SUMMARY

This chapter has presented an overview of assurance services, the attestation standard-setting environment, accounting services, and professional ethics. Familiarity with this information, in particular the authoritative pronouncements that exist, will aid the practitioner in the research process.

In researching an accounting or assurance services issue, the practitioner will be called upon to use professional judgment in the decision-making process. Experience is undoubtedly the primary factor in developing good professional judgment. However, this text presents a research methodology that should aid in the application of professional judgment.

DISCUSSION QUESTIONS

1. What is an assurance service engagement?
2. Define an attest engagement. Is an audit engagement an attest service?
3. Identify three other attest services in addition to the normal financial statement audit.
4. Differentiate between auditing standards and attestation standards.
5. a. Utilizing PricewaterhouseCoopers' Edgarscan, locate the most recent 10-K filing for a public company and summarize its Management's Discussion and Analysis Section (MD&A).
    b. For the company selected in (a), utilize the benchmarking tool of Edgarscan and report the results of five different ratios for the most current quarter and full year.
6. a. Select a publicly traded company in the airlines industry. Using Pricewaterhouse-Coopers' Edgarscan and the selected company's homepage, prepare a listing of management's mission and business strategies by highlighting the entity's business units, product lines, customers, competition, joint ventures, and any other pertinent information as to business strategies. (Hint: use Edgarscan to find the most recent 10-K filing for the company in addition to the company's homepage).
    b. Utilizing the benchmarking tool of Edgarscan, select three competitors to the company selected in (a) and prepare a benchmarking report on five attributes comparing the selected company with its competition.
7. What guidelines exist for the performance of accounting and review services?
8. Differentiate between auditing standards and auditing procedures.
9. Discuss the relationship between generally accepted auditing standards (GAAS) and Statements on Auditing Standards (SAS).
10. Discuss the applicability of the first and third general standards of GAAS to accounting and auditing research.
11. Discuss the historical relationship of the Auditing Standards Board, Auditing Standards Executive Committee, and Committee on Auditing Procedure. Also, list the authoritative pronouncements issued by each body.
12. State the objective of the Single Audit Act. When is this act applicable?
13. List the primary auditing guidelines for public sector auditing.
14. Explain the importance of the Code of Professional Conduct in the performance of an audit.

15. Explain the significance of Rules 202 and 203 of the AICPA's Code of Professional Conduct.
16. How may accounting or auditing research aid the practitioner in complying with Rules 202 and 203 of the Code of Professional Conduct?
17. What role does professional judgment play in the daily activities of the accountant or auditor?
18. What authoritative auditing literature that has general applicability in practice is considered primary authoritative support?
19. What guidelines are available for the accountant in serving the needs of the non-public client?
20. What authoritative body exists as to the development of international auditing standards?
21. Utilizing Figure 2–3 (Universal Elements of Reasoning), identify the eight elements for the following:

    You have been approached by a prospective client that has requested a report as to the reliability of its electronic commerce activities on the Internet. You are trying to decide the type of assurance service engagement this would be.
22. Access the Web site *www.riskmetrics.com*, and report on three benchmarking and best practices surveys in progress.
23. Access the Web site *www.Benchnet.com*, and report on three different riskmetrics products available.

CHAPTER 10

Introduction to Tax Research

LEARNING OBJECTIVES

After completing this chapter, you should understand the following:

- The different perspectives of tax research.
- The definition of tax research.
- The sources of tax authority.
- The overview of the tax research process.
- The use of computers in tax research.

In the United States we have what is often proclaimed to be a self-assessment system of federal income taxation. However, as a practical matter, many, if not most, higher-income taxpayers routinely seek professional help in attempting to fulfill their tax obligations at minimum cost. The complexity of current tax law and its administration are undoubtedly important factors in accounting for the widespread use of professional tax advisors. Complexity in tax rules and their application have thus rendered skill in tax research a marketable expertise, providing the basic economic justification for the study of tax research methodology. The purpose of this chapter is to present an overview of the steps involved in conducting tax research.

PERSPECTIVES ON TAX RESEARCH

Having established that tax research is an economically rewarding activity, let us now examine what the term *tax research* includes and, perhaps even more importantly, what it does not include. At the outset, note that the objective of tax research is not necessarily to produce the lowest possible tax liability for the taxpayer. Rather, the objective is to maximize the taxpayer's after-tax return or benefits, which may even take noneconomic forms. This difference in viewpoint—maximizing after-tax benefits as opposed to minimizing tax—is important when one realizes that many tax-saving strategies involve some tradeoff with pretax income, either in the form of incurring additional expense, receiving less revenue, or both. Consider the extreme case of a taxpayer avoiding all forms of income and thus achieving the ultimate in tax savings, i.e., a zero tax liability. Obviously, such action would not be considered economically optimal despite the zero tax obligation. Noting such an extreme example, it is readily apparent that tax savings should not be the sole objective of tax research.

Another distinction important to the tax research process is the one between tax evasion and tax avoidance. Both activities seek the same end; the lowering of one's tax payments on a certain level of income. However, they differ importantly with respect to the means employed to achieve that end. Tax evasion consists of illegal acts, such as the making of false statements of fact. Tax avoidance seeks to avoid the creation of facts that would result in a tax obligation under the law. Tax avoidance is unquestionably a legal activity, at least in concept. It is often the objective of tax research. In addition, most people would also deem it morally correct since Congress chose to tax income, not one's capacity to produce income.

The prevailing view on the concept of tax avoidance was perhaps best expressed in the often-quoted words of Judge Learned Hand:

> Over and over again courts have said that there is nothing sinister in so arranging one's affairs as to keep taxes as low as possible. Everybody does so, rich or poor; and all do right, for nobody owes any public duty to pay more than the law demands: taxes are enforced extractions, not voluntary contributions. To demand more in the name of morals is mere cant.[1]

Before discussing the process to conduct tax research, it is necessary to make one final distinction to clarify the perspective from which tax research is viewed in this chapter. That distinction is the difference between policy-oriented tax research and application-oriented tax research. Policy-oriented research is conducted with the objective of providing information that will bear on the fundamental issue of deciding what tax law ought to be. On the other hand, application-oriented research addresses existing tax law, with the objective of determining its impact on a given situation. In this book, the term **tax research** is used solely in the application sense of determining what the law *is*, while questions of what it *ought to be* are not addressed. In short, the type of research discussed relates to the tax problems of specific taxpaying entities rather than to those of society at large.

TAX RESEARCH DEFINED

Thus far, several distinctions have been drawn for the purpose of putting tax research into perspective. But what exactly is tax research? It can best be defined as **the process by which one determines the defensibly correct economic impact of tax laws on a given entity or group of entities with respect to a given fact situation.**

Four aspects of this definition deserve mention. First and foremost, the economic impact of taxes derives from the application of law and law only. If the correct application of law to a given set of facts results in a situation at odds with some accounting, economic, social, or moral theory, the law still controls. Only legal authority can ever be tax authority. Of course, the practical issue is often one of locating and selecting the correct authorities from among several competing alternatives.

Second, it is important to remember that tax research is a process rather than an object, namely, the process by which tax law is applied to a given set of facts. This process consists of at least two distinctly different types of activities. First, there is the thinking or conceptualizing process by which one not

---

1 *Comm. v. Newman*, 159 F.2d 848, 47-1 USTC 9175, 35 AFTR 857 (CA-2, 1947). It should be noted that this quote is taken from a dissenting opinion and thus had no value as legal precedent. However, the same idea had been expressed by other judges in majority opinions.

only decides what research is needed but also evaluates any information located through the tax research process. Second, there is the search for relevant information on specific points from among the massive quantity of tax authority contained in a comprehensive tax library. Thus, skill in tax research requires both the ability to conceptualize problems and a knowledge of the organization of the sources of tax authority. All too often there seems to be a tendency among beginning tax researchers to rush into the search for authority without adequate conceptualization of the problem to be researched. Perhaps the following example can help illustrate the benefit of spending time in simply thinking about a tax problem.

In *John J. Sexton*,[2] the taxpayer operated refuse dumps and acquired land containing large excavations for use in his dumping business. Normally, one cannot depreciate the cost of land when only the use of surface rights is involved. In this case, however, the taxpayer successfully argued before the Tax Court that the major portion of his purchase price was paid not for the acquisition of the land but rather for the large holes in the land. As the holes were filled in, he depreciated the assigned cost of the holes and claimed such depreciation as a current deduction. By characterizing his purchase as a purchase of holes as opposed to a purchase of land, this taxpayer was able to enjoy a current tax saving less imaginative persons might have easily overlooked.

A third consideration in tax research is the determination of which alternative treatments are defensibly correct. In some situations, more than one answer may have a reasonable basis in law. The taxpayer may then be informed of his or her choice based on the relative merits and tax benefits of each defensibly correct option. At other times only one result has an appropriate weight of authority. Determination of the cutoff between a defensible tax treatment and one which is not defensible is a product of the authorities found. This requires prior experience and professional judgment.

The fourth element in this definition of tax research concerns the role of facts. Many tax disputes involve questions of fact rather than questions of law. One should realize that the term **fact** as used in the definition of tax research includes conclusions as well as individual events from which those conclusions are drawn. For example, under the law gifts received are not includable in taxable income, whereas compensation for services is taxable. Whether a receipt of property constitutes a gift or compensation is a conclusion to be drawn from all events and circumstances relevant to the case at hand. Any dispute in such a case between the Internal Revenue Service and a taxpayer would be deemed a question of fact since the law clearly states that compensation is taxable (Sec. 61) while gifts are not (Sec. 102).

The nature of facts, whether already in existence or only anticipated, distinguishes the two fundamental types of activities involving tax research—tax compliance and tax planning. In tax compliance engagements (sometimes referred to as closed-fact engagements) all the facts have already occurred. In such instances the tax researcher's job is limited to one of discovery and documentation since the factual burden of proof generally rests with the taxpayer in the event of audit and dispute. On the other hand, in tax planning engagements (sometimes referred to as open-fact engagements), not all of the relevant facts have yet transpired. In effect, tax planning is nothing more than carefully executed tax avoidance; that is, controlling the facts that actually occur so as to produce an optimal after-tax result for the taxpayer. The flexibility to control at least some of the facts in an engagement increases both the complexity of the

---

2   John J. Sexton, 42 TC 1094 (1964); Acq., 1970-1 CB 16.

tax researcher's task and its potential value to the taxpayer. Consequently, the rendering of well-researched tax planning advice is generally regarded as the hallmark of a true professional.

STEPS IN CONDUCTING TAX RESEARCH

Tax research consists of five basic steps very similar to the steps identified in Chapter 1 for accounting and auditing research:

1. Identifying and refining the tax problem to be researched.
2. Locating relevant tax authorities.
3. Assessing the relative applicability and weights of relevant authorities.
4. Arriving at a defensibly correct solution (or perhaps several alternative solutions).
5. Communicating the solution to the taxpayer.

Step 1—Identifying and Refining the Tax Problem

Often, tax problems have a way of appearing deceptively simple to taxpayers, since the taxpayer is generally interested only in the final outcome of what may be a complex chain of applicable legal authorities. For instance, a taxpayer might ask the amount of allowable deduction for making a charitable contribution of land costing $10,000 and having a current market value of $25,000. As stated, this cannot be answered except to say that the deduction lies somewhere in the range of zero to $25,000. Even the most superficial review of Internal Revenue Code Sec. 170 (the basic tax authority concerning charitable contributions) reveals that the researcher needs to determine many additional facts just to identify the potential questions upon whose answers the amount of any deduction depends. A partial list of such considerations would include whether prior contributions had been made during the tax year—and, if so, the amount, nature, and circumstances of each; the amount of the individual's adjusted gross income; whether the receiving charitable organization is a public charity as opposed to a private foundation—and, if a public charity, the use to which the charity intends to put the property; and whether or not the contributed land, while in the hands of the taxpayer, would have generated ordinary income or capital gain if it had been sold instead of being donated.

Often preliminary research causes the tax researcher to realize the need for additional facts, which in turn will trigger new questions resulting in the need for even more facts, and so forth. Assume, for example, that in attempting to ascertain whether the land contributed was ordinary income or capital gain property, the tax researcher finds that the taxpayer deemed all real estate holdings to be investments in spite of an extensive history of prior real estate transactions. Thus, there is the possibility that the taxpayer might be deemed to be in the business of selling real estate so that the land in question might be deemed to have been held for sale in the normal course of that business. If so, the land would be ordinary income property, thus limiting any possible deduction to the taxpayer's basis in the property—$10,000 in this instance. If the taxpayer's real estate activities constitute only an investment activity and not a trade or business, the taxpayer might be entitled to a deduction for the $25,000 current market value of the land, assuming all other necessary conditions have been met. The central issue to be researched in such a case is whether or not the taxpayer's real estate activities constitute a trade or business, and if so, whether or not the donated land was held for sale in the normal course of the business. Note that the purpose of this example has not been to discuss the tax law concerning contributions but rather to illustrate the continually unfolding interrelationships between tax authorities and relevant facts when identifying and refining the key issue to be researched.

Steps 2 and 3—Locating and Assessing Relevant Tax Authorities

Since taxation is a matter of law, all answers to tax questions must stem from legal authority, either directly or through reasoned implication. However, not all legal authorities are of equal weight. Authority is a relative concept. Reasonable people often disagree as to what the words of a given authority really mean when applied to an actual situation—not to mention differences in ascertaining the so-called facts, which are really often conclusions. Tax authority is often classified as primary or secondary authority. Primary authority generally comes from the following sources:

- Statutory sources—U.S. Constitution, tax treaties, or tax laws
- Administrative sources—Rulings from the U.S. Treasury Department, or the IRS
- Judicial sources—Rulings from the various courts on tax matters

   Secondary authority generally comes from the following sources:

- Tax services
- Textbooks
- Tax Journals
- Tax Newsletters

   Because of their enormous volume and the many sources of tax authorities, it is imperative that tax researchers possess a working knowledge of the authoritative tax literature. Such knowledge should include both the source and the location of numerous documents. Knowing the sources of various tax authorities within the legal system, the researcher can better assess their relative weights. Knowing the manner in which the various authorities are classified and referenced, a researcher can more efficiently locate authorities on specific topics. For these reasons, both the sources and classifications used for tax authorities are described in detail later.

Step 4—Reaching a Correct Solution

In reaching a solution to the tax issue, the tax researcher will gather relevant tax information related to the issue under investigation. In certain cases, no clear solution is apparent due to unresolved issues of law, or perhaps incomplete facts from the client. As in accounting and auditing research, professional judgment plays an important role in resolving the issue.

   In unresolved cases, the tax professional will provide possible alternatives to the client with tax justification for each alternative. The client, in discussion with the tax professional, will select the best alternative considering the associated risks. The goal of conducting research is that of tax avoidance, not tax evasion.

Step 5—Communicating Tax Conclusions

No matter how competently researched, tax research not effectively communicated to clients can have no practical impact. The client should completely understand both the risks and potential benefits of any recommended actions.

Effective communication often requires that the tax researcher tailor the presentation to the intended audience. Judgment is required in determining how much detail to express when preparing any given document or letter. Whatever the level of technical sophistication of the person for whom the research is performed, any communication should follow a well-planned format that sets forth at least:

1. A statement of the relevant facts.
2. An identification of the tax questions involved.
3. The researcher's conclusions.
4. The authorities and reasoning upon which the conclusions are based.

Guidelines for preparing each section of the research report include the following:

Statement of Relevant Facts.

1. Include all facts necessary for answering the tax question(s) at issue.
2. Include relevant tax conclusions, if not at issue, as facts, such as the amounts of prior depreciation deductions, etc.
3. State events in chronological order and give dates for each.
4. Indicate sources of facts and give references for any available documentation.
5. Have the client review the written description of the facts for accuracy and completeness.

Identification of Tax Questions.

1. State each issue to be researched as a separate tax question.
2. Arrange tax questions in a logical order, particularly when the answer to one question raises another question. The best order for presentation may not be the order in which the questions were researched.
3. Avoid over-generalization. Tax questions should be tailored to the specific situation of the client with respect to dates, amounts, and any other relevant aspects.

Conclusions.

1. State a separate conclusion for each tax question listed.
2. In addition to the single most likely result, indicate any other outcomes for which a reasonable case can be made and include an assessment of the authoritative support underlying each alternative.
3. Sign and date the document or letter.

Authorities and Reasoning.

1. Separately present the authorities and reasoning underlying each conclusion listed.
2. Concisely summarize the facts and findings, plus a complete citation, for each authority mentioned. Also note the relative strength of each authority, such as whether a court decision was unanimous or split; whether a judge's remark was essential to the cited decision or merely a passing remark; whether the IRS expressed acquiescence, non-acquiescence, or neither; and whether the cited authority has been upheld in subsequent decisions.
3. Provide a detailed, logical analysis to support each of the research conclusions, using the precise findings of the legal authorities cited. Often the process of expressing thoughts in writing aids the identification and elimination of possible gaps in the tax logic.

SOURCES OF TAX AUTHORITY

Constitutional Foundation

The source of all federal legal authorities, including tax authorities, is the U.S. Constitution (Art. I, Sec. 8, Cl. 1):

> *The Congress shall have power to lay and collect taxes, duties, imposts and excises, to pay the debts and provide for the common defense and general welfare of the United States; but all duties, imposts and excises shall be uniform throughout the United States.*

However, the Constitution (Art. I, Sec. 9, Cl. 4) also states that "No capitation, or other direct, tax shall be laid, unless in proportion to the census or enumeration herein before directed to be taken." Since incomes are not, in fact, proportionally distributed among the people of various states, any income tax would clearly not meet this proportionality test. Thus, if income taxes are direct taxes, and thereby required to be proportional, they are not permissible under the original Constitution.

Between 1861 (when the Civil War income taxes were first enacted) and 1913 (the date of ratification of the 16th Amendment), the constitutionality of an income tax remained an intermittent question before the Supreme Court. In 1913 the constitutional question concerning federal income taxation was finally put to rest with the ratification of the 16th Amendment to the Constitution. This amendment states:

> *Congress shall have the power to lay and collect taxes on incomes, from whatever source derived, without apportionment among the several states, and without regard to any census or enumeration.*

The Supreme Court affirmed subsequently that the income tax could be applied through its decision in *Brushaber v. Union Pacific Railroad Co.*[3]

Legislative Sources of Tax Authority

Since the passage of the 16th Amendment, Congress has enacted many revenue acts. Prior to 1939, each individual revenue act amounted to a complete reenactment of the entire tax law to date, including current changes. As the complexity of the tax law increased, this procedure became increasingly cumbersome. In 1939, all federal tax law was codified into Title 26 of the *United States Code*, known as the *Internal Revenue Code of 1939*. Subsequent revenue acts were used to enact changes or amendments to the 1939 Code. By 1954, federal taxation had grown enormously, so Congress decided to completely rewrite the 1939 Code. *The Internal Revenue Code of 1954* was that complete revision, rearranging many of the old provisions, omitting those that had become obsolete over the years, and adding some new ones. After 1954 all federal tax legislation was enacted through amendments to the 1954 Code. In 1986, with the passage of the Tax Reform Act of 1986, the Code was redesignated as the *Internal Revenue Code of 1986*. Therefore, today the primary statutory origin on federal taxation is the *Internal Revenue Code of 1986 as Amended*. It is the statutory foundation of all federal tax authority, except for certain international issues covered in numerous tax treaties with various foreign nations.

---

3   *Brushaber v. Union Pacific Railroad Co.*, 240 U.S. 1, 36 S. Ct. 236, 3 AFTR2926 (USSC, 1969).

To better understand statutory tax law and the committee reports that aid its interpretation, we now examine the process by which a tax bill becomes law. Under the Constitution (Art. I, Sec. 7, Cl. 1), the House of Representatives has the basic responsibility for initiating revenue bills. Before any tax bill can even be considered by the entire membership of the House, however, it must first clear the Ways and Means Committee. The House Ways and Means Committee is the practical starting point in the evaluation of proposed changes to the Code.

Tax legislative proposals are frequently received from the president or his administration as well as from individual members of Congress. On major proposals the House Ways and Means Committee will usually hold public hearings where anyone can request permission to present views. While very few individuals not representing organizations are allowed to appear in person before the Committee, all written testimony submitted is entered into the public record of the hearings. By tradition, the first witness heard at such hearings is the Secretary of the Treasury representing the president and his administration.

Upon completion of the public hearings, the House Ways and Means Committee may go into a closed session from which the public is excluded. With the assistance of its technical staff, the Committee will write up and present a proposed bill to the entire House, along with a report from the Committee. This report of the House Ways and Means Committee is useful in interpreting the Congressional intent of those provisions of the bill eventually passed into law. It typically covers present law, reasons for change, description of the proposed change, effective date, and revenue effect.

With the approval of the Rules Committee of the House, tax bills are sometimes debated under a "closed rule," whereby amendments cannot be made on the floor of the House of Representatives unless approved by the Ways and Means Committee. When the debate is not under a closed rule, however, floor amendments are permitted. On occasion, the tax researcher can obtain insights into amended portions of tax bills by consulting the transcripts of the floor debate as reported in the *Congressional Record*.

Upon approval by the House, a tax bill next goes to the Senate where its first stop is the Finance Committee. The Senate Finance Committee operates much like the Ways and Means Committee of the House, possibly holding its own hearings and preparing its own Committee report, which will accompany the revised bill when it is reported to the floor of the Senate. Since the Senate Finance Committee edition of the bill will often show numerous changes from the one passed by the House, the Senate Finance Committee Report is also of importance to the tax researcher.

Since the Senate has no closed rule, amendments on its floor are more common than on the floor of the House. Obviously, the Senate Finance Committee Report does not cover those portions of the bill added or changed through floor amendment. Hence, the tax researcher may need to refer to the *Congressional Record* to uncover the reasoning behind any amendments.

The House and Senate approved versions of a tax bill will almost always differ in specific provisions. A Conference Committee, consisting of selected members from both houses of Congress, has the task of producing a compromise. The Conference Committee will also render a report. While sometimes helpful, the Conference Committee Reports tend to be rather technical in their reconciliation of the House and Senate versions of tax bills and contain little more than references to the original sources of enacted provisions.

Upon approval of the compromise version by both houses, the bill is sent to the president for either approval or veto. If signed, the bill becomes law. If vetoed, it is returned to Congress for possible override, which requires a two-thirds majority in both houses. However passed, the result is a new or changed portion of Title 26 of the *United States Code*, known as the *Internal Revenue Code of 1986 as Amended*.

The typical legislative process of enacting a tax bill and creating documentation useful in its interpretation is summarized in Figure 10–1. In addition, the staff of the Joint Committee on Taxation, an administrative combination of the members of the House Ways and Means Committee and the Senate Finance Committee, often uses the various Congressional committee reports to prepare an explanation of each major tax act. The Joint Committee staff explanation is often a convenient means for tax researchers to locate relevant comments from the House, Senate, and Conference Committee reports on only those portions of the original bill and the various amendments that were actually enacted.

Government publications that contain the various Congressional committee and staff reports include the *Congressional Record* and the *Cumulative Bulletin*. Several tax services[4] not only publish the major committee reports

---

4   Tax services or reporters are terms that can be applied to the six or more available research services in the tax area. These publications are designed to facilitate research by identifying information that may be pertinent to a particular tax question. They are typically multi-volume, comprehensive sets of information that relate to tax problems.

Figure 10–1 Legislative Enactment of Tax Law and Resulting Documentation

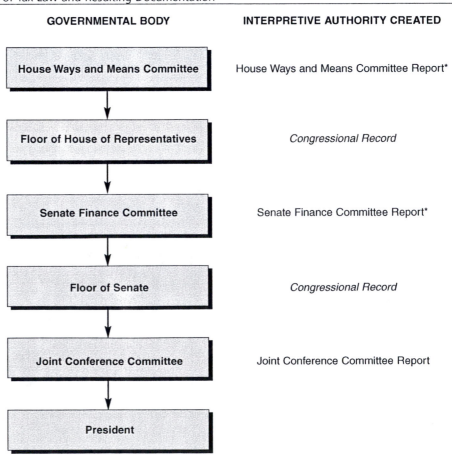

GOVERNMENTAL BODY	INTERPRETIVE AUTHORITY CREATED
House Ways and Means Committee	House Ways and Means Committee Report*
Floor of House of Representatives	*Congressional Record*
Senate Finance Committee	Senate Finance Committee Report*
Floor of Senate	*Congressional Record*
Joint Conference Committee	Joint Conference Committee Report
President	

*Items generally of greatest significance to tax researchers

as issued but also reprint relevant excerpts organized by Code section. For example, both Commerce Clearing House, Inc. (CCH) and Research Institute of America (RIA) tax services include committee report excerpts in their compilations.

To locate a given statutory provision, it is helpful to understand the organizational structure of the "law of the land." Divisions used in the *United States Code* include: Title, Subtitle, Chapter, Subchapter, Part, Section, Subsection, Paragraph, Subparagraph, and Sub-subparagraph.

A partial table of contents for Title 26 (commonly known as the *Internal Revenue Code of 1986*) is shown in Figure 10–2. Of particular importance to the tax researcher are the subdivisions called **sections** since these are uniquely numbered in a consecutive manner throughout the entire Title. In other words, each section number is used only once. Thus, one can use the citation "IRC Sec. 11" instead of the more cumbersome "Subtitle A, Chapter 1, Subchapter A, Part II, Section 11 of the *Internal Revenue Code of 1986 as Amended*." Notice also that since not all section numbers are used, additional sections may be added in the future without the need for renumbering.

In tax literature it is generally understood that, unless otherwise stated, references to section numbers concern the *Internal Revenue Code of 1986 as Amended*. Hence, it is common practice to omit the prefix IRC in citations. Also, sections are broken down as shown in Figure 10–3, in which the analysis of Sec. 217 is shown.

Ready access to the Code is required for the practicing tax researcher. Paperback editions are published after each major change in the law by Commerce Clearing House, Inc. (CCH) and Research Institute of America (RIA). In addition, the Code is included in each of the major tax services, with individual sections interspersed in the compilations, or in a separate volume or series of volumes, or both. Additionally, the Code and other tax literature are available for computer searches as discussed later in the chapter.

Figure 10–2 Partial Table of Contents of Internal Revenue Code of 1986

- Title 26—Internal Revenue Title (commonly known as *Internal Revenue Code of 1986*)
  - Subtitle A—Income Taxes
    - Chapter 1—Normal Taxes and Surtaxes
      - Subchapter A—Determination of Tax Liability
        - Part I—Tax on Individuals
          - Sections 1 through 5
        - Part II—Tax on Corporations
          - Sections 11 through 12
        - Parts III through VII
      - Subchapter B—Computation of Taxable Income
        - Parts I through XI
      - Subchapters C through V (except R, which was repealed)
    - Chapter 2—Tax on Self-Employment Income
    - Chapters 3 through 6
  - Subtitle B—Estate and Gift Taxes
  - Subtitles C through I

Figure 10–3 Analysis of a Code of a Section—Specific Citation: Sec. 217

Sec. 217. MOVING EXPENSES.

[Sec. 217(a)]

(a) Deduction allowed.—There shall be allowed as a deduction moving expenses paid or incurred during the taxable year in connection with the commencement of work by the taxpayer as an employee or as a self-employed individual at a new principal place of work.

[Sec. 217(b)]

(b) Definition of moving expenses.—

    (1) In general.—For purposes of this section, the term "moving expenses" means only the reasonable expenses—

        (A) of moving household goods and personal effects from the former residence to the new residence, and

        (B) of traveling (including lodging) from the former residence to the new place of residence.

Such term shall not include any expenses for meals.

    (2) Individuals other than taxpayer.—In the case of any individual other than the taxpayer, expenses referred to in paragraph (1) shall be taken into account only if such individual has both the former residence and the new residence as his principal place of abode and is a member of the taxpayer's household.

[Sec. 217(c)]

(c) Conditions for allowance.—No deduction shall be allowed under this section unless—

    (1) the taxpayer's new principal place of work—

        (A) is at least 50 miles farther from his former residence than was his former principal place of work, or

        (B) if he had no former principal place of work, is at least 50 miles from his former residence, and

    (2) either—

        (A) during the 12-month period immediately following his arrival in the general location of his new principal place of work, the taxpayer is a full-time employee, in such general location, during at least 39 weeks, or

        (B) during the 24-month period immediately following his arrival in the general location of his new principal place of work, the taxpayer is a full-time employee or performs services as a self-employed individual on a full-time basis, in such general location, during at least 78 weeks, of which not less than 39 weeks are during the 12-month period referred to in subparagraph (A).

For purposes of paragraph (1), the distance between two points shall be the shortest of the more commonly traveled routes between such two points.

[Sec. 217(d)]

(d) Rules for application of subsection (c)(2).—

    (1) The condition of subsection (c)(2) shall not apply if the taxpayer is unable to satisfy such condition by reason of—

SECTION 217

SUBSECTION (c)

PARAGRAPH (2)

SUBPARAGRAPH (B)

Administrative Sources of Tax Authority

Once Congress has enacted a tax law, the task of implementation rests with the executive branch of government. This responsibility is twofold. First, the Code must be interpreted and enforced. In this chapter, our concern is primarily with the former function because it is in its role as interpreter of Congressional intent that the Treasury Department (of which the Internal Revenue Service is a subdivision) creates tax authority of interest to tax researchers.

Treasury Regulations. Section 7805(a) expressly provides that "the Secretary (of the Treasury Department) shall prescribe all needful rules and regulations for the enforcement of this title." Such pronouncements are called Interpretative Regulations. In addition, several Code sections declare that certain basic concepts are to be applied under Regulations to be prescribed by the Secretary or his delegate. This second category of Regulations is referred to as Legislative Regulations. In these instances, Congress has delegated a portion of its law-making authority to the Secretary of the Treasury. Consequently, both types of Treasury Regulations are important sources of administrative law. This is particularly so for the Legislative Regulations, which are often described as having nearly the force of statutory law. This effect is further enforced by Sec. 6662, which provides that intentional disregard of either type of Treasury Regulation will invoke a 20 percent addition to any tax underpayment, even when no intent to defraud exists.

It should not be assumed that the Regulations are necessarily indisputable. Their purpose is to explain and illustrate the law as enacted by Congress. When found to be inconsistent with the intent of Congress, individual Regulations are held by the courts to be invalid. Nevertheless, any taxpayer taking a position in clear violation of a Treasury Regulation should be warned of the heavy burden of proof being assumed.

Treasury Regulations are usually first issued in proposed form by publication in the *Federal Register*. Interested parties have 30 days in which to comment. On occasion, comments received have resulted in Proposed Regulations being either withdrawn or modified. More often the Regulation will later be published as a Treasury Decision in the *Federal Register*. Later it is codified into Title 26 of the *Code of Federal Regulations*.

After major changes in the Code, the Treasury Department often issues Temporary Regulations without holding public hearings. These Temporary Regulations are legally binding and should not be confused with Proposed Regulations that are trial balloons. Most of the major tax services contain Proposed, Permanent (or Final), and Temporary Treasury Regulations. In addition, both CCH and RIA publish updated paperback editions of the Regulations each year.

In tax literature it is common practice to omit references to the phrase *Title 26 of the Code of Federal Regulations* since all such Regulations concern taxation. For example, two forms of a citation of the same Regulation are as follows:

Of particular importance to the tax researcher is the fact that the first group of numbers following the decimal in the Regulation citation identifies the section of the Code that the Regulation interprets. Thus, one can tell at a glance that the Regulation just cited applies to Code Sec. 217. However, there is no ordered relationship between the subdivisions of the Regulation and those of the Code section. The "2" after 217 in the Regulation cite means this is the second Regulation issued interpreting Sec. 217.

It is also interesting to observe that the **part number** of a Regulation citation identifies the general area to which it is related as follows.

Part 1	Income Taxes
Part 20	Estate Taxes
Part 25	Gift Taxes
Part 31	Employment Taxes
Parts 48, 49	Excise Taxes
Parts 301, 601	Administrative and Procedural Rules

Thus, any citation of an income tax Regulation begins with the part number "1" and is followed by the number of the Code section to which it pertains.

Often a considerable time lag can exist between the enactment of a tax law and the Treasury Department's issuance of related Regulations. In such instances, tax researchers are often forced to rely solely on Congressional committee reports for nonstatutory authoritative guidance. Also, they should always be careful that any Treasury Regulations being relied on are up to date, i.e., applicable to the current Code section of interest and not obsolete because of some recent change in the law. In this regard, one should be aware of the fact that the Treasury Department is frequently slow to remove or amend Regulations that have been voided by the U.S. Supreme Court.

Revenue Rulings and Letter Rulings. Revenue Rulings are issued by the Internal Revenue Service (IRS), a division of the Department of the Treasury. Revenue Rulings differ from Treasury Regulations in two important respects. First, the issuance of Rulings is the responsibility of the Commissioner of the Internal Revenue Service rather than the Secretary of the Treasury. Revenue Rulings thus represent the official public interpretation of the IRS, the federal agency responsible for the collection of the nation's tax revenue. As such, they do not carry the same force of authority as do Treasury Regulations, particularly Legislative Regulations, which constitute an administrative extension of the law-making process as directed by Congress. Second, Revenue Rulings are more limited in scope than are Treasury Regulations in that each Ruling is limited to a given set of facts. Revenue Rulings often are based upon official replies from the National Office of the IRS to taxpayers' requests concerning the tax outcomes of specific proposed transactions.

The IRS also issues Determination Letters to taxpayers. However, one should not confuse Revenue Rulings with Determination Letters. Revenue Rulings are issued by the Commissioner, whereas Determination Letters come from the District Directors. Also, Determination Letters cover only completed transactions as opposed to proposed ones. And, perhaps of most importance to the tax researcher, Determination Letters are not publicly available information.

The IRS is never obligated to respond to a taxpayer's request for an advance Letter Ruling. In fact, there are many areas of controversy in which the Service has declared a policy of not issuing any advance Letter Rulings. Of all advance Letter Rulings issued to taxpayers, only a small fraction is deemed by the government to be of sufficient general interest to justify publication in generic form as Revenue Rulings. Publication occurs first in the weekly *Internal Revenue Bulletin* and later in the semiannual *Cumulative Bulletin*. Most of the major tax services print summaries, but not the entire text, of selected published Revenue Rulings. However, the Mertens service, *Law of Federal Income*

Tax, does contain a series of volumes in which all Revenue Rulings published by the government since 1954 are reprinted in full text. Since Revenue Rulings are first published in the *Internal Revenue Bulletin* (IRB) and later in the *Cumulative Bulletin* (CB), one might encounter either of the following citations for the same Ruling:

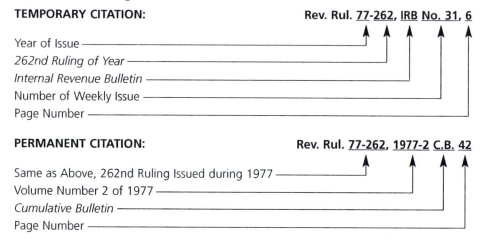

TEMPORARY CITATION: Rev. Rul. 77-262, IRB No. 31, 6

Year of Issue
262nd Ruling of Year
Internal Revenue Bulletin
Number of Weekly Issue
Page Number

PERMANENT CITATION: Rev. Rul. 77-262, 1977-2 C.B. 42

Same as Above, 262nd Ruling Issued during 1977
Volume Number 2 of 1977
Cumulative Bulletin
Page Number

Before relying on a Revenue Ruling, one should always check to determine that it was not revoked nor modified subsequent to publication. For this purpose, several of the major tax services provide tables by which one can quickly look up the number of any Revenue Ruling to determine its current status.

Unlike Revenue Rulings, Letter Rulings issued by the National Office of the IRS to individual taxpayers are not published by the government. However, as a result of the *Freedom of Information Act* as limited by IRC Sec. 6110, this information is open for public inspection although not published by the Government Printing Office. In 1978 two tax services began offering subscriptions to their Letter Rulings loose-leaf services. Letter Rulings have also been added to the data banks of LEXIS and WESTLAW commercial computerized legal data retrieval services, available on a time-sharing basis to subscribers. Letter Rulings are binding on the IRS only with respect to the requesting taxpayer.

Revenue Procedures. Revenue Procedures are used by the Internal Revenue Service to announce administrative procedures to be followed. Revenue Procedures can be regarded as being the same as Revenue Rulings in that they are issued by the same authority, can be located in the same sources, and are cited in the same manner except that the prefix "Rev. Proc." is used instead of "Rev. Rul."

Judicial Sources of Tax Authority

Note that in any legal question, while Congress sets forth the words of law, and the administrative branch of government is charged with the enforcement of those words, it is the judiciary that has the final say with respect to what the words really mean. Thus, one can seldom determine the practical impact of any area of law on a given set of facts without investigating what those words of law have been held to mean under similar factual circumstances. The Court's role as the final interpreter of language can hardly be overemphasized, as shown by the following example.

As noted earlier, Congress derived its power to tax income in 1913 from the 16th Amendment to the Constitution, which states in part that "Congress shall have power to lay and collect taxes on incomes, from whatever source derived . . . ." Shortly thereafter, Congress enacted a law which clearly declared stock dividends to be a form of taxable income. However, in the now classic case of *Eisner v. Macomber*,[5] the Supreme Court held stock dividends not taxable on the grounds that they do not fall within the meaning of the word *income* as used in the 16th Amendment. Despite the facts that the Constitution contains no definition of income and Congress declared the term to include stock dividends, the Court held to the contrary. In short, under our legal system the word *income*, and every other word in the law for that matter, means whatever the Supreme Court says it means—nothing more or less. Thus, the tax researcher must look to prior judicial decisions in determining the consequences of the words of a given Code section when applied to a particular contemplated or completed transaction.

By consistently treating similar cases in a similar way, the courts establish their interpretations of the statutes as laws in themselves. The principle that governs the use of prior decisions is called **precedent**. The courts use precedents to build stability and order into the judicial system. Decisions concerning prior similar cases are used as guides when deciding current cases. The process of finding analogous cases from the past and convincing the tax authorities of the precedential value of those cases is what judicial tax research is all about.

To appraise the relative authoritative weights of decisions rendered by the various federal courts that hear tax cases, a basic knowledge of the judicial system is necessary. An outline is presented in Figure 10–4. Each of the courts identified in Figure 10–4 will be discussed along with the systems of publication by which those court decisions are made available to tax researchers.

U.S. Tax Court. While technically a single court, the United States Tax Court consists of 19 judges, each appointed by the president for a 15-year term. Hearings are held in several cities throughout the nation, usually with only a single judge present who submits an opinion to the chief judge. Juries are not used in the Tax Court. Only rarely does the chief judge decide that a full review is necessary by all 19 judges. Rather, in most instances, the opinion will stand and be issued as either a regular or memorandum decision of the Tax Court. In theory, **memorandum** decisions concern only well-established principles of law and require only a determination of facts. On occasion, however, the appellate courts have cited memorandum decisions also. Hence, both series of Tax Court decisions should be regarded as having precedential value.

Since 1970, the Tax Court has adopted the position that within a circuit it will follow precedents of the Courts of Appeals (sometimes referred to as the *Golsen* rule).[6] As a result, the Tax Court may rule differently on identical fact patterns for two taxpayers residing in different circuits in the event of inconsistent holdings between the circuits. This problem will be explored further when the Courts of Appeals are discussed.

The jurisdiction of the Tax Court covers only tax deficiencies, not claims for refunds. Claims for refunds must be tried in either a U.S. District Court or the U.S. Claims Court. In effect, the taxpayer can elect either the Tax Court (by refusing to pay the IRS-assessed deficiency), or the District Court or Claims Court (by making payment and having his or her claim for refund denied). Unlike all other federal courts, the Tax Court hears only tax cases; consequently, Tax Court judges are usually well acquainted with tax issues.

---

5   *Eisner v. Macomber* 252 U.S. 189, 40 S.Ct. 189, 3 AFTR 3020, 1 USTC 32 (USSC, 1960).
6   *Jack E. Golsen*, 54 T.C. 742 (1970).

Figure 10–4 Judicial System for Federal Tax Litigation

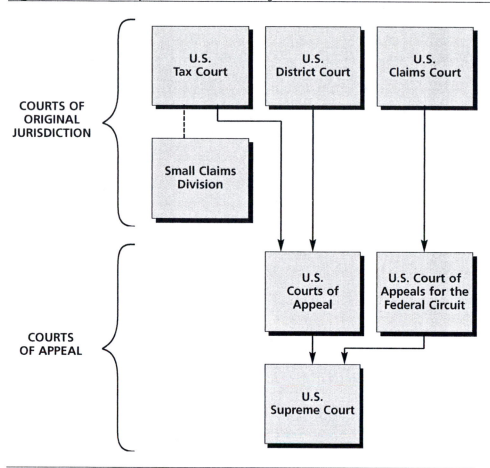

For most, but not all, regular Tax Court cases that the IRS has lost, the Commissioner will announce either **acquiescence** or **nonacquiescence**. This policy of expressing the current position of the IRS is limited to the regular decisions of the Tax Court. It covers neither the memorandum decisions of the Tax Court nor any decisions of any other courts. An acquiescence is not legally binding on the Service and can be retroactively withdrawn at any time. In *Dixon*,[7] the Supreme Court upheld the IRS's right to retroactively withdraw its announced acquiescence even after it had been relied on by a taxpayer. Thus, announcements of either acquiescence (A or Acq.) or nonacquiescence (NA or Nonacq.), as published in the *Internal Revenue Bulletin* and *Cumulative Bulletin*, can be regarded only as indicative of the current thinking of the Service and are subject to change at any time.

The reporting system for Tax Court decisions is somewhat confusing at first glance. Beginning tax researchers can save themselves considerable time and effort by paying close attention to details at this point. First, citations containing the letters USTC do *not* refer to Tax Court cases. USTC refers to *United States Tax Cases*, which is a special reporter service published by CCH containing all of the tax cases decided by all federal courts other than the Tax Court.

---

7   *W. Palmer Dixon*, 381 U.S. 68,85 S.Ct. 1301, 65-1 USTC 9386, 15 AFTR2d 842 (USSC, 1965).

Both CCH and RIA publish such reporters; the RIA series is called *American Federal Tax Reports* (AFTR, AFTR2d, AFTR3d). Note that neither of these special tax case reporters includes any Tax Court decisions, either regular or memorandum, although they do contain all other federal court decisions concerning taxation. Also, USTC, AFTR, AFTR2d and AFTR3d contain no cases other than tax cases.

Second, regular and memorandum decisions of the Tax Court are reported separately. The Government Printing Office publishes bound volumes of only the regular decisions under the title *United States Tax Court Reports*, cited TC. The government provides only mimeograph copies of the memorandum decisions. However, these are published in bound volumes by both CCH and RIA in reporters separate from those in which they report other tax cases. The Tax Court memorandum decisions are published by CCH under the title *Tax Court Memorandum Decisions* (TCM), while the RIA series is called *RIA, TC Memorandum Decisions* (RIAT.C. Mem.Dec.). In addition to these bound volumes, several of the major tax services provide loose-leaf copies of both regular and memorandum Tax Court decisions when issued.

Third, one should be aware of the fact that prior to 1943, the Tax Court was known as the Board of Tax Appeals. Both regular and memorandum decisions for years prior to 1943 were published by the government under the title *United States Board of Tax Appeals* (BTA).

The following citations indicate three locations where Tax Court decisions can be found in a professional library.

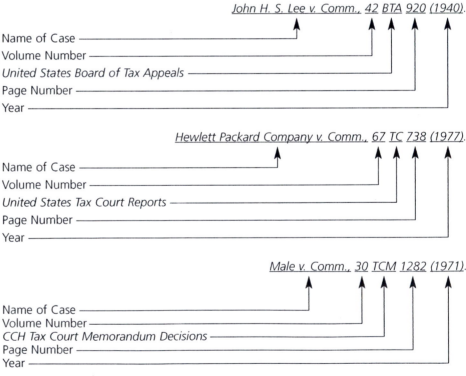

Interestingly, many of the decisions of the Tax Court, namely, those of the Small Claims Division, are of no value in tax research. These decisions cannot be used as precedents. If a taxpayer elects to have his or her case handled by the Small Claims Division of the Tax Court under an expedited and rather informal procedure in which no appeal is permitted by either side, such decisions are not even published. The tax in dispute cannot exceed $10,000 per year for the Small Claims Division of the Tax Court to have jurisdiction.

U.S. District Courts. A taxpayer can take a case to the U.S. District Court for the district in which he or she resides only by first paying the tax deficiency assessed by the IRS and then suing for a refund. Each state has at least one District Court in which both tax and nontax litigation are heard. Only in a District Court can one obtain a jury trial, and even there a jury can decide only questions of fact, not those of law. Appeals of both District Court and Tax Court decisions are made to the U.S. Court of Appeals for the circuit in which the taxpayer lives.

Published decisions of the U.S. District Courts, for tax and all other types of litigation, are contained in the *Federal Supplement* (F.Supp.) In addition, the tax decisions of the District Courts are also published in the two special tax reporter series, CCH's *United States Tax Cases* (USTC) and RIA's *American Federal Tax Reports* (AFTR, AFTR2d or AFTR3d). If only one location is to be disclosed in citing a District Court decision, common practice is to refer to the *Federal Supplement*. In consideration of their readers' convenience, however, most thoughtful tax writers use a multiple citation to all three sources as shown in the last example of the following series.

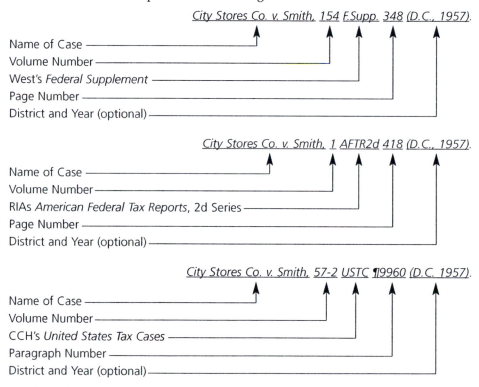

City Stores Co. v. Smith, 154 F.Supp. 348 (D.C., 1957).

Name of Case

Volume Number

West's *Federal Supplement*

Page Number

District and Year (optional)

City Stores Co. v. Smith, 1 AFTR2d 418 (D.C., 1957).

Name of Case

Volume Number

RIAs *American Federal Tax Reports*, 2d Series

Page Number

District and Year (optional)

City Stores Co. v. Smith, 57-2 USTC ¶9960 (D.C. 1957).

Name of Case

Volume Number

CCH's *United States Tax Cases*

Paragraph Number

District and Year (optional)

Complete citation: *City Stores Co. v. Smith*, 154 F.Supp. 348, 1 AFTR2d 418, 57-2 USTC fl9960 (D.C., 1957).

U.S. Claims Court. Prior to October 1, 1982, decisions of a court called the U.S. Court of Claims could be appealed only to the U.S. Supreme Court. Under the Federal Courts Improvement Act of 1982, however, that court was merged with the Court of Customs and Patent Appeals and is now called the U.S. Court of Appeals for the Federal Circuit. At the same time, a new trial court called the U.S. Claims Court was established. Decisions of the new trial court (U.S. Claims Court) may be appealed to the new appeals court (U.S. Court of Appeals for the Federal Circuit). Thus, tax researchers need to carefully distinguish between decisions of the prior U.S. Court of Claims and the current U.S. Claims Court as only the latter's decisions may be appealed to the Court of Appeals.

Since 1929, both tax and nontax decisions of the Court of Claims have been published by West Publishing Company. Decisions rendered between 1929 and 1932 and after 1959 appear in the *Federal Reporter—2d Series* (F.2d), while those issued between 1932 and 1960 are in the *Federal Supplement* (F.Supp.) In addition, the tax decisions of the Court of Claims are published in the CCH (USTC) and RIA (AFTR) special tax reporter series. A typical citation to a tax decision by the Court of Claims would be as follows:

> *McCandless Tire Service v. U.S., 422 F.2d 1336, 25 AFTR2d 70-870, 70- 1 USTC $9284 (Ct.Cls., 1970).*

U.S. Courts of Appeals. As a matter of right, decisions of the Tax Court and the District Courts may be appealed by either the IRS or the taxpayer to the U.S. Court of Appeals of jurisdiction.

Normally, a Court of Appeals' review, made by a panel of three judges, is limited to the application of law, not the determination of facts. The Court is obligated to follow the decisions of the Supreme Court but not those of the other Courts of Appeals for the other Circuits. However, the Court of Appeals for the 11th Circuit has ruled that it will follow the case precedent of the Court of Appeals for the 5th Circuit for those cases decided prior to its creation on October 1, 1981. The 11th Circuit is composed of three states previously included in the 5th Circuit.

When conflicts develop between circuits, District Courts of each individual circuit must follow precedents set by the appellate court of their own circuit, i.e., the Court of Appeals to which their decisions may be appealed. Also, as noted earlier, the Tax Court follows the policy of observing precedent set by the appellate court of the circuit in which the taxpayer resides. In this way, consistency in the application of law is maintained between the Tax Court and the District Court of jurisdiction even though an inconsistency may exist in the law's application to taxpayers residing in other circuits. The effect of this system is clearly seen in two cases concerning whether the same corporation qualified for Subchapter S status—the Tax Court effectively said "yes" to one 50 percent shareholder[8] and "no" to the other 50 percent shareholder[9] solely because of the difference in where they resided.

All decisions, both tax and nontax, of the various Courts of Appeals are published by West Publishing Company in the *Federal Reporter—2nd series* (F.2d or F.3d). In addition, tax decisions of the Courts of Appeals are also contained in CCH's *United States Tax Cases* (USTC) and RIA's *American Federal Tax Reports* (AFTR, AFTR2d, or AFTR3d). The following citation refers to a 1973 decision of the U.S. Court of Appeals of the 7th Circuit:

> *L. C. Thomsen & Sons, Inc. v. U.S., 484 F.2d 954, 32 AFIR2d 73-5718 73-2 USTC $9637 (CA-7, 1973).*

U.S. Court of Appeals for the Federal Circuit. Although the U.S. Court of Appeals for the Federal Circuit functions at the same level as the regional courts of appeal, its jurisdiction is defined by the trial court chosen by the taxpayer rather than by geography. It will hear appeals on tax issues only if they arise from decisions of the United States Claims Court. Still its decisions have nationwide precedential value.

U.S. Supreme Court. While either the IRS or the taxpayer can request the Supreme Court to review decisions of the U.S. Claims Court and those of any

---

8   *K.W. Doehring v. Comm.*, 33 TCM 1035, TC Memo. D 74,234.
9   *P.E. Puckett v. Comm.*, 33 TCM 1038, RIA TC Memo. Dex. 74,235.

of the Courts of Appeals, such requests rarely have been granted in tax cases in recent years. Appeal is by "Writ of Certiorari." If the Court agrees to hear the case, it will grant the Writ (reported as "Cert. Granted"). If the Court refuses, certiorari is denied (reported as "Cert. Den."). It should not be inferred that denial of a Writ of Certiorari necessarily means the Supreme Court agrees with the decision of the lower court. Rather, the Supreme Court simply does not wish to review the case.

Most tax cases reviewed by the Supreme Court involve conflicts between decisions of the Courts of Appeals. Once an issue has been ruled on by the Supreme Court, all Courts of Appeals are thereafter required to follow this precedent as long as the statute remains unchanged.

All Supreme Court decisions are published by the U.S. Government Printing Office in *U.S. Supreme Court Reports* (U.S.) and by West Publishing Company in its *Supreme Court Reporter* (S.Ct.). In addition, the tax-related decisions of the Supreme Court are contained in CCH's *United States Tax Cases* (USTC) and RIA's *American Federal Tax Reports* (AFTR, AFTR2d, or AFTR3d). A typical citation to a tax decision of the Supreme Court follows:

> *Eisner v. Macomber, 252 U.S. 189, 40 S.Ct. 189, 3 AFTR 3020, 1 USTC $32 (USSC, 1920).*

Figure 10–5 provides a summary of tax authority.

Evaluating Different Sources of Tax Authority

Once tax researchers have located authority relevant to a given tax question, they then face what is often the most difficult portion of the task: its assessment. A basic point to remember is that "authority" is a relative concept. Only very general guidelines can be given, as listed below.

1. The Code is the prime authority. However, many questions arise in attempting to apply the words of a Code section to a given fact situation.
2. Treasury Regulations are a strong authority. Legislative Regulations are of greater weight than interpretive Regulations.
3. Court decisions are a strong authority. Generally the higher the court, the greater the weight of the precedent.
4. Published IRS Rulings are binding on IRS personnel but not on the courts. Such rulings represent the current official policy of the IRS. They often carry considerable weight, even more than some court decisions, when dealing with employees of the IRS. In effect, the perception of the weight of authority may vary between the IRS and the courts.

Figure 10–5 Sources of Tax Authority

Legislative:	**Internal Revenue Code** Congressional Committee reports

Administrative:	Treasury Regulations—Proposed Regs
	                          Temporary Regs
	                          Final Regs
	Revenue Rulings
	Letter Rulings
	Revenue Procedures

Judicial:	Tax Court Regular Decisions Tax Court Memorandum Decisions

5. Letter Rulings are binding on the IRS only with respect to the particular tax-payer requesting the ruling. Sec. 6110 expressly prohibits their use as legal precedents by either the IRS or other taxpayers.

6. Only rarely is weight placed by either the IRS or the courts on editorial material in the various tax services. Mertens' *Law of Federal Income Taxation* is the one exception in that this service is often quoted in judicial decisions.

In addition to his or her tax education and experience, a major asset to the tax researcher in locating and assessing relevant tax authority is the nonauthoritative or general literature of taxation. This literature is not authority itself, but it is often useful in gaining insights on tax questions and in locating relevant authority bearing on those questions. In addition to tax services, this literature consists of many books and magazines reporting the opinions, analyses, and research already performed by others on a wide variety of tax issues. See Figure 10–6 for a brief listing of selected unofficial tax literature. By consulting the tax literature, one can often gain helpful insights. The ability to effectively use both the authoritative and general literature of a professional tax library is a necessary skill for the tax researcher.

Figure 10–6 Selected Examples of Unofficial Tax Literature

TAX TEXTBOOKS

Bittker & Eustice: *Federal Income Taxation of Corporations and Shareholders*	Warren, Gorham & Lamont
McKee, Nelson, and Whitmire: *Federal Taxation of Partnerships and Partners*	Warren, Gorham & Lamont
Lerner *et al.*: *Federal Income Taxation of Corporations Filing Consolidated Returns*	Matthew Bender & Co.

SINGLE-VOLUME TAX REFERENCE BOOKS

Master Federal Tax Manual	Research Institute of America
Master Tax Guide	Commerce Clearing House

CONDENSED TAX SERVICES

Federal Tax Guide	Commerce Clearing House
Tax Guide	Research Institute of America

COMPREHENSIVE TAX SERVICES

United States Tax Reporter	Research Institute of America
Federal Tax Coordinator 2d	Research Institute of America
Tax Management Portfolios	Bureau of National Affairs, Inc.
Standard Federal Tax Reporter	Commerce Clearing House
Mertens' Law of Federal Income Taxation	Callaghan & Company

TAX JOURNALS

Journal of Taxation	Warren, Gorham & Lamont
Journal of the American Taxation Association	American Taxation Association
Taxation for Accountants	Warren, Gorham & Lamont
TAXES—The Tax Magazine	Commerce Clearing House
The Tax Adviser	American Institute of CPAs

TAX NEWSLETTERS

Daily Tax Report	Bureau of National Affairs, Inc.
U.S. Tax Week	Matthew Bender & Co.
Tax Notes	Tax Analysts & Advocates

DOCUMENTING TAX RESEARCH

An important part of tax research is establishing in writing which sources were used, the results of each use, and the communication of the reasoning and conclusions. Often the research must be communicated to someone who in turn communicates it to a client. Also, the research process applied is important if the client is audited on this issue. Frequently the person preparing this year's tax return is not the person who did last year's return. Documenting research also makes pragmatic sense in today's highly litigious environment.

A structured format for describing the research done can also facilitate a logical approach and help ensure that all relevant sources of authority have been consulted, or at least, considered. Figure 10–7 illustrates such a structured format for researching tax questions.

Figure 10–7 Record of Tax Research Procedures

Date _____

Client: _____

Subject (Tax Issue(s)): _____
_____
_____

Preparer: _____ Reviewer: _____

Basic Authorities Consulted:

Internal Revenue Code _____

Regulations _____

Committee Reports _____
_____

Additional Authorities Consulted:

Tax Services (e.g., CCH or RIA):
_____
_____
_____

Tax Periodicals:
_____
_____
_____

Citator:
_____
_____

Computer-Assisted Tax Research (e.g., LEXIS or WESTLAW):
_____
_____

Other (cases, rulings, etc.):
_____
_____

Conclusions: _____
_____
_____
_____
_____

COMPUTERIZED TAX RESEARCH TOOLS

As stated in previous chapters of this text, the computer has significantly changed how the professional accountant conducts research, including tax research. In addition to the traditional hard copy of the Code, the following three tools utilizing the computer have provided fast retrieval of tax information for the tax researcher: CD-ROM systems, On-line systems, and the Internet.

CD-ROM Systems

These systems provide an inexpensive means of accessing and researching large amounts of tax information. Commerce Clearing House and Research Institute of America are examples of two CD-ROM systems. Following is an example of RIA's OnPoint system included on a CD that is an optional supplement with this text. The OnPoint Main Menu as shown in Figure 10–8 allows the tax researcher to access the various segments of the system.

After loading OnPoint onto your computer, you should be at the main menu screen as shown in Figure 10–8. A variety of items are available as listed on the menu screen. Choose and double-click on the **Code, Regs, Com Rpts, Tax Treaties** icon. A new submenu will appear to the right as shown in Figure 10–9. This submenu displays the materials available under the main heading. Double-click on the **Internal Revenue Code** icon in the submenu and the search screen shown in Figure 10–10 is displayed.

Click on the **Query** icon on the toolbar. This opens the "Query Box. Inside the "Query Box," is a smaller box labeled "Query For." Inside the "Query For" box, type "moving expenses." After you type "moving expenses," you'll see a results map appear in the center of the "Query Box." Click "OK," and the results of the search will appear in outline form as illustrated in Figure 10–11. (Please note that your outline may not look exactly like the outline in Figure 10–11, but it will function identically.)

Figure 10–8 OnPoint System Main Menu

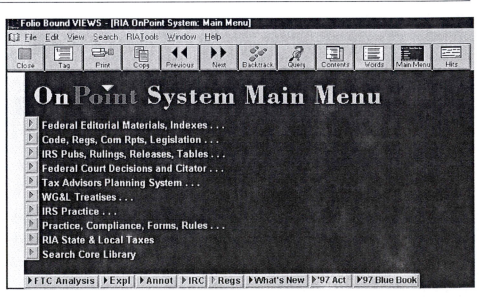

Figure 10–9 Code, Regs, Com Rpts, Legislation… Submenu

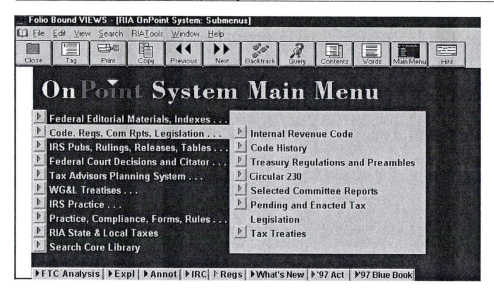

The plus signs indicate your outline can be expanded. The minus signs mean that there are no additional levels to this part of the outline. Clicking on the plus signs will expand your outline and will present results indicating that moving expenses are located in Section 217 of the Code. If you have access to this optional supplement, enjoy investigating the capabilities of this computer product. The end-of-chapter questions will ask you to use this product again.

Figure 10–10 Internal Revenue Code Search Screen

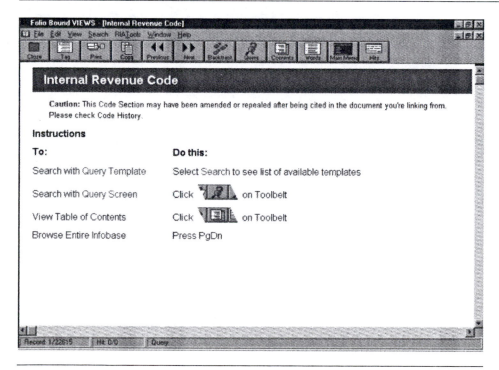

Figure 10–11 Search Results

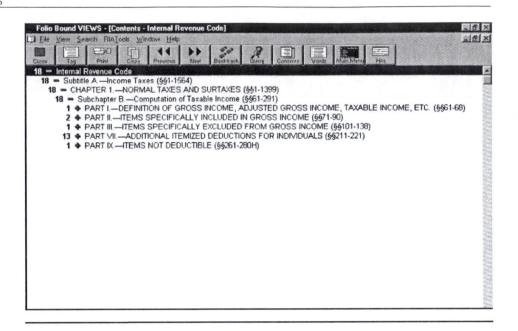

Please note that, with any CD product, updates occur rather frequently. The figures and explanation of OnPoint previously discussed are for the 1999 version. Newer versions will undoubtedly have changes to the materials and screen menus. Therefore, the Web site for this text will attempt to keep the reader current as to the new features of newer versions of OnPoint.

On-line Systems. These systems provide the tax researcher with on-line connection to a central mainframe computer that provides subscribers with the most up-to-date tax information. One example of on-line tax systems is LEXIS-NEXIS, discussed earlier in this text regarding conducting accounting research. In addition to accounting and other databases, this system contains all federal and state legal and tax research material. Also, LEXIS-NEXIS Academic Universe provides the tax researcher the capability to conduct limited tax research. Another example is the CCH Access on-line system, which contains tax information including government documents such as IRS publications and tax court cases.

Internet. You should be familiar with the use of the Internet after having read Chapter 4. Some popular Internet sites for the tax researcher are presented in Figure 10–12. Various tax resources can be located by utilizing the Internet. One can obtain primary tax research documents, IRS publications, as well as federal and state tax forms. In addition, one can access different tax preparation software packages and stay current by reading recent tax developments or participate in tax discussion newsgroups.

Figure 10–12 Internet Tax Sites

Internal Revenue Service	www.irs.ustreas.gov
Commerce Clearing House	www.cch.com
Research Institute of America	www.riatax.com
Tax and Accounting Sites Directory	www.taxsites.com
Tax Library	www.taxlibrary.com
Tax Court Opinions	www.ustaxcourt.gov
Tax Planning	www.smartmoney.com
Tax Software	www.intuit.com

DISCUSSION QUESTIONS

1. Explain the difference between tax evasion and tax avoidance.
2. Define tax research.
3. What are the basic steps of the tax research process?
4. Which of the following are primary tax research authorities:

   a. Tax services
   b. Tax court rulings
   c. Tax newsletters
   d. Internal Revenue Code
   e. Treasury Regulations

5. Primary tax research authority can be classified into three groups. Describe each group.
6. Access Internet Web site www.taxsites.com, and complete the following:

   a. Obtain a copy of Michigan's 1040 tax form.
   b. Obtain a copy of Publication 597—"Information on the United States–Canada Income Tax Treaty," located under "International tax sites."
   c. Under "Tax legislation" locate three proposed taxation bills and briefly summarize each.
   d. Under "Tax help, tips and articles," locate two tax articles and briefly summarize.

7. If you have the OnPoint CD supplement, access RIA's OnPoint CD and answer the following:

   a. What is the general content of IRS Code Sec. 61?
   b. What is the general content of IRS Code Sec. 166?
   c. Using the IRS Code as the source, define "net long-term capital gains."
   d. Using the IRS Code as the source, determine if the gain on the sale of a home is taxable.

8. Many universities or accounting firms subscribe to the on-line computer tax service, LEXIS-NEXIS. If your university or accounting firm has this service answer the following questions after accessing LEXIS-NEXIS, or as an alternative use LEXIS-NEXIS Academic Universe:

   a. Conduct a search of the U.S. Treasury Regulations using the keyword "moving expenses." Review all available dates and list three documents from your search and their dates.
   b. Conduct a search of the Internal Revenue Bulletin/Cumulative Bulletin using the keyword "qualified scholarships." Review all available dates and list the most recent IRS pronouncement published and its date.

    c. Conduct a search of the Internal Revenue Bulletin/Cumulative Bulletin using the keyword "tuition credit." Review all available dates and list three documents produced from your search.

9. Access the U.S. Code at the Web site http://uscode.house.gov/usc.htm and answer the following:

    a. What is the U.S. Code?

    b. What is the name and number of the U.S. Code section that identifies and contains the Internal Revenue Code?

    c. Search the Internal Revenue Code for a discussion of tuition credits. Did you find any information?

10. Access the Code of Federal Regulations (CFR) at the Web site http://www.access.gpo.gov./nara/cfr and answer the following:

    a. How may titles are there in the CFR?

    b. Scroll down and search the CFR for IRS Section 217. What did you find?

CHAPTER 11

Fraud and Other Investigative Techniques

LEARNING OBJECTIVES

After completing this chapter, you should understand:

- The impact of fraud on society.
- The definition of fraud.
- Different types of fraud.
- The components of the Fraud Triangle.
- An overview of a fraud examination and business investigation.
- The use of computers in fraud examinations/investigations.

Picture yourself being requested by a client to determine if evidence of vendor kickbacks to certain employees in the purchasing department exists. Or, you have been hired by a company's legal counsel to determine whether an officer of the company has any hidden assets as a result of an embezzlement scheme he or she carried out. Or perhaps, you have been engaged to conduct background checks (due diligence checks) on potential strategic partners of a newly talked-about joint venture. Sound like interesting assignments? Want to be a Sherlock Holmes? These are just a few examples of engagements of value added services offered by accounting firms to their clients. Other common engagements of a fraud auditor/examiner in relation to an audit client could include the following:

- Providing assistance to the audit team in assessing the risk of fraud and illegal acts.
- Providing assistance to the audit team in investigating potential fraud or illegal acts.
- Conducting fact-finding forensic accounting studies of alleged fraud that could include bribery, wire fraud, securities fraud, money laundering, retail fraud, theft of intellectual property, and other fraud investigations.
- Conducting due diligence studies that could include public record checks or background checks on individuals in a hiring situation or on entities in a potential acquisition.
- Consulting as to the implementation of fraud prevention, deterrence, and detection programs.

The above examples of fraud engagements demand that the investigator possess unique research skills in addition to the traditional skills presented in the previous chapters of this book.

In addition to the typical accounting, auditing, and tax services rendered by accountants, the profession is rapidly moving into additional value-added services known as fraud investigations (or litigation support), or the broader, more comprehensive term of forensic accounting. The terms "forensic accounting" or "litigation support" generally imply the use of accounting in a court of law. Thus, the services of an accountant in a court case or fraud investigation are often referred to as forensic accounting or litigation support services.

It is common knowledge that fraud is a major problem for most organizations. Newspapers and business periodicals provide plenty of stories about major frauds. A review of such articles would reveal that fraud is not perpetrated only against large organizations. One report in a business magazine has estimated that 80 percent of all crimes involving businesses are associated with small businesses. Although the full impact of fraud within entities is unknown, various national surveys have reported that annual fraud costs to U.S. organizations exceed $400 billion (or 6 percent of their revenues) and are increasing!

Fraud examinations and background, (due diligence) checks are not easy tasks. One must have the proper training and experience to conduct a successful fraud investigation. Many fraud investigators currently working in CPA firms obtained their experience working with various federal and local agencies, such as the Internal Revenue Service (IRS), the Federal Bureau of Investigation (FBI), or various levels of police work. Others obtained their knowledge of fraud examination skills by attending conferences or seminars conducted by organizations such as the Association of Certified Fraud Examiners.

The objective of this chapter is to present a basic overview of fraud and common red flags that may indicate its occurrence. Additionally, the chapter will focus on the basic steps of a financial fraud examination, and the investigation techniques a forensic accountant may use. Since no two fraud investigations are alike, an overview of a typical examination and techniques only are presented in the following pages. This chapter will not make you a fraud examiner. However, it will provide you with a heightened awareness of the environment of fraud, and present basic techniques of a fraud investigation. Also, with advances in technology, fraud examination is becoming more high tech. As in previous chapters, this chapter will also highlight the use of the computer and the Internet as tools in a fraud or other investigation engagements.

DEFINITION OF FRAUD

In its simplest terms, fraud is commonly defined as intentional deception, or simply lying, cheating, or stealing. Fraud can be perpetrated against different parties, such as investors, creditors, customers, or government entities. Black's Law Dictionary defines fraud as:

> *A generic term, embracing all multifarious means which human ingenuity can devise, and which are resorted to by one individual to get advantage over another by false suggestions or by suppression of truth, it includes all surprise, trickery, cunning, dissembling, and any unfair way by which another is cheated.*

The various laws related to fraud are many and often complex. The fraud examiner should be aware of the different types of frauds and request the legal assistance of an attorney in the interpretations of the laws. However, the different fraud-related laws have a common legal definition. As defined by the U.S. Supreme Court, fraud includes the following elements:

- A misrepresentation of a material fact,
- The perpetrator knew was false, and
- Made for the intention that the misrepresentation would be relied on, and, that
- The victim did rely on the misstatement, and as a result of such reliance, incurred a loss.

Thus, a fraud examination involves the procedures of obtaining evidence relating to the allegations of fraud, conducting interviews of various witnesses and related parties, writing reports as to the findings of the examination, and, in many cases, testifying in a court of law as to your findings. Predication is the basis for beginning a fraud examination. That is, there should be sufficient reason or suspicion (predication) based upon the circumstantial evidence to believe that a fraud has likely occurred. An employee complaint, or unusual or unexplained trends in financial ratios may rouse a suspicion that something might be wrong. The fraud examination is conducted to prove or disprove the allegations.

TYPES OF FRAUDS

Statement on Auditing Standards No. 82, *Consideration of Fraud in a Financial Statement Audit*, distinguishes between two categories of financial statement fraud. The first category is referred to as *fraudulent financial reporting*, which is usually committed by management in order to deceive financial statement users. These fraudulent acts primarily benefit the company rather than an officer or employee of the company. The second category is referred to as *misappropriation of assets*, more commonly known as employee fraud. These are acts perpetrated by employees of a company, in which the individual committing the fraud derives the principal benefits of the acts.

Fraudulent financial reporting (management fraud) refers to actions whereby management attempts to inflate reported earnings or other assets in order to deceive outsiders. Examples of management fraud would include overstating assets/revenues, price fixing, contract bidding fraud, or understating expenses/liabilities in order to make the financial statements look better than they really are. Figure 11–1 presents details of two examples of enforcement actions by the SEC relating to management fraud.

Misappropriation of assets (employee fraud) refers to actions of individuals whereby they misappropriate (steal) money or other property from their employers. Various employee fraud schemes could include embezzlement, theft of company property, kickbacks, and others as listed in Figure 11–2.

In addition to the two general categories of financial statement fraud identified in SAS No. 82, Albrecht, et al.[1] categorized fraud into six types:

- **Employee Embezzlement**—Fraud in which employees steal company assets either directly—stealing cash or inventory, or indirectly—taking bribes or kickbacks.
- **Management Fraud**—Deception by top management of an entity primarily through the manipulation of the financial statements in order to mislead users of those statements.

---

[1]   Albrecht, W. Steve, Gerald W. Wernz, and Timothy L. Williams. *Fraud: Bringing Light to the Dark Side of Business*, Richard D. Irwin, Inc., 1995.

Figure 11–1 Examples of Management Fraud

The SEC alleged that senior officers of Scientific Software-Intercomp, Inc. engaged in fraudulent schemes to inflate revenues by recognizing premature and fictitious revenue from license agreements that were subject to cancellation or otherwise contingent as of period-end and from sales of products that were not delivered by period-end.

The Commission alleged that Scientific Software improperly recognized revenue by the following methods: executing license agreements with valued added resellers with simultaneous letters excusing payment of allowing for the resellers to treat the contacts as ineffective until they resold the software. Secondly, Scientific Software routinely backdated contracts and shipping documentation so as to recognize revenue prematurely. Thirdly, Scientific Software recorded revenue before persuasive evidence of a contract existed and also recorded revenue when products had not yet been delivered. Finally, Scientific recorded revenue for work on long term projects that had not been completed.

The Commission concluded that Scientific Software engaged in a financial fraud that violated the anti-fraud, periodic reporting, books and records, and internal controls provisions of the federal securities laws.

Source: Accounting and Auditing Enforcement Release No. 1056, July 30, 1998.

The SEC brought an enforcement action against the senior management of Livent, a Toronto based company that produces live theatrical entertainment, such as *Ragtime, The Phantom of the Opera,* and *Show Boat*. The company registered its common stock with the Commission in May, 1995 in order to trade its stock on the NASDAQ.

The Commission alleged that senior management engaged in a multi-faceted and pervasive accounting fraud which included: a multi-million dollar kickback scheme designed to misappropriate funds for their own use; improper shifting of preproduction costs to fixed assets; improperly recording of revenue for transactions that contained side agreements which were concealed from Livent's independent auditors. In addition, while in possession of material nonpublic information concerning the fraudulent conduct of Livent, two senior officers and three accounting staff members of Livent engaged in insider trading of Livent securities.

The kickback scheme involved two of Livent's vendors who artificially inflated invoices. Livent would pay the inflated invoices and the vendors would return most of the excess money, totally more than $7 million, directly to Livent's senior officers directing the scheme. The accounting manipulations included transferring preproduction costs for show to fixed assets, which significantly decreased their show expenses. In addition, Livent would simply remove certain expenses and the related liabilities from the general ledger by literally erasing them and then re-entering them in the next period.

The SEC concluded that Livent's financial statements filed with the Commission were materially misstated.

Source: Accounting and Auditing Enforcement Release No. 1095, January, 13, 1999.

- **Investment Scams**—The sale of fraudulent and often worthless investments. Such frauds would include telemarketing and Ponzzi type frauds.
- **Vendor Fraud**—Fraud resulting from the overcharging for goods purchased, shipment of inferior goods, or the nonshipment of inventory even when payment has been received.
- **Customer Fraud**—Fraud committed by a customer by not paying for goods received, or deceiving the organization in various ways to get something for nothing.
- **Miscellaneous Fraud**—This category is a catch-all category for frauds that do not fit into one of the previous five categories. Examples would include altering birth records or grade reports.

Figure 11–2 Common Examples of Fraud Activities

Misappropriation of Assets:

Account	Schemes
Cash	Skimming
	Forgery
	Kiting
	Phony Refunds
	Larceny
	Fraudulent Disbursements
Accounts/Rec.	Lapping
	Fictitious Write-offs
Purchases/Inventory	Duplicate Payments
	Non-existent Vendor
	Kickbacks
	Misdirected Shipments
	Theft
Fixed Assets	Unauthorized Personal Use of Assets
	Fictitious Burglary
Payroll	Phantom Employees
	Falsified Time Cards

Fraudulent Financial Reporting:

Fictitious Revenues —recording of sales of goods or services that never occurred
—timing differences, recognizing revenue in improper periods

Asset Overstatement—recording certain assets as market values rather than the lower of cost or market

Unrecorded Liabilities and Expenses— not recording an environmental contingency that is probable and reasonably estimable

Improper Disclosures— not disclosing related party transactions or other significant events

Corruption:

Conflict of Interest
Bribery
Illegal Gratuities
Economic Extortion

Frauds can also be categorized by industry classification, such as financial institution fraud, health care fraud, or insurance fraud. Although there are many different types and categories of fraud, the fraud examiner should approach each engagement in a systematic manner, as highlighted in the following sections of this chapter.

THE FRAUD TRIANGLE

Why do individuals commit fraud? Probably the most common reason is that they are greedy and believe that they will not get caught. Various researchers, including criminologists, psychologists, sociologists, auditors, police departments, educators, and others, have studied this issue and have concluded that there exist three basic factors that determine whether an individual might commit fraud. These elements of the fraud triangle include (1) perceived pressure, (2) perceived opportunity, and (3) rationalization.[2] All three elements generally exist in the typical fraud.

An individual's motivation can change due to external forces. An individual who is honest one day may be a criminal committing fraud the next due to external pressures. One type of pressure could be financial in nature. Typical financial pressures include excessive debt resulting from unexpected high medical bills, uncontrolled spending with credit cards, lifestyles beyond one's means, or outright greed. A second group of pressures can be categorized as vice pressures, such as addiction to gambling, drugs, or alcohol. The individual in this case is motivated by these pressures to commit a fraud act in order to support his or her addiction. A third group of pressures is work-related. These pressures could include not receiving the job recognition an employee thinks he or she deserves, being overworked and underpaid, or not getting an expected promotion. Thus, the once honest individual turns to fraud in order to get even with the employer.

Top management might be motivated to commit financial statement fraud (management fraud) in order to obtain a bonus or stock option based on the company's financial results, manipulate the company's stock price, or meet regulatory requirements. Similarly, when there are dramatic changes in the organization, such as re-engineering or a potential merger, such changes can lead to uncertainty as to the future and therefore motivate an individual to become dishonest in order to survive within the organization.

The second element of the fraud triangle is perceived opportunity. All employees have opportunities to commit fraud against their employers, suppliers, or other third parties, such as the government. This element is driven by the access an individual has to the entity's assets or financial statements, the skill of the individual to exploit the opportunity to commit fraud, and, in certain cases, by the individual's seniority and trust within the organization. Many corporate frauds have occurred due to breaches of trust by employees and management to whom access privileges were granted. If an individual believes that the opportunity exists to commit a fraud, conceal the fraud in some way from others, and avoid detection and punishment, the probability of the individual committing fraud increases. When an individual's professional aspirations are being met by legitimate opportunities, generally the individual is content. However, when the aspirations cannot be met by legitimate opportunities, unconventional means that may include fraud will often be sought if the other two opportunities also exist.

Conditions (red flags) that may provide the opportunity for fraud include:

- Negligence on the part of top management to enforce ethical standards, or to discipline an individual who commits a fraud.
- Major changes in an entity's operating environment.
- Non-enforcement of mandatory vacations for employees allowing others to fill in during absences.
- Lack of supporting documentation for transactions.
- Lack of physical safeguards over assets.

---

2 More detailed discussion of the fraud triangle can be found in the following: Bologna, G. Jack, and Robert J. Lindquist, *Fraud Auditing and Forensic Accounting*, 2nd Edition, (New York, John Wiley & Sons, Inc., 1995); Albrecht, W. Steve, Gerald W. Wernz, and Timothy L. Williams, *Fraud: Bringing Light to the Dark Side of Business*, (Burr Ridge, IL, Richard D. Irwin, Inc., 1995); and *Guide to Fraud Investigations*, Volume 1, 2nd Edition, (Practitioners Publishing Co., Fort Worth, Texas, 1998).

An important factor in limiting a fraud is effective internal control. The fraud examiner must be cognizant of the entity's internal controls and be able to evaluate the weaknesses or red flags that provide the opportunity for fraud.

The third element of the fraud triangle is an individual's rationalization of the actions taken. If an individual can rationalize that the action taken was not wrong, he or she has just justified in his or her mind the illicit behavior. Common rationalizations for fraud activity include such statements as: "I work long hours and am treated unfairly by my employer; the company owes me more." "I will use the funds only for my current financial emergency and will pay them back later." or, "The federal government foolishly wastes my money and therefore I will not report my extra income this year on my tax return—besides, no one gets hurt." What the individual is attempting to do is to rationalize away the dishonesty of the wrongful action.

There are many other rationalizations that individuals use when committing fraud. However, an important factor that the fraud examiner will evaluate to minimize illicit actions is an individual's personal integrity. An individual's strong personal standards of ethics can offset the desire to rationalize the fraud activity. The tone set by top management as to proper ethical conduct can have a major impact as to actions taken by employees.

Most frauds result when the three elements of the fraud triangle, pressure (motivation), opportunity, and rationalization are present. It therefore follows that if any of the three elements can be denied or controlled, the likelihood of the occurrence of fraud decreases. Knowledge of these three elements provides the fraud examiner with a better understanding of different approaches to take in the investigation.

Fraud comes in many forms and thus the fraud examination must be tailored to the specific circumstances. Following is an overview of a typical financial statement fraud examination.

OVERVIEW OF A FINANCIAL FRAUD EXAMINATION

Over the years, independent auditors have been accused of not meeting the expectations of third parties in the detection of material fraud when conducting audits of financial statements. Fraud auditing is the creation of an environment that encourages the detection and prevention of fraud. In such an environment, the fraud auditor possesses the skills of a well-trained auditor combined with the skills of a criminal investigator. To further clarify the auditor's responsibility, SAS No. 82 provides guidance as to the treatment of and responsibility for the discovery of fraud in a financial statement audit. This standard specifically states that the auditor has a responsibility to plan and perform the audit in order to obtain reasonable assurance that the financial statements are free of material misstatement, whether they are caused by error or fraud. Therefore, the auditor/fraud examiner must understand the characteristics and types of frauds, be able to assess fraud risks or red flags, design an appropriate audit, and report the findings relating to the possible fraud to management, or the appropriate levels of authority. Specifically, the auditor needs to assess the risk of material misstatement of the financial statements due to the possibility of fraud. The assessment would include attempts to answer the following questions: What types of fraud risk exist? What is the actual and potential exposure to the fraud? Who are the perpetrators? How difficult is it to identify and prevent the fraud? What is the company doing to prevent it now, and how effective are these measures? This risk assessment then aids the auditor in designing the audit procedures to be performed.

In conducting the risk assessment of material misstatement due to fraud, the auditor would evaluate fraud risk factors (red flags) that relate to the two basic categories of financial statement fraud—fraudulent financial reporting, and misappropriation of assets. A fraud risk factor is a characteristic that provides a motivation or opportunity for fraud to occur, or an indication that fraud may have occurred. The risk factors that relate to financial reporting fraud can be classified into the following three groups:

1. **Management's characteristics and influence over the control environment.** This group of risk factors relate to management's abilities, pressures, operating style, and attitude to such issues as internal controls and the financial reporting process. Examples of risk factors or red flags would include the following: significant reliance on stock options or bonuses for management compensation; excessive interest in increasing the organization's stock price or earnings; the use of unrealistic forecasts; or management's disregard of regulatory requirements.

2. **Industry conditions.** These factors include the economic, global, technological, and regulatory environment of the organization. Examples would include new accounting requirements that have a negative impact on earnings; a decline in the organization's market share; or rapid product obsolescence within the industry.

3. **Operating characteristics and financial stability.** These factors relate to the nature and complexity of the organization, and its transactions and financial condition. Examples here would include complex accounting transactions such as derivatives, the inability to generate positive cash flow; or threat of bankruptcy.[3]

Risk factors relating to misstatements arising from the misappropriation of assets can be classified into two groups: **susceptibility of assets to misappropriation**, which relates to the nature of the organization's assets and the probability of theft; and **controls**, which relate to the lack of controls for preventing or detecting the misappropriation of assets. Examples of red flags for the susceptibility of assets include large amounts of cash on hand, easily convertible assets, such as bearer bonds or diamonds, or lack of ownership identification of fixed assets that are very marketable.

Although fraud is usually concealed, the presence of risk factors (red flags) may alert the fraud auditor to the possibility that fraud may exist within the company. If such conditions exist, and a risk assessment warrants, discussions would take place with management and/or legal counsel. If the conclusion reached is that there exists the likelihood of fraud, a fraud examination would commence. The basic steps of the fraud examination consist of the following:

1. Identify the Issue/Plan the Investigation
2. Gather Evidence/The Investigation Phase
3. Evaluate Evidence
4. Report Findings to Management/Legal Counsel

Step 1—Identify the Issue/Plan the Investigation

Based upon predication, or the circumstances indicating the possibility of fraud, the client and/or the client's legal counsel would usually contact the fraud examiner to conduct a fraud examination. Management's suspicions as to the possibility of fraud could come from a number of sources, such as

---

3   AICPA, SAS No. 82, *Consideration of Fraud in a Financial Statement Audit,* 1997.

improprieties noted by fellow employees, an observation of an employee's lifestyle that is inconsistent with his or her income, or issues resulting from an internal or external audit that has identified missing documents. Not all suspicions result in a finding of fraud, but by pursuing the anomalies and evidence, the fraud examiner can make a reasoned determination as to its existence. If fraud exists and is not pursued, it will probably continue and more likely increase over time. Based upon the circumstantial evidence, the fraud examiner would create a hypothesis as to *when* the potential fraud occurred, *how* it was committed, and by *whom*.

Step 2—Gather Evidence/The Investigation Phase

Although different investigation methods exist, the objective of the investigation step is to gather appropriate evidence in order to determine whether a fraud has occurred or is occurring. Most investigations can be contentious and generate a great deal of uneasiness for all parties involved. Each investigation is different and the suspects and witnesses will often react differently. One mistake in the investigation can jeopardize the entire process.

Also included in this step is the identification of resources to utilize in the investigation. The examiner would need to know what resources are available—secondary, primary, or third parties. Various types of resources are discussed later in the chapter.

The investigation technique used will often depend on the type of evidence the fraud examiner is attempting to gather. One approach is to classify the evidence into four types with the related investigative techniques to gather the evidence as follows:[4]

Type of Evidence	Investigative Technique
1. Documentary Evidence (hardcopy or electronic)	Examination of documents, Searches of public records, Searches of computer database, Analysis of net worth, or Analysis of financial statement
2. Testimonial Evidence	Interviewing, Interrogations, or Polygraph tests
3. Observational Evidence (Investigator's personal observation)	Physical examination—counts/inspections, Invigilation (close supervision of suspect during examination period), or Surveillance
4. Physical Evidence (i.e., tire marks, or fingerprints)	Use of forensic expert

Two examples of gathering evidence as to the existence of fraud are presented below.

Case 1. Management has experienced lower profit margins than expected. In this investigation, the fraud examiner might review inventory procedures to determine whether employees are stealing inventory. The investigation might identify shrinkage in actual counts of high-dollar inventory items, and a review of surveillance records may show whether anyone has been removing inventory during off hours.

---

4   Albrecht, *et al.*

Case 2. A co-worker has reported that an employee appears to be living well above his known means. In such a case, the fraud investigator might review payment records to determine whether sales proceeds are being diverted into an employee's personal account. A net worth analysis can also identify inconsistencies, and a review of the suspect's brokerage statements (with legal permission) may show whether the deposit dates correspond to the dates when questionable business transactions occurred.

The investigation step of the examination requires good analytical skills. These skills are important in the analysis of the financial information and other data for any trends or anomalies.

In the gathering of testimonial evidence, the fraud examiner would rely in many cases on his or her interviewing skills. These skills require an ability to extract testimonial evidence from collaborators, co-workers, or others related to the case, as well as the suspect in hopes of obtaining a confession. These interviews are carefully planned question-and-answer sessions designed to solicit information relevant to the case.

Also, information technology skills are required in order to search public records and other electronic databases in the gathering of evidence for the investigation. The use of computers in evidence gathering for a fraud investigation is discussed beginning on page 177.

Step 3—Evaluate Evidence

Once a thorough investigation has been completed, the fraud examiner will evaluate the evidence in order to determine whether the fraud has occurred or is occurring. Sound, documented conclusions can be drawn only when the information has been properly collected, organized, and interpreted. Once fraud is discovered, the fraud examiner attempts to determine the extent of the fraud. Was it an isolated incident? Was there a pattern connecting each incident? When did the fraud begin? By identifying how long and to what extent the fraud occurred, the investigator may be able to provide critical information to help the client recover missing funds from the perpetrator or an insurance company.

Step 4—Report Findings

Upon completion of the evaluation of the evidence, the fraud examiner needs to document the results of the investigation and prepare a report as to his or her findings. A report needs to be written with the concepts identified in Chapter 3 in mind. The report should consist of the following characteristics: coherent organization, conciseness, clarity, use of standard English, responsiveness, and appropriateness to the reader.

At times, the fraud examiner may be requested by the client's legal counsel to serve as an expert witness in a court case against the perpetrator. This court case can be won or lost depending upon the accuracy and technical rigor of the investigation and report. However, in the report the fraud examiner needs to avoid rendering his or her opinion as to the guilt or innocence of the suspect. The report need only state the facts of the investigation and findings. The report should present answers as to *when* the fraud occurred, *how* it was committed, and by *whom*.

Since fraud investigations are considered litigation support services, which are considered consulting services as identified in Chapter 9, the CPA/investigator needs to adhere to the following standards during the investigation as well as in developing the report. These standards and guidance have been issued by the AICPA's Management Consulting Services Committee and related subcommittees.

- Statement on Standards for Consulting Services No. 1, *Consulting Services: Definition and Standards.*
- Consulting Services Special Report 93-1, *Application of AICPA Professional Standards in the Performance of Litigation Services.*
- Consulting Services Special Report 93-2, *Conflicts of Interest in Litigation Services Engagements.*
- Consulting Services Practice Aid 96-3, *Communicating in Litigation Services: Reports.*
- Consulting Services Practice Aid 97-1, *Fraud Investigations in Litigation and Dispute Resolution Services.*

BUSINESS INVESTIGATIONS

In addition to a fraud examination, professional accountants can provide a related service to help management minimize their business risks. This service is referred to as business or due diligence investigations. At times a client may need help to verify information about an entity before entering into a joint venture or corporate merger. Or perhaps, the client needs a background information check before hiring a new corporate officer or other employee. In other situations, the client may need to know of any related parties associated with the corporation or the reputation of a potential new vendor. In each of these examples, a business or individual background investigation might prove valuable in obtaining desirable information in managing business risks.

In most types of investigative work, one needs to have what is referred to as a "documents state of mind." Many types of documents, or "paper trails," exist that the investigator can use to gather facts about the issue under investigation. Such documents often can be classified as either secondary or primary sources. A typical secondary source would be a newspaper article about a company acquiring a subsidiary or doing business in a certain country.

Primary documents are readily available in many types of investigations. For example, if you are attempting to gather background information on a new corporate executive, typical primary sources would include voter registrations, tax records for property ownership, civil and criminal lawsuits, and divorce and bankruptcy records. Corporations have similar types of paper trails. For example, an entity's articles of incorporation would be equivalent to an individual's birth certificate.

In gathering background information, the investigator typically follows a technique referred to as "working from the outside in." This technique can be depicted as concentric circles, with the larger circle representing the secondary sources as illustrated in Figure 11–3. The middle circle would contain the primary sources that often substantiate the secondary information. The inner circle could include human sources who have been interviewed for facts concerning the target or issue under investigation. In many investigations, the investigator needs to be creative in gathering and analyzing the data.

COMPUTER USAGE IN FRAUD INVESTIGATIONS

In the information technology age, fraud has widened its scope. However, new tools and techniques have been developed to detect and combat this expansion of fraud. Uncovering signs of fraud among possibly millions of transactions

Figure 11–3 Investigative Technique—"Working from the Outside In"

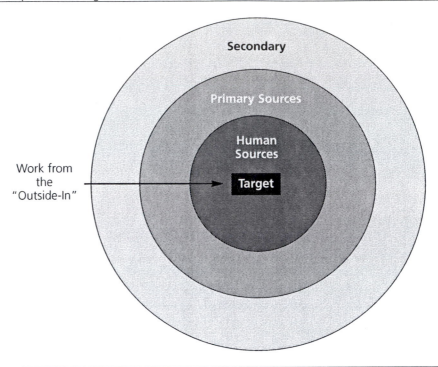

within an organization requires the fraud examiner to use his or her analytical skills and work experience to construct a profile against which to test data for the possibility of fraud. Three important tools for the fraud examiner are data mining software, public databases, and the Internet.

Data Mining Software

Data mining software is a tool which models a database for the purpose of determining patterns and relationships among the data. This tool has been an outgrowth of the development of "expert systems." Computer-based data analysis tools can prove invaluable when examining for possible fraud. From the analysis of data, the fraud examiner can develop fraud profiles from the patterns existing within the database. Through identifying and understanding of these patterns, the examiner can uncover fraudulent activity. The use of this software also provides the opportunity to set up automatic red flags that will reveal discrepancies in data that should be uniform. Some of the common features of data mining software include the following:

- **Sorting**—arranging data in a particular order such as alphabetically or numerically.
- **Occurrence selection**—querying the database to select the occurrences of items or records in a field.
- **Joining files**—combining selected files from different data files for analysis purposes.
- **Duplicate searches**—searching files for duplication, such as duplicate payments.
- **Ratio analysis**—performing both vertical and horizontal analyses for anomalies.

Following is a brief description of some of the more common commercial data mining software products used by fraud examiners.

WizRule. This software package is used for many different applications, such as data cleaning (searching for clerical errors) or anomaly detection as in a fraud examination. The program is based on the assumption that in many cases, errors are considered as exceptions to the norm. For example, if Mr. Johnston is the only salesperson for all sales transactions to certain customers and a sales transaction to one of the customers is associated with salesperson Mrs. Allen, this would be considered a "deviation" or a suspected error.

WizRule is based on a mathematical algorithm that is capable of revealing all the rules of a database. The main output of the program analysis is a list of cases found in the data that are unlikely to be true in reference to the discovered rules. Such cases are considered suspected errors.

Financial Crime Investigator. This is a program that is a systematic approach for investigating, detecting, and preventing contract and procurement fraud. The software, using artificial intelligence, provides instructions on how to query databases to find fraud indicators and match them to the appropriate fraud scheme. It provides a detailed work plan for each scheme in order to proceed with the investigation, converts probable schemes to the related criminal offenses, outlines an investigative plan based on the elements of proof for each offense, and generates interview formats for debriefing anonymous informants for each contract fraud scheme.

IDEA (Audimation Services, Inc.). This product is a powerful software package that allows the user to display, analyze, manipulate, sample, or extract data from files generated by a wide variety of computer systems. The software provides the power to select records which match your criteria, check file totals and extensions, and look for gaps in numerical sequences or duplicate documents or records. The investigator can conduct fraud investigations, do computer security reviews by analyzing systems logs, file lists, and access rights, or review telephone logs looking for fraudulent or inappropriate use of client facilities.

ACL for Windows. ACL Services Ltd., the developer and marketer of ACL for Windows, is considered the market leader in data inquiry, analysis and reporting software for the auditing profession. ACL's clients include many of the Fortune 100 companies, governmental agencies, and many of the largest international accounting firms. In the software category of fraud detection and prevention, ACL for Windows is the most commonly used software package.

This software product allows the fraud examiner to perform various analytical functions without modifying the original data. The software can sort data on multiple levels as well as locate numerical gaps in the sequencing of data. Graphical display options allow the investigator to create graphs from the Histogram, Stratify, Classify, or Age commands. ACL is very beneficial in fraud detection due to its ability to quickly and thoroughly analyze a large quantity of data in order to highlight those transactions often associated with fraudulent activity.

As a world leader in data inquiry, analysis, and reporting software, ACL is very effective in such areas as identifying trends and bringing to the auditor/fraud examiner's attention potential problem areas, highlighting errors or potential fraud by comparing files with end user criteria, and identifying control concerns. Specifically in fraud detection, ACL can identify suspect transactions by performing such test as follows: matching names between employee and paid vendor files, identifying vendor price increases greater than an acceptable percent, identifying invoices without a valid purchase order, or identifying invoices with no related receiving report.

As the forensic accountant attempts the task of sorting through a massive volume of data in order to detect the possibility of fraud, ACL for Windows is a major software product available for the fraud examiner. Accompanying this text is a CD that contains a demonstration of how ACL can be used in fraud detection. Please review this demo as selected end of chapter questions will quiz you as to the use of ACL for fraud detection.

Monarch. This is a software program for the investigator that can transform electronic editions of reports from programs such as Microsoft Access into text files, spreadsheets, or tables. Monarch can then break down this information into individual reports for analysis.

Analyst's Notebook. This software package, developed by i2, Inc., is a visual investigative analysis product that assists investigators by uncovering, interpreting, and displaying complex information in easily understood charts. The features of the software provide a range of visualization formats that find the connections between related sets of information and then in chart form reveals significant patterns in the data. This visual presentation is a powerful tool to use in discussions of the case with legal counsel and in presenting findings in court. For example, if the fraud examiner has a complex investigation chart of individuals and locations of suspects and legal counsel is interested in one particular individual, the software can immediately produce a smaller chart showing only the information relating to that one individual. The software is excellent for extracting sections from large and complex investigation charts in order to produce smaller, more manageable presentation charts.

In a fraud investigation, the Analyst's Notebook can aid the fraud examiner in developing building blocks that support the key issues of how and why. The software can help manage the large volume of information collected; help in understanding the information by providing a link analysis to build up a picture (chart) of the individuals and organizations involved in the fraud; help in the examination of the fraudsters' actions by developing a timeline analysis as to the precise sequence of events in the fraud case; and help in the discovery of the location of the stolen money or assets. Accompanying this text is a demonstration CD provided by i2, Inc. that presents an excellent overview of this unique product for the fraud examiner.

Public Databases

Given the enormity of public records (including information sold to the public for a fee), the fraud examiner or investigator in certain cases may not need anything else in gathering evidence. These public databases include, among other information, records of lawsuits, bankruptcies, tax liens, and judgments and property transactions from all over the United States and, in certain cases, from around the world. If the examiner cannot locate the information via computerized databases, he or she can still locate the necessary information by personally visiting courthouses, recorder's offices, or city halls.

The fraud examiner/investigator relies on public records/databases for several reasons; the primary reason being that they are in the public domain, and therefore there usually are no restrictions in accessing the information. Business intelligence literature commonly cites the fact that 95 percent of spy work comes from public records/databases. Additional reasons for utilizing public records include the quick access time and the inexpensiveness of the search costs.

Some of the commonly used public records/databases are discussed in the following paragraphs. Figure 11–4 presents a summary listing (not all-inclusive) of typical records/files or databases available to the investigator.

"Courthouse" Records. Every county has a courthouse and a place to file real estate records. In both small towns and large cities, suits, judgments, and property filings are found at the courthouse. In addition to county records, those same types of records are filed at federal courts, which also contain bankruptcy filings. These records address the basic questions of a business investigation: Is the subject currently in a lawsuit? Are there unsatisfied judgments? Is there a criminal history? Has the subject filed for bankruptcy?

The existence of these records tells the investigator something, but buried within the case jackets and docket sheets is even more information. Looking for financial information, the investigator can examine the mortgage on a subject's home. Divorce filings and bankruptcy filings are business investigations themselves. They will contain records on assets and liabilities, employment, and pending suits.

Company Records. The common starting point in many business investigations is filings made with the Securities & Exchange Commission. Unfortunately, the great majority of privately held companies do not file with

Figure 11–4 Investigative Resources

State Records
Driving Records
Workers' Compensation Claims
Department of Education Records
Licensing Boards (*i.e.*, bar and
　　accountancy boards)
Corporation and Securities Commissions
　　Filings
UCC Records—documents the record of a
　　loan or lease with secured assets
State Tax Liens
Vehicle ID
Ownership/Property Records
Criminal and Civil Records
Social Security Number Records
Vital Statistics—birth, death, marriages
Driving Records—MVR
Bankruptcy Records

Locator Records
Phone Directories
Zip Code Directories
Surname Directories

Federal Records
Military Records
Federal Aviation Records
SEC Filings
UCC Filings
Library of Congress
Federal Tax Liens

Educational records
Degrees Awarded
Attendance Records
Teacher Certification

Databases
Full Text
　　Lexis-Nexis
　　Dow Jones/*The Wall Street Journal*
　　DIALOG
　　Datatimes

Public Records
　　PACER
　　Information America
　　CDB Infotek

Credit
　　Experian (formerly TRW)
　　Trans Union
　　Choicepoint (formerly Equifax)

Other
　　Demographic
　　Biographical
　　Internet

the SEC. This leaves two primary sources for company information. First, Dun and Bradstreet compiles data on millions of companies. Experienced investigators recognize D&B's shortcomings, but know the reports make great starting points. Second, all businesses file some form of report within either the state or the county where they are located. Proprietorships and partnerships typically file local "assumed name" "d/b/a" or "fictitious name" filings. Corporations, limited partnerships and limited liability companies (LLC's) file annual reports in their states of registration. These reports will typically identify the officers and registered agent of the company, but most reports will not list ownership data or financial information.

Other sources of company information include the various public records and courthouse records discussed previously. Uniform Commercial Code filings (UCCs) and real estate filings can provide details lacking in basic business filings. An investigator may tie an individual to a company because both the individual and the company are co-debtors in a secured agreement. Detailed financial information on private companies often can be gathered from litigation over contracts, trade secrets, and other issues. Different regulatory bodies may have information on companies, even when they are closely held. State insurance commissions, for instance, have files for the public on companies that sell insurance in their states. Companies awarded government contracts may also have to make certain information public. Investigators should try a variety of public records to get the right company information.

On-line Databases. Many investigators use commercial databases for the majority of their information. As described above, commercial databases give investigators the ability to quickly pull information from all over the world without alerting the subject. The speed and depth of commercial databases makes them a "must have" for business investigators.

On-line databases come in four formats. The first type of database is the "full text" database. Full text means the database stores, for retrieval, the full text of articles. Databases now have articles from newspapers and magazines from around the world. Databases also carry the full text of transcripts of television and radio broadcasts. Lexis-Nexis, Dow Jones News Retrieval, and Datatimes are examples of full text databases.

The second type of database is the public record database. Database companies provide access to many different types of courthouse records as well as company records. Access to federal litigation and bankruptcy records can be obtained through the "PACER" system. Major vendors of public record databases include Information America, CDB Infotek, and Lexis.

A third type of database is the credit and demographic database. The Fair Credit Reporting Act (FCRA) restricts the use of consumer credit information, but the credit bureaus also offer data not covered by the FRCA. Other databases act as national phone books, providing names and addresses across the country. Credit Bureaus include Experian (formerly TRW), Trans Union, and Choicepoint (formerly Equifax). Suppliers of demographic data like names and addresses include Metronet and DNIS.

Finally, there are databases that do not fit the three main categories. Vendors like Dialog and Lexis provide, in addition to full text articles, company directories, abstracts, and biographical records such as Who's Who. The on-line database world provides the majority of information now used by the business investigator.

The Internet. Fraud examiners/investigators utilize the Internet, but currently not as much as the other sources. Searching the Internet is not as precise as searching most commercial databases. Thus, investigators tend to stick with Lexis and Dialog. However, Internet on-line magazines often provide breaking news stories not covered elsewhere. Newsgroups and mailing lists contain raw (but often erroneous) data on companies. Finally, the first source of information on a company these days is often its Web site. Companies put detailed background information on themselves as well as profiles of their key executives on their Web sites.

A few of the Internet Web sites utilized by fraud examiners/investigators include those listed in the following paragraphs.

KnowX (www.knowx.com). Many of the previously listed public documents are currently accessible via the Internet. KnowX, an on-line public record service, is available via the Internet. This Web site provides the fraud investigator inexpensive searches, and, depending on the search no fee is charged. Typical searches available include aircraft ownership records, a business directory, corporate records, date-of-birth records, lawsuits, real estate tax assessor records, stock ownership records, and watercraft ownership records.

Switchboard (www.switchboard.com). Switchboard is a free white- and yellow-pages service that contains primarily U.S. listings. Anyone can use this to search the database for people or businesses by going to the Switchboard's homepage and clicking on **Find a Person**, then typing the information into the respective fields and clicking **search**. Business searches are similar to individual searches.

The Web sites in the Switchboard search engine are gathered by an intelligent search tool that helps one find information related to any topic or Web site address (URL) specified. Information can be found in the following ways: (1) by entering keywords in the search fields; (2) by entering a URL in the search field; or (3) by using the A-Z letter bar to browse through topics. A user can also click the **more** button, which will provide a list of Web sites with similar content. This Switchboard Web site is a quick way for the fraud examiner/investigator to search for individuals and/or a business that are under investigation.

Other specific Internet fraud sites include:

* Association of Certified Fraud Examiners (www.cfenet.com). Web site providing information on fraud and the Certified Fraud Examiners Program.
* Online Fraud Information Center (www.fraud.org)
* Prolific Fraud Scams (www.tustinpd.org/scams.html)
* Fraud Information Center (www.echotech.com/fmenu.htm)

FRAUD INVESTIGATION REGULATIONS

Many different types of fraud investigation information exists. The information should be gathered legally in order to be good evidence in a court of law. Two federal acts that limit access to information are the Freedom of Information Act (FOIA) and the Fair Credit Reporting Act (FCRA).

The Freedom of Information Act governs the availability of government records that can be accessed by the general public. Typical information available under the Act include tax rolls, voter registration, assumed names, real property records, and divorce/probate information. Information not available under the Act includes such items as banking records, telephone records, or stock ownership.

The Fair Credit Reporting Act regulates what consumer information can be provided to third parties by consumer-reporting agencies. Under the Act, an individual cannot obtain information about one's character, general reputation, personal characteristics, or mode of living without notification to the individual in advance. Thus, a fraud examiner/investigator needs to be careful as to the legality of evidence gathered.

SUMMARY

As discussed in this chapter, fraud is a major risk to society. As fraud increases, businesses are turning to fraud examiners/investigators to help fight it. Therefore, professional accountants are offering additional services to clients in the area of forensic accounting or litigation support services. This chapter presented an overview of fraud and the steps involved in a fraud examination/investigation in order to help the professional gather some basic knowledge for such engagements.

DISCUSSION QUESTIONS

1. Describe four different examples of fraud engagements.
2. Define "forensic accounting."
3. Define fraud and identify four examples of fraud.
4. What are the three components of the fraud triangle? Of what concern are they to the fraud examiner?
5. What is a risk factor or red flag?
6. Differentiate between management fraud and employee fraud.
7. What are some risk factors associated with management fraud and employee fraud?
8. Identify the basic steps of a fraud examination.
9. Provide two examples of a business/due diligence investigation.
10. Describe three computerized tools used by the fraud examiner/investigator.
11. Explain the difference between data mining software and public databases.
12. Access the following Web site (www.i2inc.com) and find examples of how investigators can use The Analyst's Notebook software. Also, review the Analyst's Notebook CD.
13. Access the KnowX Web site (www.knowx.com) and enter a free search. Discuss what you searched for and what you found. Provide two examples of how the fraud examiner/investigator can utilize this Web site.
14. Access Switchboard (www.switchboard.com) and search for a business. What were your results?
15. Access the Fraud Information Center (www.fraud.org) and locate and describe three types of fraud reported by the Center.
16. From the CD accompanying this text, review the ACL and Fraud Detection demo and explain how an auditor can utilize ACL for:
    a. Purchase fraud
    b. Vendor fraud
    c. Inventory fraud
17. Access ACL's Web site (www.i2inc.com) and locate three examples of how ACL assists in fraud detection.